T0384070

Global Lean for Higher Education

Education

A Themed Anthology of Case Studies, Approaches, and Tools

Global Lean for Higher Education

A Themed Anthology of Case Studies, Approaches, and Tools

Edited by
Stephen Yorkstone

A PRODUCTIVITY PRESS BOOK

First edition published in 2020
by Routledge/Productivity Press
52 Vanderbilt Avenue, 11th Floor New York, NY 10017
2 Park Square, Milton Park, Abingdon, Oxon OX14 4RN, UK

© 2020 by Taylor & Francis Group, LLC
Routledge/Productivity Press is an imprint of Taylor & Francis Group, an Informa business

No claim to original U.S. Government works

Printed on acid-free paper

International Standard Book Number-13: 978-0-367-02428-4 (Hardback)
International Standard Book Number-13: 978-0-429-39968-8 (eBook)

This book contains information obtained from authentic and highly regarded sources. Reasonable efforts have been made to publish reliable data and information, but the author and publisher cannot assume responsibility for the validity of all materials or the consequences of their use. The authors and publishers have attempted to trace the copyright holders of all material reproduced in this publication and apologize to copyright holders if permission to publish in this form has not been obtained. If any copyright material has not been acknowledged please write and let us know so we may rectify in any future reprint.

Except as permitted under U.S. Copyright Law, no part of this book may be reprinted, reproduced, transmitted, or utilized in any form by any electronic, mechanical, or other means, now known or hereafter invented, including photocopying, microfilming, and recording, or in any information storage or retrieval system, without written permission from the publishers.

For permission to photocopy or use material electronically from this work, please access www.copyright. com (http://www.copyright.com/) or contact the Copyright Clearance Center, Inc. (CCC), 222 Rosewood Drive, Danvers, MA 01923, 978-750-8400. CCC is a not-for-profit organization that provides licenses and registration for a variety of users. For organizations that have been granted a photocopy license by the CCC, a separate system of payment has been arranged.

Trademark Notice: Product or corporate names may be trademarks or registered trademarks, and are used only for identification and explanation without intent to infringe.

Library of Congress Cataloging-in-Publication Data

Names: Yorkstone, Stephen, editor.
Title: Global Lean for higher education : a themed anthology of case studies, approaches, and tools / [edited by] Stephen Yorkstone.
Description: Boca Raton : Taylor & Francis, 2020. | "A Routledge title, part of the Taylor & Francis imprint, a member of the Taylor & Francis Group, the academic division of T&F Informa plc." | Includes bibliographical references and index.
Identifiers: LCCN 2019008185 (print) | LCCN 2019013514 (ebook) | ISBN 9780429399688 (e-Book) | ISBN 9780367024284 (hardback : alk. paper)
Subjects: LCSH: Universities and colleges--Administration--Case studies. | Education, Higher--Planning.
Classification: LCC LB2341 (ebook) | LCC LB2341 ,G5528 2020 (print) | DDC 378.1/61--dc23
LC record available at https://lccn.loc.gov/2019008185

Visit the Taylor & Francis Web site at
http://www.taylorandfrancis.com

Contents

SECTION I   Starting Out

SECTION II People

SECTION III Projects

SECTION VI   Culture

Foreword

The birth of lean is typically traced to the development of the Toyota Production System in the aftermath of World War II. The Toyota Production System was a necessity given the limited capital available, outdated factories, and the need for a manufacturing process that could efficiently produce a variety of automobiles demanded by a small but growing number of customers. Over time, Toyota's successful principles and practices have been extended to virtually every business and industry sector including, in the past 20 years or so, higher education. As the challenges facing global higher education have grown – loss of public confidence, calls for accountability, rising costs, increased competition, and other disruptive forces – lean for higher education provides a proven framework for universities to address these challenges and fulfill their important missions.

Following early pioneers such as the University of Central Oklahoma and the University of St Andrews, the implementation of lean for higher education continues to mature and expand around the world. This book, *Global Lean for Higher Education*, provides a useful compendium for universities exploring the possible application of lean at their own institutions; it also offers additional tools and approaches to further improve efforts at those universities currently implementing lean. *Global Lean for Higher Education* provides a broad selection of readings from lean researchers and practitioners from around the world, sharing research, approaches, tools, and case studies that offer rich information and useful insights that can guide universities seeking to adopt lean as well as suggest new ideas for continuous improvement at universities currently implementing lean.

Importantly, the chapters in this edited book, especially those describing approaches and case studies, underscore the important organizational principle of equifinality: there are multiple paths, rather than a single path, to success. The variety of initiatives and ideas discussed across the chapters show that there is no one "correct" way to successfully implement lean principles and practices at a university. As noted by lean author and luminary Jeff Liker, in his 2004 book, *The Toyota Way*, lean should follow principles that are right for your own university, which are then diligently implemented to achieve high performance and bring value to your processes and their beneficiaries. This book provides great examples of how lean efforts in higher education can be designed to accommodate various "on the ground" constraints (resources, culture, etc.) when on your lean journey.

Overall, the success of lean for higher education comes from evidence of its long-term sustainability (e.g., continuation following the transition to a new university president or rector, or the departure of the original lean champion) and long-term effectiveness (e.g., qualitative and quantitative evidence of improvements in respect for people, and a university culture committed to continuous improvement). This book is a great step in that direction, advancing our understanding of lean for higher education and the practical things lean practitioners and champions can do to bring the university closer to realizing the full benefits of lean.

Bill Balzer
Bowling Green State University, USA
Author, Lean Higher Education *(2010)*

Acknowledgments

Universities are in the business of making the world a better place. Lean practitioners in all their forms in HE are in the business of making universities even better. This work is important, but, many of those who undertake this work do so quietly, and deserve much credit. So: thank you to those working to improve universities, the community of Lean HE practitioners (particularly members of all Lean HE steering groups and networks) and their supporting organisations, for all the good work that you do.

Thank you in particular to Bill Balzer for his continuing wisdom and support; and the idea from which this book sprung. Thank you to my home institution Edinburgh Napier University, for their ongoing support.

I would like to express my gratitude to the publishing team at Productivity Press (Michael Sinocchi and Katherine Kadian in particular), to the peer review team, external referees, and most importantly all contributors for telling their stories.

You are all heroes. Ever onwards!

Stephen Yorkstone

List of Contributors

SECTION I: STARTING OUT

Chapter 1. Establishing Process Improvement Capability in Higher Education

Rachel McAssey, The University of Sheffield., UK

Rachel McAssey co-founded the award-winning Process Improvement Unit at the University of Sheffield, was a founder member of Lean HE and chairperson for Lean HE Europe. She has 22 years' experience in Higher Education, she is a Lean Six Sigma black belt, and is recognised as a global leader and mentor for Lean and process improvement. She was lead author for the Association of University Administrators Best Practice Guide "Introduction to Business Improvement for HE Administrators".

Chapter 2. Tools to Get You Started

Bonnie Slykhuis, Des Moines Area Community College, Ankeny, IA

Bonnie is a Lean/CI Consultant for Des Moines Area Community College (DMACC). She holds a M.S.E in Training & Development and launched DMACC's internal Lean program in 2006. Her responsibilities include driving Lean throughout DMACC's six campuses, designing Lean training programs and providing training/consulting services to external clients in education, government, manufacturing, and service organizations. Having delivered more than 1200 training sessions for over 150 clients, she is an Iowa Lean Consortium board member and is currently completing a book on *Continuous Improvement in Higher Education: How to Begin Your Lean Journey.*

Chapter 3. VSM as a Tool for Creating a Lean Culture in a University

Justyna Maciąg, Jagiellonian University in Cracow, Poland

Justyna Maciąg (PhD of Business Administration, and Master of Economics in specialisations: education and accountancy) is a lecturer and researcher in the Institute of Public Affairs in Jagiellonian University in Cracow. In 2015–2016, she graduated in Studies in Lean Service, in 2017 she was awarded a Green Belt certificate. Her research interests are process management, quality management and Lean management in higher education and public organisations. She participated in several projects on process management in business and public organisation. She organises the cyclic seminar and polish network for Lean practitioners: Lean higher education under her function in Lean HE Steering Committee.

Chapter 4. "Lean" into your Service Model: An Institutional Case Study using Library Systems

Tony L.H. Wai and Lenore O'Connor, Macquarie University, Australia

Tony L.H. Wai is Discovery Services and Systems Librarian at Macquarie University Library. With over ten years of experience in frontline services coordination and systems management, he takes an innovative and holistic approach towards workflow improvement by leveraging systems. Formerly co-founder of a boutique ethnic marketing agency in Sydney, "do more with less" Lean thinking runs in the heart of Tony's business. He is passionate in charitable work, serving as a charter member of a Lions Club of Sydney Selective Inc., is a Lifeline crisis supporter and NSW Justice of the Peace. He is also a loving father of an adorable girl.

Lenore O'Connor is Library Services Manager (Information Access Services) at Macquarie University Library. Her library career began as a part-time Shelver while finishing her honours thesis in 2008; she fell in love with the library world, and never left. Lenore has held many library leadership positions, culminating in her current role ensuring clients are connected to information and resources; including physical and virtual frontline services, and learning and study spaces. Her goal is to promote a culture of continuous improvement across her teams, empower staff to take ownership of the services they deliver and create positive experiences.

*Chapter 5. Developing a Continuous Improvement
Service: From Inception to Reality in 18 Months*

Katie Wall and Emma Morris, Sheffield Hallam University, UK

Katie Wall is Continuous Improvement (CI) Manager at Sheffield Hallam University (SHU) and, with her then manager Claire Ward, led the formation of the CI Service at SHU. Katie's background includes project management, project implementation and business analysis and she has been employed in roles that involve process improvement for the majority of her career, in both higher education and the public sector. Katie is vice-chair of the Lean in HE North & Midlands group and is currently working towards her BCS Diploma in Business Analysis.

Emma Morris is a Continuous Improvement Analyst at Sheffield Hallam University and has worked in process improvement and project management roles for around 15 years. Emma has a passion for helping others to improve ways of working and over recent years has become a highly skilled trainer and facilitator. Emma recently played a key role in developing a new workshop facilitation training course, designed specifically for university staff who have previously undertaken continuous improvement training. Despite her current role being focussed mainly on continuous improvement, Emma is also currently working towards her BCS Diploma in Business Analysis.

SECTION II: PEOPLE

*Chapter 6. Identity and Values to Drive Respect
for People: A Case Study based on Embedding
Kindness as an Organizational Value*

*Susanne Clarke, Laura Roper, Dr Lois Farquharson, and
Vianna Renaud, Bournemouth University, UK*

Ms Susanne Clarke is Head of Service Excellence and Organisational Change Lead at Bournemouth University. Susanne has a track record in leading transformational change programmes and has expertise in the development of organisational performance frameworks. A Chartered Global Management Accountant and Chartered Fellow of the CMI, Susanne's key research interests are in strength-based approaches to change such as appreciative inquiry, kindness and improvement methodologies.

Ms Laura Roper is Accreditation Officer at Bournemouth University; she has extensive experience in higher education and her research and practice interest focus on embedding cultural change focused on kindness. Laura has introduced Ubuntu – a philosophy of human kindness and has developed workshops in skills development for teams which include active listening and communication.

Dr Lois Farquharson is Deputy Dean for Education and Professional Practice at Bournemouth University. Lois has a strong academic background in organisational change and development, culture, HRM and leadership. Lois is a Chartered Fellow of the CMI, an academic member of the CIPD and Fellow of the HEA. Lois has worked to support a number of organisations including Merlin Entertainment, Dorset Police, Investors in People Scotland, and various NHS Healthcare groups.

Vianna Renaud is a Placement Development Advisor for the Faculty of Media and Communication at Bournemouth University supporting students during the sandwich placement in the industry component of their academic course. She is also a Trustee for ASET, the Work Based and Placement Learning Association in the UK, and the UK Regional Coordinator for the International Association of Student Affairs and Services.

Chapter 7. Inspiring Sustainable Higher Education and Lean through a Lean Ambassadors Network

Tammi Sinha, and Claire Lorrain, Winchester University, UK

Dr Tammi Sinha is Senior Lecturer in Operations and Project Management at Winchester University Business School. She is Director of the Centre for Climate Change Education and Communication. After a decade in aerospace engineering, she joined Portsmouth Business School, then Winchester Business School. Tammi is a practitioner and researcher in systems thinking, visual leadership, operational excellence and Lean Six Sigma; with public and private sector organisations. She founded and co-leads a community of practice to embed improvement theory into action. Tammi has delivered invited keynotes and workshops at international conferences on Lean, Lean in Higher Education and the public sector.

Claire is Head of Continuous Improvement at the University of Winchester. She is an experienced European Excellence Model Assessor, having embedded EFQM within Winchester: winning the British Quality Foundation UK Excellence Award. She chairs The Association of Managers in Higher Education for Post 1992 and Guild HE institutions.

She holds the Lean Competency System 2B (black belt) Qualification. Claire's MSc Business Administration dissertation: "The Implementation of Lean in Higher Education in the UK, and its challenges" was presented on at EUROMA, the eminent international operations conference. Claire manages institutional-wide Lean projects, aiming to embed a culture of transformation and Lean.

Chapter 8. Improving Performance through Engagement – the Impact of Daily Stand Ups in the University of Strathclyde

John Hogg and Heather Lawrence, University of Strathclyde, UK

John Hogg is the Director of Continuous Improvement, University of Strathclyde. John joined the University of Strathclyde in 2002 and is responsible for providing leadership and direction to the University's continuous improvement activity and national higher education agendas including Value for Money, Effectiveness and Efficiencies. John is currently a member of Lean HE Global as Chair of Lean HE (Europe), a member of Universities Scotland Efficiencies & Effectiveness Committee, and is also on the Board of Management at Glasgow Kelvin College.

Heather Lawrence is the Head of Continuous Improvement, University of Strathclyde. Heather joined the University of Strathclyde in 2009 and leads strategic continuous improvement initiatives and change programmes across the University. Heather works with senior leaders to drive enhanced organisational performance by designing processes that achieve greater alignment to strategic objectives. Heather has a keen interest in benefits management realisation and is the co-author of the Guide to Evidencing the Benefits of Change in Higher Education.

Chapter 9. Lean Transformation Management among Employees in Universiti Putra Malaysia

Siti Raba'ah Hamzah and Dalina Kamarudin, Universiti Putra Malaysia

Dr. Siti Raba'ah Hamzah is Associate Professor of Faculty of Educational Studies, Universiti Putra Malaysia. She conducts research on volunteerism, leadership, and career development, international and national HRD. Although she has published many peer-reviewed articles, she has not limited her writings to academic publications but has directly influenced the field of leadership practice in Malaysia through training modules.

Despite her current role as a senior lecturer, she has a passion for helping staff and students in the university to undertake learning and professional experience through mobility and training programmes to improve competences, linked to professional profiles across the countries.

Dalina Kamarudin is Senior Administrator Officer at Universiti Putra Malaysia. She has dedicated her work in pursuing the field of management, especially towards Lean thinking in practice. Her responsibilities including Lean in Universiti Putra Malaysia as a mentor in the Lean Project at UPM (2014–2018), providing training and consulting services to internal clients in UPM and external clients in education, government, manufacturing and service organization.

SECTION III: PROJECTS

Chapter 10. Applying Lean in Projects; from Visualisations to Process Engineering – It's Covered!

Laura Hallett, York St John University, UK

Laura leads the Strategic Projects and Change team at York St John University, having worked in transformation and change for over ten years. She has significant expertise in successfully delivering large change programmes alongside undertaking business process improvements, and has presented internationally on her approach to project management. Laura has recently designed and launched a Project Framework to her organisation, in collaboration with her colleague, Christina Nichols. The accompanying training programme will see 10% of staff at the organisation being trained within the first six months of its rollout. In her spare time, Laura is a keen runner.

Chapter 11. BOSCARD A Scoping Tool for Lean Continuous Improvement Projects

Mark Robinson, University of St Andrews, UK

Mark Robinson is Director of Lean at the University of St Andrews and Managing Director of St Andrews Lean Consulting. Mark joined St Andrews' Lean Team 2007, co-developed the "St Andrews Model" and has

considerable experience applying Lean, particularly in universities. He has
delivered Lean training, facilitated Lean Rapid Improvement Events, and
consulted on establishing Lean Teams at universities all around the globe.
He has worked with the charity, government, law, military, and philanthropy
sectors, both in the UK and internationally. Mark, a founder member of the
Lean HE, regularly writes about and presents on Lean in HE.

Chapter 12. Six Sigma as a Method of Improving University Processes, the Case of the Academic Assessment Process

Justyna Maciąg, Jagiellonian University in Cracow, Poland

See Chapter 3

Chapter 13. Lean Training to Lean Projects

Marion Malcolm, University of Aberdeen, UK

Marion joined the University of Aberdeen Business Improvement Team
in January 2013 and became BI Team Lead in April 2017. She is passionate
about business improvement and undertakes a variety of roles (e.g. strategy
setting, scoping projects, facilitating BI events, training staff in lean
methodology and philosophy) within the team to promote a continuous
improvement culture in the University. Marion has significant experience
of working in the higher education sector in both teaching and research
departments and has a strong operational background in finance, HR etc.
Marion is a member of Lean HE (Europe).

SECTION IV: TECHNOLOGY

Chapter 14. Machine Leaning: Adapting Lean into a University IT Culture

Brian Stewart, LeeAnne Klein, and Melanie Clements, University of Alberta, Canada

Brian Stewart is the Deputy CIO at the University of Alberta, responsible
for Information Services and Technology, and Project and Organisational
Change Management. Brian works with his peer executive group to

provide strategic leadership to the application of information and communications technology (ICT). Initiatives include: introduction of inclusive and responsive IT governance, development of portfolio management, organisational change management and introduction of Lean operations. Brian is active in the Post Secondary ICT Community, chairing multiple sector groups. Brian has published on ICT in printing and education and contributes to Educause forums and publications. Brian is a PMP and holds multiple degrees.

LeeAnne Klein is the Change Management Practice Lead at the University of Alberta. LeeAnne is a seasoned professional with over ten years' hands on experience managing organizational change in several industries including oil and gas, technology, and manufacturing. LeeAnne specializes in organizational change management (OCM) and business process management (BPM). She has extension certificates in Business Process Management, Business Analysis and Project Management from Mount Royal University and Prosci Change Management certification.

Melanie Clements is a process analysis and improvement specialist at the University of Alberta with notable experience in the University IT sector, and specifically the areas of IT Service Management. She is skilled in IT change management, Lean and business process improvement methods. Melanie's significant experience in process improvement initiatives originates from an ITIL background, where her work was awarded ITIL project of the year in 2012 by the prestigious Pink Elephant consultancy.

Chapter 15. Can Information Services Lead a Network of Change Agents in a HEI?

Linda Spinks, University of Cambridge, UK

Linda Spinks has worked at the University of Cambridge for over 14 years both as a business analyst and more recently as Process Improvement Manager, a role she has held for over five years. She has significant experience of business analysis for Accenture, and Sainsbury's supermarkets. A recognised expert in Business Process Improvement, Business Process Mapping and Business Analysis; she is a Lean Six Sigma Black Belt, an international speaker on Lean and kata, the chair of the Triaster (Business Process Management software) user group. Linda until recently spent many years as Chair of Governors for a local primary school.

Chapter 16. Lean, Kanban and Agile, A Story of Continuous Improvement in a University Software Team

Richard Arkless, University of Edinburgh, UK

Richard Arkless is a Senior Business Analyst at the University of Edinburgh. He has been working in higher education for 18 years and has worked as a business analyst for the last 8. It was in this role that Richard first came across different approaches to process improvement while working on software projects, and has been interested in it ever since. He believes that it is always possible to find a better way of working and endeavours to put this into practice using Lean, agile and focussing on continuous improvement.

Chapter 17. Every Organisation Needs a Mole!

Stuart Morris, University of Lincoln, UK

Stuart Morris is the Continuous Improvement Facilitator in the Vice Chancellor's Office in the University of Lincoln. Following 28 years' service in the Royal Air Force, ending as a Senior Continuous Improvement Facilitator, he is now bringing the skills he learnt throughout his military career into the University, assisting staff to become more adaptable to change and removing the fear it instils. Qualified in Lean Six Sigma and Facilitation, his responsibilities in Lincoln are to assist staff to remove waste from their processes and ensure processes only add value to customers. He is a whiz with a Twitter account.

SECTION V: SUSTAINING

Chapter 18. Head, Heart, Hands: The Three Essentials to Sustaining Lean in HE

Valerie Runyan and Jennifer Bremner, Macquarie University, Australia

Valerie is currently working in an advisory capacity to support universities implementing Lean. As Director of Business Process Improvement in Macquarie University she established the highly successful Business Process Improvement initiative, going beyond this to found the highly successful Lean HE Australasia network, and host the 2017 Lean HE conference "Implementing, Measuring and Sustaining Change.". With a background as a Director of Student Services and in marketing and communications she is an expert in the international university sector, and a passionate advocate of Lean.

Jennifer is currently the Manager, Library Planning and Administration in Macquarie University, and was formerly the Business Process Improvement Manager at Macquarie University. She has experience in quality and strategic planning, and has published widely, including on "Lean in the library: building capacity by realigning staff and resources". She is passionate about innovative practices that enrich the student experience.

Chapter 19. Lessons from Implementing Lean at the Veterinary Teaching Hospital

Chris Shannon, The University of Queensland, Australia

Chris has a wealth of experience as a higher education manager with a background in management accounting and HR. He is experienced at facilitating process improvement and cultural change primarily using Lean, with a particular interest in building capability at the individual and team levels. Chris has a degree in HR, Graduate Certificate in Executive Leadership, and Masters in Leadership, and a long-term interest in career theory and leadership development.

Chapter 20. Cardiff University: A Lean University or a Better University?

Sarah Lethbridge, Cardiff University, UK

Sarah Lethbridge, is the Director of Executive Education, Cardiff Business School. She has worked on numerous Lean projects in hospitals, universities and public and private services. Her passion is to explore the interconnection of Lean concepts and tools, helping people to understand how all of the Lean ideas support and inform each other, to bring about the pursuit of organisational perfection. Sarah was a former Senior Research Associate in the Lean Enterprise Research Centre and fully funded on the Lean University project 2006–2009.

SECTION VI: CULTURE

Chapter 21. Developing a Culture – The Essentials for Continuous Improvement

Natasha Bennett and John Perkins, Middlesex University, UK

Natasha has worked in higher education for 13 years following a career in organisational development in both the private and public sector. Natasha established the Business Enhancement Team in 2014, following her previous role as Deputy Director Staff and Organisational Development with Middlesex University. Natasha is Chair of the Lean HE Southern Regional Group, and an active member across the transformational change and organisational development communities across the sector. Additionally, she shares responsibility for the delivery of the University People and Culture Strategy in collaboration with the HR Director.

John Perkins is a Business Enhancement Facilitator. John has worked with Lean and Continuous Improvement at Middlesex University since 2015. His background is varied, his career combing a mix of experience from Students' Union leadership to student recruitment, corporate governance and project work within the student experience directorate, at the University of Bedfordshire. A Six Sigma green belt, John is currently managing a long-term change programme for the Student Timetable. His role to date has covered the successful development and delivery of training, alongside end-to-end improvement project work across Academic Registry, Student Support and other Professional Service functions.

Chapter 22. Growing a Lean Approach in a Changing University

Brent Hurley and Stephen Yorkstone, Edinburgh Napier University, UK

Brent Hurley is a project, programme and portfolio management practitioner, and business/process improvement specialist. He has experience in the voluntary, private and public sectors, initially delivering pharmaceutical projects, then as Project Manager for the Scottish online flood maps, before moving into higher education. He leads on the coordination and delivery of Edinburgh Napier University's change portfolio, and supports development of University strategy. He is passionate about the people aspect of delivering change, with particular interests in embedding a culture of continuous improvement through building communities of practice; strategic alignment of change; visual communication; and generating ideas through creativity and innovation.

Stephen Yorkstone is an acknowledged authority on applying Lean in universities, leading successful initiatives in a number of institutes. He currently works applying Lean in Edinburgh Napier University, Scotland, UK. In 2016 he wrote the chapter "Lean Higher Education" in the Shingo Research Prize-winning "Routledge Companion to Lean Management". He has served as an editorial board member of the Lean Management Journal, founded and currently chairs the international community of practice for Lean in higher education, Lean HE. His current interest is in developing a framework to support facilitation for change.

Chapter 23. Making Sense of Learning, Practice and Theory

Gretel Stonebridge, Claire King, and Leanne Sowter,
Leicester University, UK

Gretel Stonebridge MCIPD is a Continuous Improvement Manager at the University of Leicester. In her role she facilitates and runs improvement interventions ranging from "process reviews" to tailored approaches and coaching. Her experience in continuous improvement and Lean originates from the manufacturing sector. She has experience of practically applying Lean and the Vanguard Method in both manufacturing and higher education. Gretel is very people-focussed and curious to understand the role of organisational culture in change and improvement.

Claire King (Member of ILM, Member of Association for Coaching) is a Continuous Improvement Specialist at the University of Leicester. Her work focuses on developing a culture of continuous improvement. Claire is an effective facilitator giving space and time to teams and individuals to improve their own process through workshops and providing coaching. Claire has experience of leading small teams, continuous improvement and designing and delivering training courses within higher education, local authorities and within the voluntary sector.

Leanne Sowter is a PRINCE2 qualified and Lean Six Sigma yellow belt certified Continuous Improvement Facilitator at the University of Leicester. She has worked in numerous high-profile transformational projects and currently delivers significant local customer-focussed process improvements. She embraces the challenge of cultivating an empowering change culture in support of the institution's strategic vision. When not covered in layers of post-it notes Leanne enjoys complaining about spending prolonged periods of time on the train and pretending that she isn't really feeding the neighbour's cat.

Chapter 24. What If We Knew the Future Could be Different!

Dr Radka Newton, Lancaster University, UK

Radka is an enthusiastic leader, coach and skilled facilitator with experience of living and working in multiple cultures. In her role as a Director of a global MSc Management in Lancaster University she has applied Lean methodology to operations process improvement and she is committed to empowering students as partners in curriculum co-creation through service design. She is a Senior Teaching Fellow in Strategic Management and Innovation and her overarching research is in the deployment of Lean methodology and service design in the HE sector, investigating the context of organisational culture and the role of resistance to change.

Introduction

BACKGROUND

Lean is a high-performance methodology, enabling organisations to focus on improvement and value. Respect for people and continuous improvement are the foundations of lean. Lean has a long history in manufacturing, more recently in service environments, health, and the wider public sector.

The application of lean in higher education (HE) has the potential to transform this sector too, and there is a growing number of lean practitioners in universities.

Higher education is regarded as amongst the hardest sectors in which to apply lean; the nature of universities resists being changed, and their organizational cultures are far from the manufacturing environment where lean was born. The way HE organisations are structured, funded, and function across the globe is far from homogenous; one size is unlikely to fit all. However, the sector is also a dynamic one; and a mature understanding of lean, as a philosophy, led by principles, suggests there are many ways HE could grow through lean.

Over the past five years, the Lean HE community of practice has brought together many people, doing many things with lean in the sector. With the title of the organisations' 2018 conference in UiT the Arctic University of Norway in Tromsø, being "Everyday Lean – from your story to my story" it was felt that now was the time for the community to create a book together, to share what they have learnt.

ABOUT THIS BOOK

This book is a collection of work that reflects the state-of-the-art in the global practical application of lean for higher education. It aims to demonstrate the diversity of how lean is applied in universities, in a way that can inspire others to deeply engage with lean thinking in their own unique context; in order to drive successful, sustainable, lean work.

Contributions are from both well-known experts in lean HE and up-and-coming practitioners. Authors live in countries such as Australia, Canada, Malaysia, Poland, the UK, and the USA. They represent all flavours of higher education, from applied teaching institutions, to research-focussed universities; from universities less than 50 years old, to universities more than 800 years old.

Contributions tend to focus on lean as applied across universities as a whole, often addressing the administrative support or professional services side of how these institutions work. The application of lean is not limited, however, purely to the administration of such organisations, but also can be applied to the primary purpose of universities: teaching and research. For deep insight into how lean can impact on teaching, not just in higher education, Vincent Wiegel's 2019 book offers a unique and valuable perspective.

This volume is not focused on lean theory, as there are already many books that unpack this. Instead it discusses how HE institutions have taken lean forward and what they have achieved with it, in a way that others can share and learn from.

It is hoped that the rich and wide perspectives in this book will enable the reader to understand the many ways that lean thinking is applied in higher education around the world, and moreover, can be applied in the readers' own work.

Making the Most of this Book

The book is comprised of six sections, namely: Starting Out, People, Projects, Technology, Sustaining, and Culture.

Each chapter is identified as either a case study, approach, or tool, and could be for example:

- A case study of how institutions have applied lean, what went well, what the challenges were, and what lessons were learned
- A description of a lean technique or approach that has been developed within HE, with a focus on how this could be applied by other practitioners
- A theme that has emerged from practice, offering practical benefits and understanding

Each contribution is also drawn from a different institution, allowing for the reader to select an area of most interest and relevance to them.

OVERVIEW

Section I: Starting Out

In the Lean HE community there are many universities seeking to begin their journey, and this section aims to outline some of the things to know and do when starting lean in this sector.

Chapter 1. Establishing Process Improvement Capability in Higher Education **[Research]:**
Rachel McAssey, The University of Sheffield, UK

Strategic questions faced include where to place a function, how many people do we need for it, how should we talk about it? These questions are addressed by Rachel McAssey in Chapter 1, where she outlines her research into how process improvement capability is established.

Chapter 2. Tools to Get You Started **[Tool]:**
Bonnie Slykhuis, Des Moines Area Community College, Ankeny, IA,

Having set off, there are a number of operational steps to take to bringing about a successful improvement initiative. This is the theme of Bonnie Slyhuis' chapter "Tools to Get You Started".

Chapter 3. VSM as a Tool for Creating a Lean Culture in a University
[Tool]:
Justyna Maciąg, Jagiellonian University in Cracow, Poland

One of the central tools used in lean and process improvement is value stream mapping, and Justyna Maciąg from the eminent Jagiellonian University in Crakow outlines value stream mapping in theory, and in how she has used it practically for her institution.

Chapter 4. "Lean" into your Service Model: An Institutional
Case Study using Library Systems **[Institutional Case Study]:**
Tony L.H. Wai, and Lenore O'Connor, Macquarie University,
Australia

This case study outlines how Macquarie University Library launched their activity to apply lean and improve their work, giving two practical examples of how it worked in practice.

Chapter 5. Developing a Continuous Improvement Service:
From Inception to Reality in 18 months **[Approach]:**
Katie Wall and Emma Morris, Sheffield Hallam University, UK

Finally, in this section Katie Wall outlines how they established the highly successful Continuous Improvement Service in Sheffield Hallam University in a timescale of just 18 months.

Section II: People

It is the experience of many lean thinkers that at the heart of success lies good people. In this section, chapters look at values, techniques, tools and ways of measuring how people engage and enable lean.

Chapter 6. Identity and Values to Drive Respect for People:
A Case Study Based on Embedding Kindness as an Organizational
Value **[Case Study]:**
Susanne Clarke, Laura Roper, Lois Farquharson, and
Vianna Renaud, Bournemouth University, UK

Bournemouth University is leading the way in the practical application of "kindness" as a concept, to enable customer service excellence. In this chapter the authors relate kindness to lean's "respect for people", and propose two experiments to apply kindness in lean initiatives.

Chapter 7. Inspiring Sustainable Higher Education and Lean
through a Lean Ambassadors Network **[Approach]:**
Tammi Sinha and Claire Lorrain, Winchester University, UK

Exploring how people are key to embedding lean, Chapter 7 describes the Lean Ambassadors Network worked in the University of Winchester, bringing together people to support their improvement work through training and networking.

Chapter 8. Improving Performance through Engagement – the Impact of
Daily Stand Ups in the University of Strathclyde **[Approach]:**
John Hogg and Heather Lawrence, University of Strathclyde, UK

Daily team huddles might seem counter to many HE cultures, but the University of Strathclyde has been successfully leading the way in applying this approach to bringing people together in universities. This chapter outlines how they've managed this, what it looks like in practice, and outlines the results they've seen.

Chapter 9. Lean Transformation Management among Employees
in Universiti Putra Malaysia **[Case Study]:**
Siti Raba'ah Hamzah and Dalina Kamarudin, Universiti Putra Malaysia

University cultures globally are not homogenous however, and the next chapter from the Universiti Putra Malaysia discusses how they used a survey approach to assess readiness for change amongst their employees, against a challenging background.

Section III: Projects

Often in university implementations of lean, people talk of lean "projects"; however, this is not without controversy. Some thinkers would remind us that seeing lean as a project, as different from business as usual, is to miss the point that lean has to be about daily work. Nevertheless, often lean begins with a series of projects, uses project tools at certain stages, learns from different project approaches, and links project work to learning to become lean.

Chapter 10. Applying Lean in Projects; from Visualisations to Process Engineering – It's Covered! **[Approach]:**
Laura Hallett, York St John University, UK

Firstly, we see an example of how lean thinking can support successful project outcomes, along with a range of techniques used to achieve this in York St John University.

Chapter 11. BOSCARD A Scoping Tool for Lean Continuous Improvement Projects **[Tool]:**
Mark Robinson, University of St Andrews, UK

Famously in the sector, the University of St Andrews proposes a project-type approach to lean, and here Mark Robinson outlines one of the key tools they use for this in the early stages of a project: BOSCARD analysis. This chapter includes developments beyond BOSCARD, and key questions to help facilitate this.

Chapter 12. Six Sigma as a Method of Improving University Processes, the Cease of the Academic Assessment Process **[Case Study]:**
Justyna Maciąg, Jagiellonian University in Cracow, Poland

Six Sigma is as a hugely successful approach to managing quality improvement and eliminating defects, applied in high volume transactional processes. There are some applications where Six Sigma has been applied to HE processes, and here we see a case study of this in relation to academic assessment.

Chapter 13. Lean Training to Lean Projects **[Approach]:**
Marion Malcolm, University of Aberdeen, UK

This section concludes with the story of how Aberdeen University in Scotland links their lean training to a project approach, and how this supports their improvement and growth towards a lean culture.

Section IV: Technology

The rise of technology is often cited as one of the biggest changes facing the world of work today. There is also a large intersection between lean and technology, and active discussion in lean about what the right relationship between lean and technology is. Can lean "fix" processes before technology automates them? Should technology functions take responsibility for leading lean?

Chapter 14. Machine Leaning: Adapting Lean into a University IT Culture **[Case Study]:**
Brian Stewart, LeeAnne Klein, and Melanie Clements, University of Alberta, Canada

The first chapter in this section looks at how the Library in the University of Alberta, Canada launched their lean initiative with work focusing on technology, and what they learned from this.

Chapter 15. Can Information Services Lead a Network of Change Agents in a HEI? **[Case Study]:**
Linda Spinks, University of Cambridge, UK

At time of writing, based in the Information Services division in the University of Cambridge, Linda Spinks is using a kata approach, among other techniques, to build a network of lean change agents; this chapter looks at how this has happened, and what the implications of a technology department leading this initiative are.

Chapter 16. Lean, Kanban and Agile, A Story of Continuous Improvement in a University Software Team **[Case Study]:**
Richard Arkless, University of Edinburgh, UK

The Student Systems team in the University of Edinburgh are passionate about lean, and passionate about their systems development. This chapter describes how they have taken lean and agile approaches, practically used them to help manage their tasks, and what the result has been.

Chapter 17. Every Organisation Needs a Mole **[Tool]:**
Stuart Morris, University of Lincoln, UK

This next short chapter focusses on one particular technological tool for supporting staff engagement, social media. Particularly the increasingly famous "Muda Mole" character in the University of Lincoln.

Section V: Sustaining

While often lean can bring about short-term improvements, the real benefits of lean are in sustaining activity across the long term. With some universities now having been applying lean for well over a decade, this section looks at taking a holistic approach, carefully scaling your activity, working across different cultures, and taking the long view.

Chapter 18. Head, Heart, Hands: The Three Essentials to Sustaining Lean in HE **[Approach]:**
Valerie Runyan and Jennifer Bremner, Macquarie University, Australia

Macquarie University in Australia is often seen as the benchmark of lean success in Australasian HE. This chapter looks at their holistic approach to lean and how it enabled their achievements so far.

Chapter 19. Lessons from Implementing Lean at the Veterinary Teaching Hospital **[Case Study]:**
Chris Shannon, The University of Queensland, Australia

Staying in Australia, this time looking at the Veterinary Teaching Hospital in the University of Queensland; this chapter looks at lessons learned when comparing an ambitious program of work across an entire institution, in contrast with a more tightly scoped intervention.

Chapter 20. Cardiff University: A Lean University or a Better University? **[Case Study]:**
Sarah Lethbridge, Cardiff University, UK

Sarah Lethbridge reflects on the ten years since the University of Cardiff launched the first lean implementation in an UK University, the context that led to the birth of that lean initiative, the lessons that have emerged, and where Cardiff University is going next.

Section VI: Culture

Culture is perhaps a theme that has emerged across all of these sections, culture as the way in which groups of people behave; and moving these behaviors towards respect for people and continuous improvement being the aim of lean. This section looks at what the key ingredients are for developing such a culture, tells the stories of cultural evolutions towards lean, looks at how we make sense of all of this, before challenging us to think differently about bringing people on a lean journey.

Chapter 21. Developing a Culture – the Essentials for Continuous Improvement **[Approach]:**
Natasha Bennett and John Perkins, Middlesex University, UK

The first chapter in this section looks at the approach that was built in Middlesex University to build a culture of continuous improvement, describing how they bring together individuals to create a consistent continuous improvement programme.

Chapter 22. Growing a Lean Approach in a Changing University **[Case Study]:**
Brent Hurley and Stephen Yorkstone, Edinburgh Napier University, UK

Edinburgh Napier University has been experimenting with lean type activity since 2009, this case study chapter describes that journey, and outlines the current approach that the university is undertaking.

Chapter 23. Making Sense of Learning, Practice and Theory **[Approach]:**
Gretel Stonebridge, Claire King, and Leanne Sowter, Leicester University, UK

The chapter "Making sense of learning, practice and theory" tells the story of now the University of Leicester created their approach, going beyond book learning to build a practical approach that met their organisations unique culture.

Chapter 24. What If We Knew the Future Could be Different! **[Approach]:**
Dr Radka Newton, Lancaster University, UK

Finally, Dr Radka Newton offers a challenge to the culture of lean itself in the context of universities, asking the question of whether we really take respect for people seriously in universities, and proposing we should take more time to think about our improvement activity, to make a genuine difference.

It is hoped that this anthology will be a helpful resource to those seeking to understand and apply lean in Universities, and further afield, in order to further improve our organisations and benefit their vital work for the world around us.

Stephen Yorkstone
Business Improvement Consultant, Edinburgh Napier University
Chair, Lean HE

Section I

Starting Out

1

Establishing Process Improvement Capability in Higher Education

Rachel McAssey

CONTENTS

INTRODUCTION

Higher education (HE) establishments across the globe have the shared aim of delivering high-quality teaching to undergraduate and graduate students alongside undertaking and delivering research. Comparing HE globally is complex, due to different funding mechanisms and approaches to delivering student experience. Universities may also seem unusual places to implement methodologies such as Lean from the private sector. However, the experience of many university staff suggests that learning from other sectors can be a highly successful way of enabling positive change.

Process improvement activity in HE is growing, partly in response to effectiveness and efficiency, partly in response to delivering better experiences to students but also as a response to today's rapidly changing political and economic environment.

This chapter seeks to evidence what higher education organisations are currently doing to embed process improvement capability and to support those considering undertaking such activity or those already doing so.

DATA

This chapter is a piece of primary-based research principally shaped by responses to a survey conducted in the spring and summer of 2018. It attracted 63 unique responses from higher education institutions, 30 from Europe, 17 from USA and Canada, 16 from Australasia. There were not any responses from universities based elsewhere. A series of short follow-up interviews also informed this research.

The format and structure are an extension of research into UK HE undertaken by the author and Stephen Yorkstone.*

A level of caution should be applied when reviewing the outputs of this research; the sample size is relatively small. It is likely that there are many other universities and colleges that have levels of process improvement capability that have not responded to the survey: due to the way the survey was publicised (primarily via Lean HE networks) and/or the timing of the survey (May–August 2018).

---

* https://www.ucisa.ac.uk/publications/pcmg_epic

WHAT ARE THE DRIVERS FOR ESTABLISHING PROCESS IMPROVEMENT CAPABILITY IN HIGHER EDUCATION?

The research identified several drivers for establishing process improvement capability. The primary driver was to drive effectiveness and efficiency within the institution, with student experience being the second most reported driver.

Within the UK the 2011 Diamond Report* is reported as having been an impetus for establishing process improvement capability. Elsewhere, there are no reports of key national reports that were fundamental to the establishment of capability. However, more generally changes in funding for universities appear to drive the imperative for effectiveness and efficiency programmes and projects.

Several respondents identified other reasons for creating capability, these include: risk mitigation, IT enabled transformation and restructuring (Figure 1.1).

WHAT IS THE CURRENT PATTERN OF ACTIVITY OF PROCESS IMPROVEMENT INITIATIVES IN HIGHER EDUCATION?

Date Established

Of the 53 Institutions that responded to this question, dates ranged from "we've always done this" to 2018. With notable peaks in 2012 (7 institutions), 2014 (9 institutions) and 2017 (10 institutions) (Figure 1.2).

Trends in Continental Areas

Australasia reported limited process improvement capability until 2013; there is a growth trend year on year up until 2017.

Europe had limited process improvement capability until 2012, there is a growth trend until 2017, with a peak in process improvement capability being established in 2017.

---

* Efficiency and Effectiveness in Higher Education, A Report by the Universities UK Efficiency Task Group, September 2011.

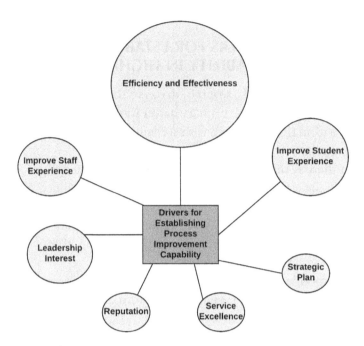

FIGURE 1.1
Drivers for establishing process improvement capability.

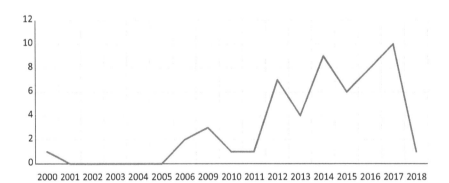

FIGURE 1.2
Date capability established.

USA and Canada show the greatest maturity in creating process improvement capability. There was statistically valid growth from 2010, with peaks in 2012 and 2015.

WHERE IS TEAM-BASED/LOCATION IN THE ORGANISATIONAL STRUCTURE?

The most frequently identified reporting position (where there is one formal team) was the Vice-Chancellor/Principal/Executive's Office (29%), with Planning second at (14%) and Human Resources third (10%). The responses demonstrate that there is huge variation in reporting structures for process improvement capability.

There is a correlation between offices that have been more recently created (post 2015) and the reporting structure to Vice-Chancellor/Principal/Executive's. In follow up interviews, respondents reported that the justification for this reporting line was to demonstrate neutrality and senior buy-in.

Follow-up interviews with institutions in the UK and USA also indicated that there appears to be a movement of standalone offices/units/staff moving into larger change offices and/or project/programme management offices.

Size of Team

There is huge variation in team sizes; there is no correlation between size of team and reporting line nor is there correlation between size and date of establishment or geographical location (Table 1.1).

Many teams have three or fewer staff (64%), with between 3.5 FTE (full time equivalent staff) and 6 FTE being the next common (16%).

47% of respondents identified that there had been a previous iteration/attempt to establish process improvement capability within the institution. 18% replied that there had not been any previous attempts to establish process improvement capability and 35% did not know. The data does not evidence a pattern of previous attempts to establish process improvement capability based on location or reporting line. The data evidences huge variation in the nature of the previous attempts to implement improvement methodologies: from implementing Total Quality Management, IT systems projects, Systems Thinking and Project Management approaches.

TABLE 1.1

Size of Process Improvement Teams/Functions

Team Size (Full Time Equivalent (FTE))	Quantity
0	2
0.25–1	11
1.01–2	13
2.01–3	15
3.01–6	10
6.01–10	4
10.01–20	7
20.01–50	1

There are several ways that universities have created process improvement capability. 56% have used consultancy to create capability: of those that used consultancy 55% used non-HE consultants and 45% used consultancy from other universities. 31% recruited skilled people, 13% used other methods (predominantly reading, external training and online resources). There is evidence of increasing use (2014 onwards) of consultants from other higher education institutions to help set up process improvement capability.

Additionally, there was a notable sub-set of respondent universities that had several small improvement teams/individuals that had been established to support key functions: Student Services; Finance Departments and specific projects being the most frequently cited.

Job Titles and Language Used within Higher Education

There is a range of titles use to describe staff who provide process improvement expertise within universities and colleges. The most frequently reported include (in order of popularity):

1. Process Improvement
2. Continuous Improvement
3. Business Improvement
4. Service Improvement
5. Lean
6. Project Manager

There are also several roles with: change; business change; business enhancement; service excellence/design.

Most frequent roles included:

1. Manager
2. Lead
3. Officer
4. Analyst
5. Head
6. Consultant
7. Director

The primary research and supporting interviews demonstrate that institutions are moving away from having job titles that are exclusively Lean. Several reasons were mentioned (including): "we want to fully represent our service offering" and "we do not want to tie ourselves to one methodology"*.

Across the three continental areas that responded there was not an identifiable pattern in Australasia – although no use of the word *Lean* in job titles. In Europe "Continuous Improvement" and "Process Improvement" are the most common trend. In the USA and Canada, "Continuous Improvement" was the most reported title although it also showed the biggest range and variation in job titles.

WHAT METHODOLOGIES ARE CURRENTLY BEING USED?

The HE sector is currently using a variety of approaches and methodologies to establish capability. The predominant sector approaches are Lean and Lean Six Sigma/Six Sigma, with the business process review (BPR) process in third place. It is clear that institutions are mainly taking a mixed model approach to improvement, with only five purists identifying as Lean exclusively (Table 1.2).

Although there is consistent application of Lean across the three continental areas that responded (probably in reflection of the way the survey was promoted), there is worldwide variation in the way that

---

* Anonymous interview respondents.

TABLE 1.2

Process Improvement Methodologies (Excludes Methodologies Mentioned Only Once)

	Australasia	Europe	USA and Canada	Total Individual Institutions that Identified using the Methodology
Agile	6	1	6	13
Business Process Review	5	10	5	20
Coaching and Mentoring	0	2	0	2
ITIL	1	4	2	7
Lean	12	22	13	47
Lean Six Sigma/Six Sigma	12	12	8	31
Operational Excellence	2	2	7	11
Prince 2	4	5	0	9
Prosci	1	5	4	10
Service Design	4	5	0	9
Service Excellence	5	3	4	12
Systems Thinking	3	6	2	11

other methodologies are used and applied. During follow up interviews, participants cited this variation as a function of factors such as: reporting line, larger remit, function of office/department and as from the interest and skill set of direct hires.

There was also a high of difference in the number of identified methodologies and approaches used institutionally, with ten being the highest (one respondent) and seven approaches (five institutions) being next highest. On average people identified 3.62 methodologies being used.

There is an apparent juxtaposition between Lean being the most popular methodology used within the services or offices surveyed and the decline in using the world "Lean" in job titles and or team names. One of the reasons cited is: in recognition of the number of different improvement approaches used by a team or office, the terms "process/business/continuous improvement" was a more accurate description rather than suggesting the function was exclusively a Lean team. This correlates with the findings on job titles.

WHAT SERVICES OR ACTIVITIES CONSTITUTE THE REMIT OF PROCESS IMPROVEMENT?

When establishing process improvement capability, clarity around services that the function will deliver and support is as an enabler for success. Frequently process improvement functions are founded with a narrow set of service offerings, and as these functions become more established the variety of service offering tends to increase.

Initially functions tend to focus on the process mapping workshops and the delivery of localised and/or institutional process improvement projects as a primary purpose and then grow the offering based on institutional need/demand. Delivering training, both general process improvement training and practitioner training is also popular.

The survey respondents indicated that the following top ten services that they offer are, in order:

1. Business Process Mapping Workshops (92%)
2. Process Improvement Projects (84%)
3. Internal Consultancy (82%)
4. Training (76%)
5. Rapid Improvement Events (58%)
6. Practitioner Training (54%)
7. Working with Institutional Programme/Project Management Offices (34%)
8. Teaching (20%)
9. External Consultancy (20%)
10. Communication Cells (14%)

Other service offerings of note included: robotic automation and IT development, coaching, communities of practice, 5S interventions and demand workshops. The survey showed that many functions/offices are offering a range of services (Table 1.3).

There is no correlation between unit/team size and number of services offered, and the range of services is consistent across the three continental divisions. There is some correlation between maturity of the team/office and the provision of external consultancy.

TABLE 1.3

No. of Services Offered

No. Services Offered	Percentage of Respondents
1	6%
2	2%
3	6%
4	18%
5	16%
6	26%
7	12%
8	12%
9	2%
10	2%

Key Areas of Success

There is a pattern of successful activity primarily amongst the institutional secondary processes (not teaching or research). The most common areas for success included:

- Finance
- Human Resources
- Academic Registry/Student Administration
- Library
- Estates and Facilities
- Student wellbeing/counselling
- IT

WHAT ARE THE CHALLENGES AND SUCCESS FACTORS FOR ESTABLISHING PROCESS IMPROVEMENT CAPABILITY?

Survey respondents identified several challenges to establishing process improvement capability, the top three challenges are:

- Absence of continuous improvement culture
- Getting leadership buy-in
- Lack of staff time to participate in improvement activities (Figure 1.3)

Challenges						Success Factors		
Absence of continuous improvement culture						Leadership endorsement		
	Getting leadership buy-in					Customer/staff satisfaction		
		Lack of staff time to participate in improvement activities				Continuous Improvement Culture		
			Insufficient change management/staff resistance		Establishing Process Improvement Capability	Involving people		
				No/insufficient budget		Expert process improvement staff		
		Silo working				Examples/ case studies		
			Activity not linked to strategy			Training		
				Not evidencing benefits		Strategic alignment		
				Lack of ownership		Solid framework		
					Time to build expertise	Funding		

FIGURE 1.3

Challenges and success factors for establishing process improvement capability.

CONCLUSIONS

There is a trend to move improvement capability away from operational areas such as Information Services. However, there also appears to be growing interest in enhancing improvement activities with technology, for example using robotic process automation. It will be interesting to review whether the growing interest in automation and university digital strategies affect reporting lines of the future.

There is a strong trend for small, neutral teams supporting universities with continuous improvement activities at both strategic and local level. Respondents cited the placing of functions with reporting lines to senior university staff as leadership recognition of the importance and effectiveness of process improvement capability. Increasingly, offices and functions are applying a more rigorous approach to evidencing the benefits of process improvement activities. Also, continuous improvement is a more widely used/recognised approach in other sectors; it is likely that higher education is learning from the experiences of other service sectors.

BIBLIOGRAPHY

Balzer, W.K. (2010). *Higher Education: Increasing the Value and Performance of University Processes*, Productivity Press.

Yorkstone, S. (2016). Lean universities. In: Netland, T. & Powell, D. *The Routledge Companion to Lean Management*, Routledge, ISBN: 978-1138920590.

2

Tools to Get You Started

Bonnie Slykhuis

CONTENTS

WHAT IS LEAN AND CONTINUOUS IMPROVEMENT?

When people hear the word Lean they often think of a reduction in staffing and doing more with less. Lean is not an acronym, it's a term that was first used by John Krafcik, an MIT graduate student, in an article he published in 1988. Jim Womack and Daniel Jones picked up the term and used it in their 1990 book *The Machine That Changed the World* making the word synonymous with process improvement. Lean focuses on using tools or step by step methods to remove waste from work processes so information and/or product flows more efficiently throughout a process.

In Lean, all work steps are sorted into two basic categories, value-added (VA) and non-value-added (NVA).

Value-added steps are steps that are necessary to provide a product or service. We like to say it changes the form, fit or function of a product or service. We determine VA steps based on their value to the customer. These include both internal and external customers. If given a choice would the customer be willing to pay for the step if they could see the whole process? Does it create value for them? Examples of VA steps in higher education would include students filling out an application, submitting it, Admissions reviewing the application for completeness and eligibility, Admissions processing the application in the system, and students receiving letters or emails informing them of their status.

Non-value-added steps are those that create no value in the process. Also called wastes, these activities consume valuable time, money, personnel and materials. If given a choice, customers would not be willing to pay for these. Staying with the example of students submitting an application, non-value-added steps would include reentering a paper application into an electronic system, re-formatting addresses, searching or calling for missing information, rechecking the same information multiple times, printing and filing copies. Let's use another example to show non-value-added work. Imagine your department or workgroup is holding a big meeting. Someone is assigned to make the big pot of coffee for the group. In this example the person whose job it is to make the coffee does not drink coffee and has not seen it done. Much like a new employee who doesn't receive proper training. These might be the steps the person goes through (Figure 2.1).

In looking at the steps, how long would it take this person to make coffee compared to someone who drinks coffee and makes it regularly?

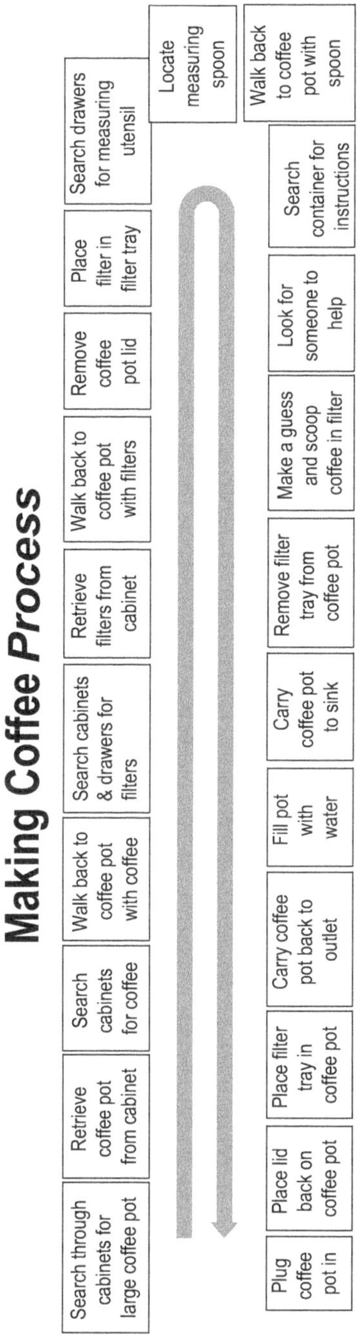

Making Coffee *Process*

Search through cabinets for large coffee pot	Retrieve coffee pot from cabinet	Search cabinets for coffee	Walk back to coffee pot with coffee	Search cabinets & drawers for filters	Retrieve filters from cabinet	Walk back to coffee pot with filters	Remove coffee pot lid	Place filter in filter tray	Search drawers for measuring utensil	Locate measuring spoon

Walk back to coffee pot with spoon

Plug coffee pot in	Place lid back on coffee pot	Place filter tray in coffee pot	Carry coffee pot back to outlet	Fill pot with water	Carry coffee pot to sink	Remove filter tray from coffee pot	Make a guess and scoop coffee in filter	Look for someone to help	Search container for instructions

FIGURE 2.1

Coffee-making process.

Likely much more time. Next question, what is the quality expectation? Can you be guaranteed a good cup of coffee? Probably not. In the case of Lean we would use the process mapping tool to map out all the steps in the process and then evaluate each one to determine whether it is VA or NVA (Figure 2.2).

These NVA steps delay service to the customer, create extra work that costs money and diminishes the quality. The goal of any process improvement is to remove waste from the process to improve efficiency and quality. To do that we use simple Lean tools and methodologies such as visual controls, point of use storage, replenishment triggers and more. It's important to train people how to recognize waste, because if you can recognize it you can work to reduce or eliminate it (Figure 2.3).

Lean, continuous process improvement, rapid process improvement, kaizen or whatever other term you want to use is not important. What is important is that you've made the decision to start. There is no magic bullet, instruction guide or one method for doing continuous improvement. It varies greatly by institution and you must find, build and adapt methods that work for you. In the following paragraphs are steps to guide you through getting started based on years of experience working with many organizations.

If you're considering embarking on a continuous improvement journey of any kind you should first research what others are doing. Find others who are already doing formalized continuous improvement and how they are doing it. This book contains several case studies and approaches from people whom I'm confident would be willing to share their knowledge. You will find that Lean is not standard across institutions. It needs to be customized to fit each environment. By researching others, you can begin gathering best practices and building a network of Lean resources to draw from when needed. Things to look for and take note of in your research:

- Internal support structure:
  o Who's leading the charge?
  o Do they have staff dedicated to continuous improvement?
  o What responsibility does each level of the organization have in supporting Lean activities?
- Methods and models used:
  o How do they educate staff and faculty about Lean?
  o What tools are used to evaluate processes, organize workspaces and solve problems?
  o Are their methods standardized or do they vary each time?

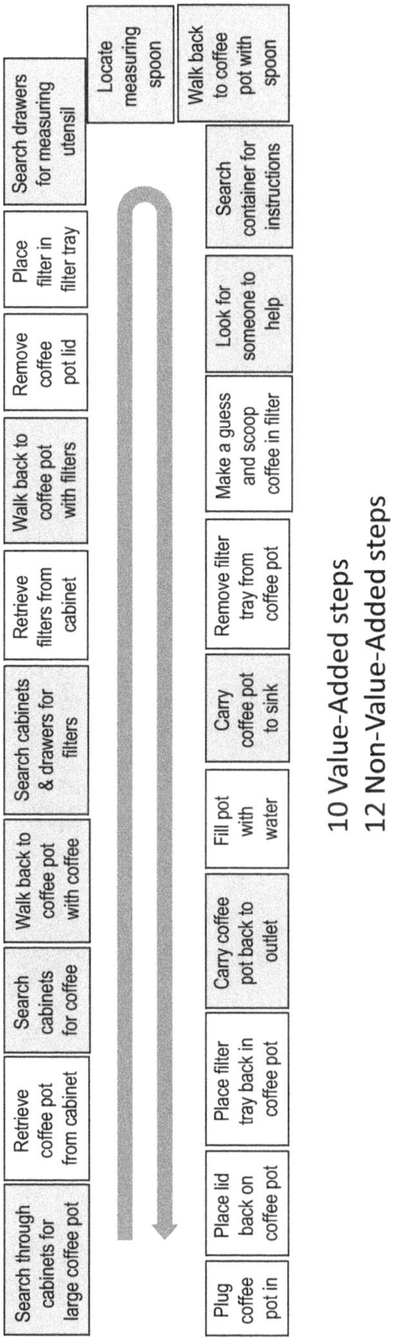

Search through cabinets for large coffee pot	Retrieve coffee pot from cabinet	Search cabinets for coffee	Walk back to coffee pot with coffee	Search cabinets & drawers for filters	Retrieve filters from cabinet	Walk back to coffee pot with filters	Remove coffee pot lid	Place filter in filter tray	Search drawers for measuring utensil	Locate measuring spoon

Plug coffee pot in	Place filter tray back in coffee pot	Carry coffee pot back to outlet	Fill pot with water	Carry coffee pot to sink	Remove filter tray from coffee pot	Make a guess and scoop coffee in filter	Look for someone to help	Search container for instructions	Walk back to coffee pot with spoon

Place lid back on coffee pot

10 Value-Added steps

12 Non-Value-Added steps

FIGURE 2.2

Identifying value.

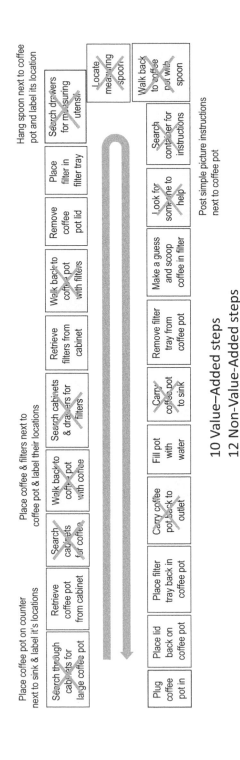

FIGURE 2.3
Removing non-value-added.

- Performance metrics:
    - Are metrics collected?
    - If so, what's the expectation?
    - For example, are their goals on cost savings/cost avoidance or are they expected to align with strategic initiatives?
- Case studies:
    - Do they have specific examples of projects, successes and challenges they're willing to share?
- Resources:
    - Do they utilize internal staff, external consultants or a combination to facilitate, train or support Lean activities?
    - For example, do they use consultants, faculty or internal staff to help design and deliver training?

Research institutions similar to yours and also some that are different. Look for common themes, methods, best practices and advice. It's helpful to have a variety of information in your toolbox for when you begin designing your lean roadmap.

WHERE ARE YOU GOING?

So, your institution is considering (or should consider) actively pursuing a continuous improvement program. The first question you should be asking is, "Why do it?" You're probably thinking, "Well why not as the benefits are so numerous." Still, it's important to have clear goals and expectations from the beginning and to be able to communicate the *why* to everyone. It's difficult to give people direction if you don't know where you're going. If you've done your homework of researching what others are doing you can gain a better insight as to their reasons for doing Lean, which may mirror your own. Take time to identify what's driving your need to change? In other words, what's your sense of urgency? Read the book *Our Iceberg is Melting,* by John Cotter. If there is no urgent need to change, it will be tough to get employee buy-in and support to make changes. Work with leadership to identify the need for Lean so it can be effectively and consistently communicated. One method to do this is through a half or full day group work session. Have key leaders work through answering the following questions.

Why Lean and Why Now?

What's driving the decision? Is it budget, growth, low enrollment, technology, etc.? As an example, Des Moines Area Community College's sense of urgency was due to several factors. Student enrollment had grown 43% in five years, the state of Iowa drastically cut college funding, numerous experienced employees were at retirement age, student and technology needs were rapidly changing, and they were preparing for an accreditation renewal. Have the group prepare and agree on a *why* statement.

What Do You Expect to Achieve?

In addition to identifying the sense of urgency, leaders should also identify high level goals or outcomes they are striving for. Examples: improve student access to quality services, reduce cost, all departments actively working on continuous improvements, prioritization of initiatives, standardize how we evaluate and prioritize college improvements, and standardize operations across locations. What will this initiative help the college to achieve?

What Are the Benefits to the Organization?

These can mirror what you identified previously but will hopefully narrow in on what the values are to your customers and students. Examples: reduce need for (or amount of) tuition increase, reduce costs, improve service, increase retention, expand technology, reduce workload, upgrade technology, and become proactive vs. reactive in meeting customer/student needs.

How Will It Benefit Employees?

Employees need to know how this initiative will impact them, their WIIFM (What's In It For Me). What can they expect and why should they care? Examples of common benefits to employees include: reduce frustration, minimize or eliminate errors, save time, eliminate unnecessary steps, better understanding of work processes, and improve communications between and within departments.

Potential Impact to Students, Employees, Customers, and the Institution If You Do Nothing

Sometimes the best way to convince the masses is by giving them a choice. Give them something to say no to. In this case provide a perspective of how inaction will also impact the college, students, staff and faculty. Change is happening faster now than at any time in history. Those institutions that are reluctant to change or are slow to change will get left behind or cease to exist all together as budgets grow tighter, learning methods and resources change, and competition improves. Loss of students, accreditation, funding, services, benefits and reputation become a real threat.

Once your leaders have identified the needs and benefits for a Lean/continuous improvement approach, have them agree on a unified statement that everyone can use to explain the "why are we doing this" to employees. Make it easy for them to share the message.

PLANNING THE TRIP

Once you know why you are making the journey now it's time to plan the trip. It's time to put more detail into where you are going and how you plan to get there. Lean is a vehicle to help drive your continuous improvement efforts. Ideally, it is a standard, systematic process for identifying, evaluating and implementing change. It's important and daunting to look at the long journey ahead. However, let's keep it simple and first focus on how to just get out of town. Instead of focusing on three-, five-, and ten-year goals, I recommend focusing on a first-year plan. Then, in the spirit of continuous improvement, you can continue to re-evaluate and adjust your plan and goals as you move forward.

Begin by Evaluating Your Current Condition or Current State

An evaluation of your current state can be done through employee surveys, focus groups or leadership discussions. I like to have leaders participate in a planning session, the same one I mentioned earlier. During the session we discuss change management, what Lean is and is not, educate them on common types of wastes and more as they're led through elements of creating their first-year plan. The *why* statement (developed earlier) can be created during this session as well, before proceeding to the next step.

Identify and Prioritize Improvement Opportunities

During the Lean overview presentation, leaders learn about common types of work wastes. Have the group discuss and brainstorm where they see inefficiencies or wastes in their current work environment. I like to refer to these as *improvement opportunities*. Don't worry about how small or minuscule some of their items might sound. All problems are wasteful. Take care of the little problems and some of the larger ones diminish or go away. Have the group write each waste or opportunity down on separate sticky notes. Next, have the group categorize the items into common themes. They can rewrite, add to or combine items as they see fit. Lastly, have the group prioritize the items within each category. To keep it simple use 1–3 with 1= high priority, 2= medium priority and 3= low priority. High priority items should be worked on immediately, medium items should be address within two to three semesters and low priority items can be worked on later within the year or delayed until the next year (Figure 2.4).

Determine Tools or Approaches for Each Priority 1 Opportunity

Once you have your top priorities identified, the next step is to create actions or next steps for acting on each priority 1 opportunity. In other

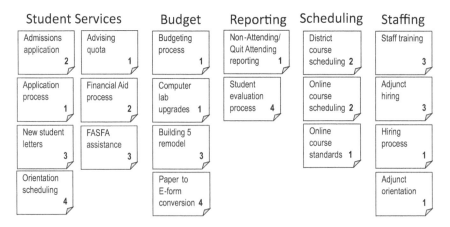

FIGURE 2.4
Prioritizing opportunities.

words, if you were put in charge of a specific priority what actions would you take to address it? Does it require training, a task team, research, etc.? How will you approach it? The actions might involve evaluating a process, investigating equipment issues, researching software, conducting time studies, tracking occurrences, conducting observations or any number of other steps. Think about what needs to happen, who should be involved and what method or tool will be used. Work with the group to write action steps for each top priority item. Make sure that each action begins with an action verb. For example, if the issue is payroll overtime, what do you want to have happen with the overtime? Potential action statements could be to determine the reasons for overtime, evaluate the payroll process to reduce the number of errors Payroll receives each pay period, or reduce the amount of overtime Payroll staff spends correcting errors. One college I worked with identified several problems with new student communications. Issues included students receiving multiple letters with confusing or conflicting information, untimely receipt of letters, and duplicate letters being sent from different campuses. The college identified it as a priority 1 opportunity. One of their actions was to *create a continuous improvement team to evaluate the content and timing of new student communications.* Another priority 1 opportunity involved staff vacancies. Their action was to *evaluate and improve the hiring process for fulltime staff.*

When identifying actions, it's helpful to also identify appropriate Lean tools to help achieve those actions. Lean tools are just like tools in a tool box. Tools make the job easier, but you also must select the right tool for each job. You can use pliers, a socket wrench or crescent wrench to turn a bolt but finding the best fit depends upon the task. If you are evaluating processes, then value stream mapping or process mapping tools are appropriate. However, determining which mapping tool to use depends on what your focus is and what you want to achieve. If you are looking at organizing workspaces 5S is an appropriate tool, but know there are differences when organizing physical workspaces versus electronic workspaces.

Familiarize yourself with popular Lean tools or include someone with Lean tool knowledge to help provide direction. Once again, research what others are doing, what tools they're using and why they chose them. My guess is they will have only a couple frequently used tools. Most colleges can accomplish a great deal using a mapping tool (process map or value stream map) and 5S. In short, Lean tools are simply a standardized step by step approach to addressing a problem.

Mapping tools evaluate processes, 5S organizes workspaces, A3's focus on problem-solving and there are many more. Use and learn the tools but know how to pick the right tool for the job.

FUELING UP AND WHO'S DRIVING

Any effort worth doing is worth doing right. Anything worth doing right usually requires funding. A critical question to ask is, "Is your institution willing to invest dollars and staff time to fuel this initiative?" If not, your journey ends right here. If the answer is yes, the journey continues. As you begin to make decisions and build your first-year plan start gathering potential costs along the way so you can adequately fund your effort.

Let's assume you've established a budget and you've worked through the initial planning steps outlined in the previous sections; you should have:

- Leadership agreement that there is a need to create a formal, and hopefully structured, process improvement approach.
- The leadership team, or others, have identified current opportunities within the college and prioritized them.
- Broad action steps have been created for each of the top priorities.
- Hopefully some Lean tools have been identified to aid in addressing each priority opportunity.

So what's next? Now is the time to buy the fuel and decide who is the driver or drivers of your activities. Think seriously about what is needed to move your process improvement activities forward. Let's start with whose responsibility it is to make these Lean activities happen? It doesn't happen automatically, and please do not to assign a Lean champion who is not passionate about working with people, process improvement or problem-solving. That is the surest way to stop your program before it even starts. Let's look at options for establishing the Lean driver or facilitator. Do you plan to hire someone new or use an internal staff person or team of people to lead your Lean activities? If using internal resources are they experienced in leading process improvement and/or eager to learn?

Internal Staff

If your plan is to utilize internal employees to coordinate and deliver your Lean activities consider these options.

- Hire new staff experienced in process improvement.
- Use existing staff who already have Lean/process improvement skills.
- Train an existing employee in process improvement skills.

Keep in mind that option three can be time-consuming and cause issues with getting your initiative started. It's also more difficult than people realize to find good quality training and training materials to help train staff. Whomever you hire for the position should have strong facilitation (not just teaching) skills, the ability to multi-task, strong relationship skills, be flexible, able to adapt to participant needs, and excellent problem-solving skills.

Other things to consider are whether the person is fully dedicated to process improvement or if it's a percentage of their job. If it is not a dedicated position be cautious. If continuous improvement is not their passion, if the other duties take higher priority or those duties require more attention your initiative will run out of gas. If you don't have a fully dedicated person consider using multiple people to lead the charge to help ensure it stays a priority. I also reiterate, whomever is responsible make sure they have a passion for problem-solving and working with people!

External Consultant

If you do not have internal staff with adequate time and skills to lead your activities your other option is to hire an external consultant and trainer. Make sure the person or persons have a solid background in continuous improvement *and* have proven experience working with colleges. There have been many instances of colleges hiring process improvement experts from manufacturing to lead activities in higher education. Although a few have been successful many more have been left with negative feelings about the experience. Working and training many years in both manufacturing and higher education I will tell you they are *not* the same. The tools, methods, focus, culture and terminology are different. Continuous process improvement is hard enough, don't make it harder by trying to fit a square peg (manufacturing methods) into a round hole (education needs).

Depending on who's available and your budget you may need to use a combination of various consultants/facilitators based on the different skill sets needed. Maybe use external trainers and consultants to train the masses or fill the gaps for what your internal Lean staff can't provide. In another scenario; maybe someone is good at leadership development and strategy deployment, another at process mapping, and possibly your internal person is good at meeting facilitation. You are the client, get them to work together to build a training program that works for you. A good group to help coordinate this and other efforts might be a Lean Advisory Team.

Advisory Team or Steering Committee

In addition to someone to lead your events I would also encourage you to consider forming an advisory team that includes your internal facilitator and cross-functional members to help drive continuous improvement throughout the college. The team's responsibility would also be to ensure efforts align with college goals. Their charge could include helping plan and drive ongoing activities, monitor outcomes, communicate to the masses and look for ways to continually improve and expand the institution's Lean effort. Ultimately the goal is to achieve a true Lean culture where everyone in the organization is using and actively promoting process improvement behaviors. However, that's a way down the road and we're just trying to get out of the driveway. So be realistic in your creating your first-year plan.

LEADERS ON THE BUS

Hopefully by now you've identified a skilled driver (facilitator). But what's the point of driving if no one is on the bus? The driver cannot do it alone. It takes a team effort with everyone working towards the same goal or destination. It's time to get the leaders or coaches on board. Leadership support is critical. You can't do this without it. Like any team, if one or more players fail to perform to the level that is needed it brings the whole team down.

Support for this type of initiative requires more than saying you support it and allocating funds. Too often I see top senior leaders deciding to support continuous improvement or other initiatives, then expect their staff to somehow make it happen with very little direction. For many things this works. But consider this: How often do we hire leaders and assume with a leadership title or promotion comes instant knowledge of how to lead people and make things happen? The personal initiative might be there but the knowledge of how to lead effectively, especially in a Lean environment, is commonly absent. So, the leader starts somewhere, muddles through what they think needs done. If there are no complaints the assumption is that everything is working, the boss is satisfied and eventually things die down and the person quietly goes back to what was comfortable and familiar. That is not Lean and it's not efficient or effective. Be purposeful in how you want all employees to behave and create a plan to adequately prepare them.

If you want to start with a true Lean journey start by educating your leadership. Help leaders learn the game of continuous improvement. Let them practice and coach them on expected behaviors. Not in just what you plan to do but "how" to do it daily. Begin by identifying coaching opportunities and create trainings where leaders can model specific behaviors to support and encourage Lean thinking. If you expect people to follow your lead then lead by setting a good example, through your actions. If you expect people to learn, teach them, then set expectations for them to practice the new skill. I've had situations where top leadership, sometimes having successfully applied Lean to their previous organization, gives the directive that their current organization is going to embark on a Lean journey. Often driven by cost, lack of growth, competition or whatever challenges are on the forefront. They make the announcement and set the expectation for results by a given timeframe. Middle level leadership accepts the directive, and each goes their separate direction to figure out how to make it happen as best they can in their area, which is often siloed. They each try to do the right thing but because the *process* of how to lead in the new environment is unclear, and probably non-existent, it's frustrating, difficult, confusing and inefficient. Lean is also about standardization which has just been thrown out the window by not creating standard processes for your leaders, and you're just getting started.

Take time to start building a clear process for how you want your leaders to support and promote Lean behaviors within their areas (Table 2.1). As you learn more build on it. One way to start is to allocate time to establish standard work elements for leaders, also known as *leader standard work (LSW)*. If you are conducting a leadership workshop like the one I mentioned earlier, include the following activity.

TABLE 2.1

Supportive Lean Leadership Behaviors

Organization Level	Action/Behavior	Frequency
President	Request project updates at senior leader meetings	Weekly
	Request written status updates to share with Board of Directors	Monthly
	Communicate initiatives and celebrate successes at district meetings	Bi-yearly
	Address leader/director performance issues	As needed
	Work with senior leaders to select district-wide projects	Bi-yearly
	Visit departments to show support and gather feedback	Monthly
Vice Presidents	Outline Lean expectations for the college	Bi-yearly
	Meet with direct reports to align and monitor Lean activities, address barriers and secure resources/funding	Monthly
	Establish and monitor communication methods (postings, reports, websites, announcements)	Monthly
	Work with departments to set performance standards and goals	Yearly
	Participate, observe or be present at a Lean event	Quarterly
	Attend project meetings	Monthly
	Address direct report performance issues	As needed
Deans/Directors	Hold weekly department meetings, review performance status, request improvement ideas and assist with problem-solving	Weekly
	Post and update improvement ideas and status	Weekly
	Provide status updates to Senior Leaders	Monthly
	Coach staff in problem-solving tools	Weekly
	Establish yearly department performance goals	Yearly
Staff	Identify and submit process improvement ideas	Quarterly
	Assist in tracking errors	Yearly
	Attend a minimum of two training events to update skills	Yearly
	Work on implementing process improvement ideas	Monthly
Faculty	Analyze (program and course) evaluations for improvements	Bi-yearly
	Work with program faculty to standardize course content	Yearly
	Identify and submit process improvement ideas	Quarterly
	Work on implementing process improvement ideas	Monthly

- List the different organizational levels on a flipchart, whiteboard or screen.
- Pose the question, "What actions and behaviors must each level do to support Lean within the organization?"
- As a group, start identifying items under each level.
  - State each item as an action, because we want action and not just empty words that go nowhere.
- Identify the frequency of the actions (daily, weekly, or monthly).
- For each action identify accountability steps.
  - How do you know it's being carried out? In other words, who is responsible for monitoring the actions and how will they do it? Will there be a form, updates to supervisors or other checks? List the monitoring steps at each level.
- Identify the corrective actions for failing to perform the "standard work."
  - What happens if a person, area or group fail to perform the action? What are the consequences? If a leader fails to follow through with one or more actions and there is no corrective action for the behavior it's like punching holes in the side of a ship. Soon the support structure will weaken, the problem will spread and eventually the Lean ship will struggle to stay afloat.
- Determine how the steps and actions will get communicated and implemented.

There is no need to create long lists of activities at this stage. The goal is to once again *start* building the support structure and support behaviors that drive improvements.

You may decide to conduct leadership training on change management or even basic supervisory skills. Once again, you are asking them to act and behave in a different manner. Be purposeful in preparing them.

Hold training and planning sessions with leaders in the beginning to develop needed skills and a unified approach to your Lean rollout. Teach them specific behaviors and tools they will use with employees and colleagues to create the desired Lean culture. Doing so will help reduce significant NVA during your journey.

More feedback and coaching in the beginning will be required until the new behaviors become routine. Even after putting all this in place you will still find people who refuse or are reluctant to get on the Lean bus. Prepare a clear plan for dealing with those people. Ignoring them flattens the bus tires and causes the engine to sputter. Taking even difficult actions shows people that adherence to expectations is important. Work on raising the bar at all levels instead of lowering it to accommodate non-conforming, marginally productive and negative staff.

ALL ABOARD

Let's assume now that you've created a sound and supportive plan up to this point including preparing your leaders. Now it's time to plan on how this new focus on process improvement is going to be communicated to the masses. One mass email to everyone is not going to be enough. Try not to make people a victim of change. A victim of change is when change is suddenly forced upon you with no warning, no preparation time, and no opportunity to ask questions or provide input. It's the surest way to anger and alienate the masses. It's what gives the word *change* such a bad name.

Now is the time to plan your initial rollout. Consider how you want to introduce this new initiative to all faculty and staff. If you decide to begin with a mass email, design it so it includes the what, why, how, when and scheduled times to ask questions. Consider holding info sessions, department meetings, an all staff meeting, forums, or training sessions to get everyone up to speed and allow them time to ask questions. Educate them on the definition and purpose of Lean to start building a common vocabulary. Many organizations that I work with schedule a short three to four hour Lean Overview to accomplish this. The session includes:

- What is Lean and what it is not
- Why the organization is deciding to do Lean
- How Lean benefits both employees and the organization
- Review of common types of work wastes
- Lean tools to help reduce waste
- A group activity in which participants break into small groups and identify wastes, or we like to call them opportunities for improvement
- Sharing and discussion about the list of wastes/opportunities
- Expectations of employees and what employees can expect over the next year
- Question and answer period

If your institution is large (several thousand) you might choose to roll out these initiatives one area at a time. For example, if you are a large university start with selected colleges within the university, but have a plan and a timeline for incorporating all others.

TRIP ACTIVITIES – FIRST-YEAR CALENDAR

By now you should have a plan for the initial rollout and communication. Now it's time to start building your schedule of activities for the next year incorporating all the items we've discussed so far. Begin by adding your rollout dates and related communications. From discussions and prior planning steps, start adding projects to the calendar. When colleges first begin focusing on formal process improvement projects there are usually a plethora of large cross-functional projects to select from. I recommend selecting only four to six large scale projects per year. More than that affects the quality and completeness of implementation. Don't focus on counting projects, focus on making positive change, the implementation. I have experience working with a Vice President who after two months on the job kicked of five large scale district projects. After ten weeks of training and team work sessions each project group reported out their recommendations for improvements to senior leaders. The report outs were celebrated with plaques for each team member but ironically, six months later only a couple teams had implemented tangible improvements. Five months after the first groups ended six more district teams were kicked off with similar results. Remember, it's non-value-added activity unless you can make things better.

When scheduling your projects be conscious of key people. Try to choose projects in different areas or with different focuses so that key people don't get pulled into more than one major project at a time. Also, try to incorporate different people rather than always using the same few from a department. Remember, the goal is to get everyone involved in process improvement.

As you schedule projects remember to refer to your initial list of priorities and tools/methods for addressing them. When starting out try to limit your tools or methods to a select few to start. My college uses process mapping and 5S (organizing workspaces) for most of its projects. Get good at using a few select tools and standardize your delivery of them before adding too many other tools to the toolbox. Also, involve your trainer/ facilitator in the scheduling process. If you are using an internal (on staff) trainer/facilitator determine if they need training or developmental time to prepare. If using external consultants set up a meeting with them to work out a schedule.

In addition to trainings, add into the calendar specific communication dates, status updates and report-outs. Consider adding formal accountability and project checkpoints throughout the year with individuals assigned responsibility for the activity. For example, part of the President's responsibility in our earlier example was to request project updates weekly. Those updates might be less formal, but you may consider scheduling a specific meeting time dedicated to more formal project updates, maybe once a quarter or semester.

Other dates to include on your calendar might be strategic planning meetings and dates in which the next round of projects will be selected and started. One college that I reviewed for accreditation used an all staff day in which a full day was dedicated to discussing and identifying process improvement opportunities. In this college ideas were submitted, and a review committee evaluated each based on specific criteria (budget, student impact, cost savings, etc.). Those that met the criteria were prioritized and received funding/support. Eventually, these might be things to add to your yearly calendar down the road once you have your continuous improvement system established.

Daily Announcements – Communication Plan

We've discussed communication and identified some communication responsibility, but how do we make sure we are communicating effectively? Ask any institution what they would like to see improved and communication will always be on the list. Because it is so multi-faceted and fluid it's difficult to do it well but, by the same token, it can't be ignored. Lack of communication causes all sorts of inefficiencies, so you must make a conscious effort to do better at it. Communication doesn't just happen automatically. Quite the reverse, it *doesn't* happen automatically. Therefore, in building your Lean support structure you need to include a communication plan (Table 2.2). Once again, this plan is a starting point to make sure you are being purposeful and not letting things happen by chance.

Report Card – Importance of Metrics

In education we have report cards or grades that measure how we are doing throughout the year. Midterm grades grant a warning, and an opportunity,

TABLE 2.2

Communication Plan Template

Tool/Method	Purpose	Audience	Responsibility	Frequency
Level 1 - All Employees: Awareness – Intended for all levels of employees to communicate information about Lean, build basic understanding and promote Lean thinking				
Presidential email	Awareness of Lean initiatives, results and direction	All employees	College President, Lean staff	Bi-annually
All staff presentation	Awareness of Lean initiatives, results, direction, success stories	All employees	College President, Lean staff	Bi-annually
Website	Communicate details on future, current and past projects	All employees	Lean staff, team sponsors	Monthly
Team Sites/team boards	Monitor and communicate department CI/Lean activities	Department staff	Department leaders	Monthly
Level 2 - Leadership: Awareness and Responsibility – Keep leadership informed of initiatives, requires responsibility on their part to help incorporate changes into work areas				
Leadership meeting CI/Lean updates and presentations	Keep leaders informed of each other's projects, promote collaboration and assess project alignment with college goals	All leaders	Deans/directors, VPs	Monthly
Dean/director meeting updates	Provide awareness of activities and gain support	Deans, directors, provosts, VPs	Executive VP	Monthly
Level 3 - Senior Leadership & Governing Board: Awareness, Monitoring & Direction – Intended to keep senior decision makers and governing bodies informed to help direct strategic planning activities				
Senior staff updates	Awareness	Senior leaders	President	Quarterly
				(Continued)

TABLE 2.2 (CONTINUED)

Communication Plan Template

Tool/Method	Purpose	Audience	Responsibility	Frequency
Project report-outs by teams	Provide status updates on current and newly implemented projects	Senior leaders	Project lead	Quarterly
Board meeting update	Awareness of Lean initiatives and results	Board of trustees	VP, President	Semi-annually
Yearly report	Share status of all projects so institutional leaders can monitor progress towards strategic goals	All area leaders, Sr. Staff	Departmental leadership	Annually

to adjust behavior before the end of the term. Having measurement systems that monitor processes serve the same purpose. For-profit businesses do a much better job of tracking costs, productivity, sales, error rates, etc. than institutions of higher education. Colleges are good at tracking things like retention, graduation rates, persistence and applicants but typically fail to track business processes as effectively. This is especially true of public institutions. As a result, colleges are typically slower to adapt to changes that affect their financial health. Start at the top and begin building your Lean report card to align with institutional goals and objectives.

Work with Leaders to Build Lean into the Strategic Plan and Job Performance Expectations

Consider adding continuous improvement expectations into everyone's job descriptions whether that includes participation in continuous improvement events, attending trainings or simply providing improvement suggestions throughout the year. Ensure the expectations support key initiatives of the institution. Each level of the organization should have metrics which evaluate their continuous level of performance.

Align Projects with Strategic Initiatives

As you begin to identify projects, it's always good to give priority to those projects that support strategic initiatives. To help ensure alignment I've seen project scope documents require the project lead to indicate which strategic goal the project aligns with. I've also seen a rating system where by points were assigned based on how well the proposed project aligned with strategic goals. Those projects that scored higher received priority and, if needed, funding.

Gather Baseline and Progress Metrics for Each Project

Identifying and tracking metrics provides feedback for how projects and processes are performing, much like the guages, warning lights and dials in your car. They help to monitor on-going performance and alert us before things get really bad. Identifying metrics for your Lean activities operates in much the same way. Several years ago, I was working with a city government on reviewing different work processes. Throughout the project the group continued to dismiss gathering the appropriate metrics mostly because of the time it would have taken staff to find, collect and analyze the data. Once implementation was complete the team had to report their project and outcomes to the City Council. The report went well until one of the council members asked for proof that the changes really worked. The team knew that the changes were good but had no way of showing it leaving the Council with doubt about the true benefits of the project and potentially jeopardizing future funding approval.

Identifying appropriate metrics and determining how to gather them is not always easy. If you are not currently tracking performance data in your existing process it may be necessary to track performance measures manually for a period of time. Be sure to capture baseline data, before you start making any changes, then again after changes have been implemented. Ideally, its best if you can establish long-term metrics that departments can use to monitor on-going performance. Whether it's short term or long-term, measurements should be easy to collect, read, interpret and provide timely information that serves as an alert for when action needs to be taken.

CONCLUISION

Benjamin Franklin once said, "Failing to plan is planning to fail." Anyone can make changes and solve problems. But working proactively to solve problems in an efficient and effective way that provides better service to both internal and external customers takes a plan. Lean is about identifying waste, analyzing and improving processes to remove waste, standardizing work steps, and engaging people to solve problems. It's called continuous improvement because you start somewhere and keep moving forward, continuously improving. Start by building your support structure, one that drives the actions and behaviors of the entire organization towards a true Lean culture.

BIBLIOGRAPHY

Harris, Adam, (June 5, 2018). Here's How Higher Education Dies. *The Atlantic*, https://www.theatlantic.com/education/archive/2018/06/heres-how-higher-education-dies/561995/.

https://en.wikipedia.org/wiki/Lean_manufacturing.

Holweg, Matthias, (2007). The genealogy of Lean production. *Journal of Operations Management.* 25(2): 420–437.

Kotter, J. P. & Rathgeber, H., (2006). *Our Iceberg is Melting: Changing and Succeeding Under Any Conditions*, (1st St. Martin's Press ed.). New York: St. Martin's Press.

3

Value Stream Mapping (VSM) as a Tool for Creating a Lean Culture in a University

Justyna Maciąg

CONTENTS

INTRODUCTION

The application of Lean Management is at present one of the major issues raised within the process of reforming higher education institutions. It is assumed that Lean Management will be as effective in universities as it is in business organizations, despite the fundamentally different character of the former. Research conducted in public organizations indicates that Lean Management generates positive results in organizational and technical systems, but there are doubts about the permanence of such results (Radnor and Bucci 2011). Resistance and the impermanence of introduced changes are explained by too little attention being paid to the development of an organizational culture of Lean Management – a Lean Culture (Francis, Krehbiel and Balzer 2017) as well as the specific character of universities themselves. The lack of connections between the implementation of Lean Management and a change in an organizational culture decreases the permanence of the effects of restructuring and in the long term does not contribute to the improvement of processes in universities (Radnor et al. 2006).

Thus, the discussion on the shaping of a mature Lean Culture in institutions of higher education continues. Value Stream Mapping (VSM) is one of the most popular tools used in Lean Management. The purpose of this chapter is to show how the application of VSM can influence Lean Culture. This chapter is based on the results of an analysis of the literature on this particular subject, the author's own research conducted within the frame of the "Miniature 1" project financed from an National Science Centre, Poland grant (The Conditions for the Maturity of the Lean Management Culture in Higher Education Institutions in the period from 25 September 2017 to 25 September 2018, nr DEC. -2017/01/X/HS/00619) as well as her experience gained during the execution of various Lean projects.

PART 1: LEAN CULTURE IN A UNIVERSITY – APPROACHES TO DEFINING AND CREATING

As an organizational culture, Lean Culture is multidimensional; hence a large number of research approaches, definitions, and interpretations are connected with it. Lean Culture can be defined based on a philosophical (Yorkstone 2016), enumerative (Parkes 2017), normative (Liker 2005, Liker and Morgan 2006, Robinson and Yorkstone 2014), or psychological (Mann 2014) approach, as well as based on oppositions or gaps (Mann 2014).

The attempt to define the idea of Lean Culture for the purpose of this paper is based on Schein's concept (Schein 2004). In this approach, Lean Culture can be defined as an organizational culture which is the result of learning together how to solve problems in the process of external adaptation and internal integration based on the continuous pursuit of excellence and respect for people. Since people are at its centre, Lean Culture has an important universal and humanistic dimension. It manifests itself on the following three levels (Schein 2004):

- The level of artefacts: material artefacts (e.g. process maps), behavioural artefacts (e.g. Kaizen events), linguistic artefacts (the Lean language)
- Espoused beliefs and values (which may appear through surveys)
- Basic underlying assumptions (taken for granted unconscious beliefs and values; they are not visible)

As Schein emphasizes, it is these invisible elements, lying, as it were, under the surface of an organization, that play the essential role in the shaping of attitudes, relations, and functioning of a whole organization (Schein 2004). Their change is the most difficult because they constitute the most permanent element of any organizational culture. They are determined by academic traditions, university models, the culture of a society in which a university functions, the nature of actions undertaken by a university (teaching, research, social missions), its environment, beliefs, values, and principles of its founders and dominant leaders (Ott 1989). Therefore, the shaping of Lean Culture in higher education institutions has a unique character.

Since ancient times the mission of the university has been evolving from the creation of pure knowledge to the domination of social, political, and economic functions. This has exerted considerable influence on the transformation of university organizational culture and approach towards change.

Observing contemporary universities, one can notice that their organizational cultures are diversified and characterized by a certain dominant aspect determined historically, mentally, or politically. University organizational cultures can be collegial (with the dominant role of an academic oligarchy), bureaucratic (with the dominant role of the state), corporate (with the dominant role of the top management), or entrepreneurial (with the dominant role of the market) (McNay 2006, Lacatus 2013). Another emerging type is a virtual culture (Bergquist and Pawlak 2008).

In the collegial model, a university is ruled by an academic oligarchy whose members are elected for a particular term of office from among members of the academic community. Such an oligarchy makes all decisions concerning the management of a university. Because of collegiality, decision making processes are very long and require the approval of numerous bodies and teams whose changes made in proposed decisions can frequently distort their original character. Effectiveness and efficiency are measured with respect to the achievement of objectives established by the academic oligarchy.

In the bureaucratic model, many areas of academic activities are under strict control of the state (e.g. tuitions, types of job positions, allocation of funds, salaries, teaching loads, forms of employment). Funds for regular functioning are distributed mainly on the basis of algorithms (e.g. academic categorization). The main objective of a university is to comply with the law, which determines its effectiveness and efficiency. Compliance with various legal regulations frequently does not have an economic justification (e.g. public procurement procedures).

It should be noted that the principles of the Lean concept are the most compatible with the enterprising culture of a university. Its actions are oriented towards customers and meeting their expectations. This model, however, assumes the high flexibility and short-term nature of made decisions. This can be perceived as inconsistent with the unique character of higher education institutions and their didactic and scientific processes, as well as the social and culture-formative missions attributed to them.

Therefore, implementing the Lean concept, one should take into consideration the existing organizational culture of a university as an element determining the process of implementing changes and its effectiveness. The example presented next shows how VSM can influence the process of changing an organizational culture at all levels.

PART 2: VSM – THE BARRIERS AND BENEFITS OF USING THIS TOOL IN A UNIVERSITY

Value Stream Mapping (VSM) is the basic technique and tool used in Lean Management. VSM helps to analyse all actions within a process, starting from a customer and moving along the value stream towards resources necessary for conducting a process, producing a product, or providing a service. The essence of mapping is to show these actions which create value and to eliminate or minimize these which do not contribute to the creation of values (are sources of waste). Thus the mapping of a value stream allows the successful application of all Lean principles by (Robinson and Yorkstone 2014):

- Determining precisely the value of a particular product/service
- Identifying a value stream for every process/service
- Ensuring an undisturbed flow of value
- Creating value when it is expected by the customer
- Pursuing continuous improvement

The Key Notions in VSM Include Value and Waste

Value is created in a value stream which comprises all actions (both those that add value and do not add value) necessary in the process of providing a service from its designing to its delivery to the customer (so-called flows) (Rother and Shooka 1999). Value is defined by the customer (the end user of the effects of performed actions who can be a person outside the organization, e.g. a student, or a person within the organization, e.g. another employee in the process). From the business point of view, value is benefits expressed by means of a monetary measure which the customer receives in return for the paid price (for services or products, economic or social values) (Orzen 2014). Added value can be analysed based on the subjective approach (who it is created for) or the objective approach (what constitutes value, in what terms value can be expressed).

According to the Lean concept, waste is every action which uses resources, but does not add value for the customer (A Lean Lexicon 2010).

The sources of waste include two categories of actions: actions which do not generate value, but are indispensable for the correct performance of a service (e.g. actions required under the law or a university's internal regulations, customs, or traditions) and actions which do not generate value and are unnecessary from the point of view of an organization's external or internal customers. A typical classification of waste sources includes the following categories (Douglas, Douglas and Anthony 2013): transport, inventory, motion, waiting, overproduction, over-processing, defects, skills (TIMWOODS).

Such classifications of waste sources cannot be unquestioningly transferred from production enterprises to the service sector, and in particular to higher education institutions. They need to be broadened by such categories as legal regulations, bad organization and management, or improper communication – this issue requires further research. Balzer proposes the following division of waste sources in higher education institutions (Balzer 2010): waste of human resources, waste in processes, waste of information, and waste of assets.

Processes are mapped by means of a value stream map, i.e. a drawing presenting the characteristic features of the course of a given process, with a particular emphasis put on the flow of values. Value stream mapping can consist of the following stages (Balzer 2010):

- Diagnosing the present state (an analysis of the current value stream) – *Value Stream Mapping* (VSM)
- Creating a vision of the future state (designing a target value stream) – *Value Stream Designing* (VSD)
- Preparing a solutions implementation and improvement plan – *Value Stream Work Plan* (VSP)

VSM was developed for business enterprises in the production sector. Therefore, the use of this tool in higher education institutions can result in numerous dilemmas and problems. The most important of them are as follows:

a. Defining values
b. Determining which actions and activities make up value stream flows
c. Measuring time and other quantities used in process mapping

a. Defining Values

With respect to processes/services performed by higher education institutions, value is defined very generally as a set of tangible and intangible benefits which meet customers' requirements in a timely, efficient, and effective manner (Makkar, Gabriel and Tripathi 2008).

Value carriers are tangible effects (micro-products) created in particular actions making up a process (e.g. a class schedule, didactic materials, prospectuses, certificates, resolutions) and intangible effects whose carriers are students, alumni, and employees (knowledge, skills, social competencies). Therefore, values can be expressed by means of abstract categories such as trust, respect, commitment, responsibility, etc., referred to as Lean values, and measures of an operation character such as quality, satisfaction, compatibility, costs, time, and other measures of services and processes.

It should be noted that in the case of higher education institutions, value can be perceived in what business enterprises would classify as waste (e.g. time dedicated to an individual student, actions rooted in academic traditions). Therefore, it is very important to determine what is the product of a process and what is a unit of flow – an object in a value stream, e.g. a customer (a student, a graduand), documents (a student's file), a dean's group, etc.

b. Determining Which Actions and Activities Make up Value Stream Flows

Processes taking place in universities are usually very complex. A customer often fulfils simultaneously the functions of a supplier and recipient (e.g. a doctoral student submits a complete set of documents – the function of a supplier in a process; a doctoral student receives a diploma – the function of a customer in a process). What is important for the course of a process is a customer's level of commitment (time, number of errors, etc.). Balzer emphasizes that in view of its specific character, a value stream map of an educational process may contain (Balzer 2010) a beneficiary stream and a provider stream (unlike a standard map which takes into consideration the perspective of an organization – provider only, value streams can be presented separately or jointly).

Another problem which appears in relation to determining which actions make up a process is to establish a proper level of detail ensuring the possibility of measuring time (if applicable). VSM is a tool used in very detailed process analyses; therefore, in the case of large or complex processes, it is possible to divide them into smaller units such as stages or subprocesses. Such a division can be also determined by the course of a given process, e.g. between particular units, or by the status of process owners (the division of scopes of responsibilities). However, it is necessary to exercise care in order to avoid strengthening the existing unwanted arrangements. Such divisions can become visible automatically during the execution of a restructuring project.

According to another proposal, a process can be divided into operational, warehousing, transport, and control actions. As Czerska emphasizes, operational, warehousing, and control actions can become the main area of improvement in a process undergoing a mapping procedure (Czerska 2009).

c. Measuring Time and Other Quantities Used in Process Mapping

In business, the most important process measures are the total duration of a process (L/T Lead Time – L/T is understood as the nominal time of carrying out a process as determined by applicable regulations, P/T Processing Time – P/T is understood as the factual time of carrying out a process, VAT Value Added Time), costs, compliance, and quality (including customer satisfaction).

Time is a basic measure used in standardized and repeatable production processes. However, time is not always suitable for measuring processes in higher education institutions because of the frequent lack of work standards and the existence of considerable diversification and individualization of processes (the same action can be performed in different amounts of time, e.g. consultations with a student, and generate the same value). The duration of processes can be different because of internal organizational (e.g. the availability of employees, infrastructure, students' punctuality) and legal conditions. Furthermore, frequently there are no standards determining precisely the (maximum and minimum) duration of performing an activity; in such circumstances, only general guidelines included in general legal regulations or university by-laws can provide some help.

That is why, in measuring added value in process mapping, it is possible to use other objective (time, a monetary measure, the number of performed actions, costs, compliance with legal and normative requirements, the number of errors, the number of corrections) and subjective (e.g. student or employee satisfaction indicators) measures.

The majority of processes taking place in higher education institutions are of a seasonal character and consequently there occur limitations in their counterbalancing. Therefore, calculating the customer's tact time can constitute a problem (the customer's tact time is understood as a rhythm in which a process should be carried out in order to meet a customer's requirement) (Czerska 2009). Furthermore, not all processes within a stream will continue in the same rhythm determined by the customer's tact time. This may result from overburdening IT systems or overburdened employees in the so-called peak season (e.g. an examination session). Additionally, various employees often fulfil other functions in the process (e.g. they handle students' affairs, answer the phone, provide answers to urgent questions from managers or lecturers, etc.), which may extend the duration of particular actions and cause difficulties with a precise determination of such duration (e.g. preparing a document usually lasts approximately ten minutes, but this time may be extended up to one hour if an employee has to perform any other actions simultaneously).

Measuring inventories in the process of education can be conducted on the basis of tangible measures (e.g. the number of diploma papers, the number of grade sheets, the number of applications) and on the basis of the number of customers waiting for the performance of a particular action (e.g. the number of students waiting in a queue for the issue of a student ID card).

It should be remembered that universities do not take some measurements because of difficulties with access to data, or with the time and cost of acquiring data. Data and information are often scattered all over a university's structures; they are located in various databases, departments, and organisational units; there is a lack of comprehensive information about educational processes. Therefore, interviews and reviews of documentation are a useful method of measurement.

Despite the barriers just described, VSM is a useful tool for the process-oriented restructuring of a university and its continuous improvement; it also exerts considerable influence on the building of a mature Lean Culture. The methodology of using VSM and its impact on the Lean Culture will be presented in the following example.

PART 3: A CASE STUDY – SIMPLIFYING THE PROCESS OF AWARDING DOCTORAL DEGREES IN THE UNIVERSITY

The objective of this project was to restructure the doctoral dissertation processes (the commencement and completion of a doctoral dissertation). This process is important for the University because of its prestige in the academic community, the promotion of the academic personnel, the maintenance of the academic powers, and the academic category determining – among other things – the amount of public funds allocated to the University.

The process under analysis is complicated, stretched in time, and strongly regulated by the provisions of the law. Any non-compliance with the legal requirements entails a serious risk of complaints, inspections carried out by external bodies, litigation, and – in extreme cases – the suspension or revocation of the academic powers.

From the administrative point of view, the main process quality indicator is compliance with legal regulations (deadlines and formal requirements).

The project was carried out in the period from October to December 2017. It should be emphasized that it was the first project of this type executed in the University. Therefore, it was combined with a series of intensive training, which considerably extended its duration. Table 3.1 presents the stages of the project.

The particular stages of the project are described in detail next.

Stage I Preparing for Project Execution

The project was initiated by the Vice Dean for Research Affairs. After defining the objective and scope of the project, the first step was to define the main features of the process and the problems occurring in it. During the course of the meeting the project members identified the following characteristics of the process:

- The process is very complicated.
- It can take a long time (from one year to ten years) (duration depends mainly on a doctoral student's progress with work; generally, there are no restrictive guidelines).
- Changes in the law (the relevant acts can change every year). (This causes a situation in which doctoral students can conduct a

TABLE 3.1

The Project Execution Stages

	Timeline	Participants			Work Methods	Outcome
		Dean, Vice Dean	Project Leader – Lean Facilitator	Project team		
START	1 hour	Project initiation			meeting	Project plan (no record)
Stage I Preparing for project execution		Establishing the objective and scope of the project, the composition of the project team, and the project execution schedule				
	3 hours	Collecting information on the characteristic features of the project and the main problems connected with it			online work, meetings	Description of process (record)
	1 hour	Selecting tools for process restructuring			meeting	Set of tools (no record)
Stage II Training and project execution	3 hours		Training – introduction to LM and VSM		workshop	Knowledge and competence
	2 hours		Identifying internal and external customers in the process and their requirements		workshop	Table with characteristics of customers (record)
	5 hours		Mapping and analysing the process		two workshops	Map of process (documented)
	3 hours		Preparing a process map (VISIO)		work on VISIO	Electronic version of map (record)
	1 week (10 hours)		Preparing a detailed table with descriptions of each step in the process		online work	Table with detailed characteristics of each step in the process (record)
	2 hours		Preparing four versions of a simplified process		online work	Four versions of the new process (record)

(Continued)

TABLE 3.1 (CONTINUED)

The Project Execution Stages

	Timeline	Participants			Work Methods	Outcome
		Dean, Vice Dean	Project Leader – Lean Facilitator	Project team		
Stage III Completion of the project	1 hour	December – the final meeting			meeting, Power Point presentation	The Dean's decision selecting one version of the simplified process (record)
	3 hours		Training in SIPOC and SOP		workshop	Knowledge and competence
STOP	1 week (10 hours)		Preparing a proposition about a procedure and specimen documents		online work	Procedure – proposition (record)
SUMMARY	54 hours in total for the project/3 months	13 steps, seven persons Dean, Vice Dean – 8 hours, Project leader – 54 hours, Administration staff – 39 hours/average for each person			Four work methods Meetings – 3 hours, Workshops – 13 hours, Online work – 25 hours, Work with VISIO – 3 hours	Eight different records (presentation, maps, tables)

dissertation process governed by different successive versions of the same regulation.)

- Compliance with the law is a priority (the consequence of non-compliance is the University's inability to award a doctoral degree).
- Many problems with non-compliance, lack of punctuality, incomplete documents, and others.
- The process is seasonal and unbalanced.
- The process is a source of huge stress for the administrative staff.
- The process is highly bureaucratic with extensive documentation, which is determined by the external regulations and the University's by-laws applicable to the whole HE or to particular faculties.
- Approximately 70% of students who initiate a dissertation process fail to submit a dissertation and are not awarded a degree (due to general statistics).

The preparation of a detailed description of the process was followed by the selection of a tool for its restructuring: Value Stream Mapping.

Notes and Recommendations

A preliminary survey of a process is very important from the point of view of further planned activities and the selection of methods of analysis.

Stage II Training and Project Execution

Every successive stage in the execution of the project was preceded by training.

The first training session had the character of an introduction to Lean Management. It was combined with a workshop on process mapping by means of Value Stream Mapping. Because the members of the team had never had any contact with this work method, the workshop was conducted based on the example of analysing and simplifying a coffee brewing process.

Notes and Recommendations

1. Working with the new tool caused a lot of emotions, surprise, and satisfaction as work effects were readily available (shorter time, fewer actions, saved resources, etc.).

2. A drawing of the map and coloured sheets of paper stimulated creativity and created an atmosphere of child's play. At the beginning the participants were very tense, but they quickly became interested and involved in the workshop.

3. The participants' attitude towards VSM was positive when they realized that it was a simple tool offering possibilities of finding solutions to various problems.

4. The author's personal experience indicates that at the stage of learning to work with VSM, it is better not to use examples connected with the university. If such examples are used, there occurs a mechanism consisting in participants' trying continually to refer to their specialist knowledge and work experience. They assess, criticize, find it difficult to open up, do not enjoy themselves, are not creative. They focus on the essence of a problem under analysis instead of learning how to use a particular tool. Therefore, the author chose the process of brewing coffee as an example illustrating the gist of VSM (see Chapter 2 for an example of brewing coffee process mapping). Its analysis allows one to understand completely what is value, what is waste, and what types of waste there are.

5. Project meetings should not be conducted at participants' workplace because of continual interruptions caused by urgent matters.

At the next meeting of the project team work was started on the restructuring of the selected process.

The Identification of Process Customers, Their Requirements and Expectations

The participants defined the customers of the process and their expectations, the potential measures of values, and the methods of analysing a value stream. It is a considerable challenge because of their numbers. All information was written down on the board by the project leader, who simultaneously fulfilled the function of the Lean facilitator. The results of the analysis are presented in Table 3.2.

Customer analysis increased the participant's knowledge of occurring problems and allowed them to categorize them in a certain way. It turned out that the common categories were time, process documentation, law, communication among the participants, financial matters, process organization.

TABLE 3.2

The Analysis of Process Customers, Their Requirements and Expectations

Process User	Requirements, Expectations, Problems
Doctoral student	Information on: necessary documents, deadlines, fees, the course of the process (stages), current information on the course of the process
	Expectation of short deadlines
Research supervisor/ dissertation supervisor	Information on: necessary documents, deadlines, fees, the course of the process (stages), current information on the course of the process, meeting of the committee, doctoral examinations
	Expectation of short deadlines
	Possibly specimens of documents, opinions
Reviewers	Information on: deadlines
	Possibly specimens of documents, opinions (information on defending a dissertation with distinction)
	Agreement
	Doctoral dissertation
	Contractual penalties – information (50% of reviews are submitted late)
	A cover letter – specimen
Vice Dean, committee chairperson	Information on the number of cases
	Complete documentation
	Dates of committee meetings
Committee	Scanned documents
	Dates of meetings (problems with fixing dates)
Vice Dean and Faculty Council	A well-prepared item in the agenda of a Faculty Council meeting
Administration/ Dean office	A complete set of documents – documents are not complete in 50% of cases
	Attitudes and behaviour of process participants
	Compliance with deadlines
	Effective communication with other stakeholders (they respond to emails)
	Supplementing documentation on an ongoing basis
	Necessity of appointing a secretary for a committee

Notes and Recommendations

The attitude of the Lean facilitator during a meeting is very important. The Lean facilitator has to be open to any piece of information, record everything, refrain from assessing or criticizing things, and to be 'a pen', as it were, in the hands of the project team, ask questions, e.g. Where should I write it? Anything else? Why? The technique of 5WHY is very useful to ask the asker to specify the scale or intensity of a given problem, e.g. how often the problem occurs, how intensive it is, etc.

Process Mapping

At the next meeting the participants started to map the process. First they determined the product of the process, the object in the process, and the measure of added value.

The product of the process is a resolution of the University Council awarding a doctoral degree. For such a resolution to be adopted, during the course of the process it is necessary to gather all documents certifying the performance of relevant actions (e.g. the opening of a doctoral dissertation process, submitting a dissertation for reviews, passing examinations, etc.). The participants agreed that the object of the process was a doctoral student's documentation provisionally referred to as a doctoral student's file.

Defining a process product and a process object is very important from the point of view of defining value and establishing which actions add value, and which do not. Added value is created by every action causing a change in a doctoral student's file, i.e. a change which pushes the file towards fulfilling the requirements necessary for the University Council to adopt a relevant resolution.

The actions adding value include for example creating subsequent documents, obtaining necessary signatures, receiving documents from external entities, e.g. guidelines for a doctoral dissertation, applications, reviews, opinions, resolutions of the University Council. The compliance of the process was determined to be the basic measure of added value. Added value was measured by means of a number of errors and the number of delays (an action performed or a document submitted after deadline).

Time indicators were used as auxiliary measures. Next the beginning and the end of the process were precisely defined. For this purpose, the author asked the participants about the first action initiating the process and the final action completing the process.

The next stage was preparing the map itself. For this purpose, the participants used large sheets of paper, coloured pieces of paper, and other office supplies. The meeting room was equipped with a long table. Figure 3.1 shows that analysing the particular actions within the process, the participants wrote down all problems (originally in yellow slips), sources of waste (green slips), ideas for improvement (pink slips), elements which could not be categorized

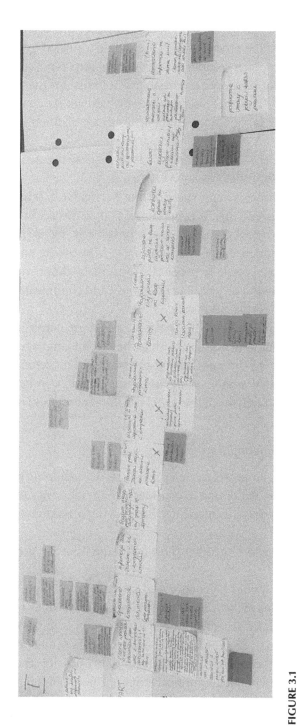

FIGURE 3.1

A handmade map of the process (note: language contained is Polish).

at a given moment (blue slips). In this particular project it was challenging to assess the particular actions in terms of created value. This resulted from the specific character of the process, which is strongly regulated by the law. The process contains very many actions which were classified as not creating value, but indispensable for its proper execution (e.g. essential for the fulfilment of legal requirements). There are also actions which do not create value but are important from the point of view of the University's tradition or a doctoral student.

On the basis of the conducted analysis, a map of the process can be prepared by means of the software i.e. Microsoft's Visio. Created in Visio programme, the process map specifies the particular actions and their characteristic features (time, the number of people involved in an action, the percentage of errors). It is additionally possible to specify L/T, P/T, the time of creating added value, the location of bottlenecks and problems within the process, as well as proposals for possible improvements. The map can be prepared in order to facilitate work and communication in the project team. But it is not necessary.

Within the framework of the project, a representative of doctoral students (a Ukrainian for whom Polish is the second language) was asked to give an opinion on the information placed by the office on its website. The student said that some notions were unintelligible to her (they had been transposed directly from the text of the relevant acts and regulations).

Notes and Recommendations

1. In the case of large and complex processes, the mapping procedure is quite arduous. An option to consider is to divide it into smaller parts as well as to prepare meetings well, paying attention to necessary breaks.
2. It is necessary to remember the whole time what the product of the process is.
3. Discussions should be encouraged because, after all, it is the team that determines what constitutes value and what does not. There is no one generally accepted model; what counts is the model worked out by a given team in particular conditions. Thus the Lean facilitator cannot play the role of the ultimate judge because it is the employees carrying out a particular project that are true experts in it.
4. Team members should be encouraged and stimulated to think analytically and creatively. They should be asked questions such as:

What? Who? How? Why? In what time? Where from and where to? What is the problem? How could actions be improved? What could be eliminated? What would happen if this action were eliminated?

5. During meetings as many notes as possible should be taken in order to record proposed ideas, diagnoses, and recommendations.

In the next stage, on the basis of the prepared map, the team created a detailed table specifying the activities in the process, responsibility, timing, the legal and other requirements, problems, suggestions for improvement (online team work). Although preparing the table took a long time, it turned out to be indispensable for grasping all details connected with the legal requirements, the university's by-laws, and the Faculty's tradition performing particular actions. The table constituted a basis for developing an operational procedure.

Eventually, the team put forward four proposals for simplifying the process together with a description of benefits and barriers related to their implementation. For this purpose, the team carried out a benchmarking analysis with respect to the execution of the same process in the other Faculty, taking advantage of suggestions offered by the University's deans and professors.

Stage III Completion of the Project

The final stage included a meeting. The participants discussed the project execution process and its effects. Taking into consideration the good practices and the University's interests, the optimum variant of the restructuring process was selected.

At present work is underway on developing new process documentation (procedures, instructions, and other documents). The final version of the procedure will have to be approved by a decision of the University Council.

The Results of the Project in the Organisational and Technical Spheres

The most important project results include the following:

- Obtaining transparency of the process.
- Identifying numerous sources of waste, presenting dozens of proposals for improving the process.

- Simplifying the process: the number of actions before restructuring: 32; after restructuring: 27.
- Improving the process in terms of its timeliness. This was achieved by excluding some actions performed at the beginning of the process in order to postpone the formal initiation of the process (altogether five actions were excluded, which postponed the formal initiation of the process by approximately 1–1.5 months).
- With respect to some actions, the pull principle was applied (e.g. previously a doctoral student was able to take examinations immediately after initiating a doctoral dissertation process; according to the new solution, a student may take examinations only after submitting their doctoral dissertation).
- In order to reduce the number of errors and improve the completeness of documentation, the project team proposed the introduction of the following:
  - SOP – a standard operation procedure.
  - Specimen documents.
  - A checklist attached to a doctoral student's file.
  - Poka Yoke (applies to electronic documents).
- The number of documents in the process was reduced (e.g. the project team proposed changing the model of an application for initiating a dissertation process – the scope of information was reduced, the number of ballots was reduced to just one; wherever possible, a voting procedure was replaced by a report).
- In order to balance the process, the project team proposed separating actions characterized by a high level of changeability from standardized ones and implementing visual management tools (competence matrices, dashboards).

All proposed improvements in particular legal and organizational conditions should result in considerable improvement in the effectiveness and efficiency of carrying out the process. They should also contribute to reducing the employees' stress and workload. The academic employees (supervisors, reviewers, committee members) and University authorities will be partly relieved of administrative duties, which will allow them to focus on the academic aspects of the process. The benefits for doctoral students include higher intelligibility and transparency of the process in which they constitute an integral part.

The execution of the project also caused changes in the employees' attitudes.

The Cultural Change of the Administrative Staff Behaviour and Attitudes at Work

Interviews conducted with the project participants confirm that a change in an organizational culture, and particularly in employees' attitudes, takes place simultaneously with becoming familiar with and using Lean Management methods and techniques. During the interviews the employees were asked about their knowledge of the Lean methodology, its strengths and weaknesses, the possibility of its application in higher education institutions, and the impact of the project on their attitudes towards solving organizational problems.

Before the initiation of the project they had not known the principles of Lean Management and some of them had been sceptical about its effectiveness. They had not expected a revolution, being convinced that nothing could be done with such an overregulated and complex process.

After the project was completed, their attitudes changed. The employees found that Lean Management introduced order into some actions and activities, indicated what was redundant, what was missing, and what had to be improved. An analysis of particular processes allowed, among other things, the more effective use of work time, for example, by shortening its duration, avoiding errors, increasing employees' mobility at workstations. They stressed that it was important to monitor processes carried out at work (many actions are performed because "it has been so decided") and not to multiply documents required for a particular process.

The respondents described also how the execution of the project influenced the relations in the group. They emphasized that working together integrated the team and allowed all team members to participate in working out and implementing ideas and solutions, with the will to change and communication being the key elements.

Another important aspect of the change in the employees' attitudes was becoming aware of barriers to process restructuring. One of such barriers is the collegial and bureaucratic organizational culture dominating in Polish institutions of higher education. It was highlighted that a university was a unique environment characterized by unchanging rules, conservatism in thinking, excessively complex procedures, and avoidance of responsibility. Attention was also drawn to time constraints and problems with time management, which could be the source of some employees' resistance to any change.

As success factors, the respondents referred to support of the authorities, determination in enforcing the adopted solutions, and good work time organization. Answering the question about benefits resulting from participation in the process, they mentioned broadening their knowledge of management issues, feeling empowered, raising awareness of the possibility of making changes. The results of the conducted interviews confirm that participating in restructuring projects based on the Lean methodology, employees became simultaneously the authors and recipients of changes. This influences changes in their attitudes, behaviour, values, and principles. Thus technical and organizational changes run in parallel to and are integrated with social changes, which increases the probability of maintaining introduced changes.

SUMMARY

It should be noted that the use of VSM in higher education institutions requires some modifications in the tool. Nevertheless, this does not belittle its significance and strength in the technical, organizational, and cultural dimensions. It is a tool which can be used successfully to build and deepen the maturity of Lean Culture at all levels of higher education institutions.

However, as it has been emphasized in the introduction, the effectiveness of building a mature Lean Culture depends also on the model of higher education in a given country and the attitude of the authorities of a particular university. Every model of an academic organizational culture contains mechanisms causing the perception of the Lean concept as something alien and incompatible with traditions. It can result in defensive attitudes, tension, and inability to get used to the process of cultural and organizational changes. Therefore, any implementation of the Lean concept requires a previous diagnosis of the maturity of a university's organizational culture with respect to planned changes. If Lean is to become a part of a university's DNA code, it has to be based on shared values and principles pursued in individual and collective actions, everyday philosophy, and management practices.

LITERATURE

Balzer, W.K. 2010. *Lean Higher Education*. New York, CRP Press: Francis & Taylor Group.

Bergquist, W.H. and K. Pawlak. 2008. *Engaging the Six Cultures of the Academy*. San Francisco: Jossey-Bass.

Czerska, J. 2009. *Doskonalenie strumienia wartości* [Improvement of value stream]. Difin.

Douglas, A., J. Douglas, and J. Anthony. 2013. *Gold in the Mine: Recognising Waste in UK HEIs using Lean Thinking*. Enhancing Process Efficiency and Effectiveness in Higher Education Using Lean Six Sigma. In: Proceedings of First International Conference on Lean Six Sigma for Higher Education. pp. 17–26.

Francis, D.E., T.C. Krehbiel, and W.K. Balzer. 2017. Lean applications in higher education. *Lean Management Journal*, no. 3: https://the-lmj.com/2017/03/.

Koch, T. and Sobczyk. 2010. *Leksykon Lean* [A Lean Lexicon]. Lean Enterprise Institute Polska.Wroclaw, Poland.

Lacatus, M.L. 2013. Organizational culture in contemporary university. *Procedia - Social and Behavioral Sciences*, 76: 421–425.

Liker, J.K. 2005. *Droga Toyoty. 14 zasad zarządzania wiodącej firmy produkcyjnej świata* [The Toyota Way. The 14 Management Rules of the World's Leading Manufacturing Company]. MT Biznes.

Liker, J.K. and J.M. Morgan. 2006. The Toyota Way in services: The case of lean product development. *Academy Management Perspective*, no. 2: 5–20.

Makkar, U., E. Gabriel, and S.K. Tripathi. 2008. Value chain for higher education sector-case studies of India and Tanzania. *Journal of Services Research*.

Mann, D. 2014. *Tworzenie kultury Lean* [Creating a Lean Culture]. ProdPublishing.

McNay, I. 2006. *Values, Principles and Integrity: Academic and Professional Standards in Higher Education*. https://www.oecd.org/site/imhe2006bis/37245044.pdf (accessed May 12, 2018).

Orzen, M. 2014. *Connecting with the Customer to Create Greater Value*. In: XV Międzynarodowa Konferencja Lean Management, Materiały konferencyjne [The 15th International Lean Management Confrerence, Conference Proceedings], T. Koch (Ed.).

Ott, S.J. 1989. *The Organizational Culture Perspective*. Chicago, IL: The Dorsey Press.

Parkes, A. 2017. *Kulturowe uwarunkowania Lean Management* [Cultural Conditions of Lean Management]. Difin.

Radnor, Z. and G. Bucci. 2011. *Analysis of Lean Implementation in UK Business Schools and Universities*. Association for Business Schools. https://www.york.ac.uk/admin/po/processreview/ABS%20Final%20Report%20final.pdf (accessed March 12, 2015).

Radnor, Z., P. Walley, A. Stephens, and G. Bucci. 2006. *Evaluation of the Lean Approach to Business Management and Its Use in the Public Sector*. Scottish Executive Social Research. Crown Copyright.

Robinson, M. and S. Yorkstone. 2014. *Becoming a Lean University: The case of the University of St. Andrews*. Leadership and Governance in Higher Education: Handbook for Decision-Makers and Administrators.

Rother, M. and J. Shooka. 1999. *Learning to See*. Brookline, MA: Lean Enterprise Institute Inc.

Schein, E. 2004. *Organizational Culture and Leadership*, 3rd Edition. San Francisco, CA: Jossey-Bass.

Yorkstone, S. 2016. *Lean Universities*. In: T. Netland and D. Powell (Eds.), *The Routledge Companion to Lean Management*. Routledge.

4

"Lean" into Your Service Model: An Institutional Case Study Using Library Systems

Tony L.H. Wai and Lenore O'Connor

CONTENTS

INTRODUCTION: WHAT WE DO MATTERS

The value of Macquarie University Library's Service Model and Quality Enhancement Framework lies in the ability of all Library staff to understand and engage with the concepts of the models in their everyday work. To ensure that the service model and quality enhancement framework is accessible to all staff, these concepts have been incorporated into the What We Do Matters programme (Figure 4.1).

What We Do Matters consists of four key elements:

- Create positive experiences – Having a welcoming, client-centred approach in all work and interactions with clients (and other staff).
- Is there a better way? – A commitment to continuous improvement.
- What I do matters – Every individual taking personal responsibility in work and processes, including raising issues and ideas.

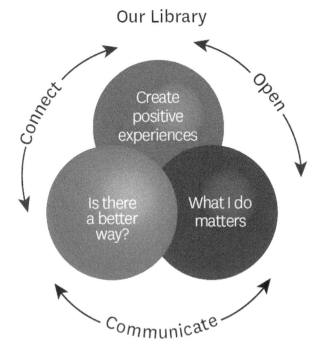

FIGURE 4.1
Macquarie University Library graphic created for What We Do Matters communications.

- One Library/What We Do Matters – All staff working together across functional boundaries to collectively deliver holistic services and workflows.

While the What We Do Matters programme supports the implementation of the service model and quality enhancement framework, the way in which it is explained to staff avoids these terms in favour of more relatable and accessible language for staff to engage (Bremner, 2016).

What We Do Matters is directly aligned with Lean principles in the broader Macquarie University environment, particularly connected to a commitment to continuous improvement and showing a respect for people that recognises that our staff are our greatest asset, experts in the processes that they undertake, with the greatest understanding of what improvements are most needed.

THE SUPPORT TOOLS

Library staff are supported in the continuous improvement process by practical tools (flowchart, visual representation of What We Do Matters, change brief and project documentation templates) to guide them through the continuous improvement process. These are displayed throughout staff spaces, available via shared drives, and included in an induction package for new staff.

A high-level flow chart provides an overview of our continuous improvement processes, guiding staff to the most appropriate course of action; from simply implementing a minor change to developing a project on a small or large scale, to a five-day intensive Rapid Improvement Event (RIE) to map and then fully redesign a process (Figure 4.2). This chapter will explore two case studies where RIEs were used and one project-based case study to show how these options bring process improvements to fruition.

Written in the language of the Library's service model and quality enhancement framework, a change brief template, titled *Is There a Better Way?* leads staff through how to clarify their process improvement ideas and expected outcomes, how to identify relevant stakeholders and how to measure success via a series of questions:

- What can be better?
- What does better look like?

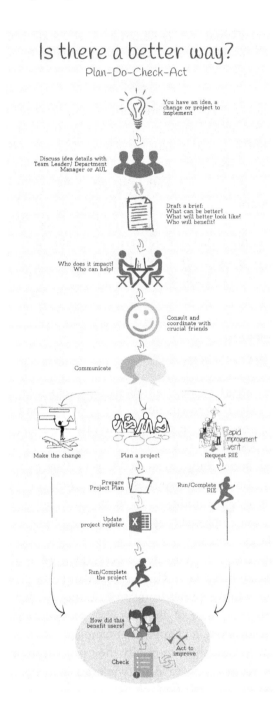

FIGURE 4.2

Macquarie University Library flow chart created to represent continuous improvement processes.

- Who will benefit?
- How will we know it's better?
- Who can help make it happen?

This change brief is the starting point for all process improvements in the Library. Through this document, the stakeholders responsible for each aspect of the process are identified and connected to enable them to consider whether the proposed improvement or a suitable alternative is feasible. More importantly, as staff need to articulate what can be improved and how, who the impacted stakeholders are and how improvement will be measured (*How will we know it's better?*) by answering the questions, the change brief ensures staff give due consideration to how the proposed change maximises value for clients.

Where a change brief indicates that a project is the required course of action and the Library Executive Team has given approval for work to commence, a project template based on a simplified Prince2 methodology is used to support staff through the completion of the project. As with the change brief, this template is written in terms that align with What We Do Matters, using robust continuous improvement methodologies in a way that relies on everyday language and a practical approach for all staff across the Library to engage in service and process improvements.

The following case studies outline how Macquarie University Library has empowered staff via the What We Do Matters programme to leverage systems and apply Lean methodology to improve workflow efficiency and improve the client experience.

CASE STUDY ONE: INVENTORY "UN-MANAGEMENT"

Macquarie University Library operates with an electronic-preferred policy, that is, whenever a new book or a journal subscription is requested, the first part of the process is to attempt to source an electronic version and only resort to purchasing of a print version if there is absolutely no alternative option. With this policy in place, there has been a steep, well-documented decline in demand for printed materials over the past five years. Even so, Macquarie University Library still has approximately 1.2 million printed materials in its collection that require managing.

Given the size of the print collection, locating a misplaced item can be problematic. In fact, at any given point of time, the Library has over a hundred items missing or misplaced from the designated bookshelves. While the number of missing books may seem trivial (100 over 1.2 million is less than 0.001%), most of the missing items are highly popular items, such as textbooks. This poses a genuine reason for the Library to have a proper process to retrieve and replace the missing items.

What Could Be Better?

The following demonstrates how misplaced items were handled before the workflow improvement process:

"When a client reports an item missing from the shelves, a library staff member will firstly perform another shelf check, just to confirm it is not simply a misread of the item's call number. Once confirmed the item cannot be found, the staff member will mark the item as missing in the library system. Collection Organisation staff will then perform shelf checks over the next three months. At the end of the period and if the item still cannot be located, then it will be considered irretrievable and the procurement process will begin, sourcing a suitable replacement. The client will be contacted to collect the item upon the arrival of the replacement copy." (See Figure 4.3.)

While the process seems straightforward, some problems with the workflow were raised. Firstly, a systematic way to communicate between the collection organisation team and procurement staff was not available, and as a result, delays in the book replacement process were documented. Furthermore, the list of missing items had grown too rapidly and was becoming too difficult to be managed manually. Lastly, some confusion in how missing items were presented in the library system occurred.

To summarise the situation, a problem statement was established:

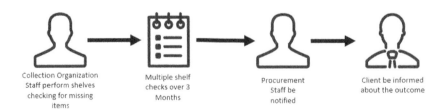

FIGURE 4.3
Missing items workflow before improvement.

"The missing/lost books process in the library is not explicitly understood and/or implemented/followed by all staff and clients and has some gaps in it."

Rapid Improvement Event (RIE)

A working group was formed and tasked with the responsibility to develop an improved workflow that tackled the problems raised. The group contained staff from departments right across the library, including system librarians, procurement staff, collection organisation staff, patron management staff and shelvers, each of whom was in some way involved in the missing book workflow. The RIE was undertaken for five consecutive days with the objective being to come up with a solution and implementation plan by the end of day five. And yes, free lunches were provided.

An objective statement, summarising the objective of the project, was created:

"To design a missing/lost item [including books & journals] process that is easily understood and complied with by all staff and patrons, that is equitable to all customers to the benefit of our collection, that utilises the functionality of our existing system."

Identifying Workflow Waste

One of the aims of Lean methodology is to achieve efficiencies by reducing the amount of workflow waste. There are seven deadliest wastes that can be identified: Overproduction, Waiting, Transport, Over-processing, Inventory, Motion and Defects (Hicks, 2007). During the RIE, a technique called Gemba Walk was adopted to walk-through the existing workflow and describe the wastes observed in personal perspective.

The first task is to identify and explain the workflow wastes from the aforementioned scenario.

i) *Over-processing* – Before collection organisation staff could perform shelf checks, they needed to export a list of items that were marked "missing" from the Library system. The export process could be tedious as it involved logging into the Library systems, manipulation of an Excel spreadsheet, including applying filters and sorting rows based on Call Number order. Furthermore, the process had to be repeated every time a new staff member was rostered on shift, just to ensure that any items found were no longer on the missing item list.

ii) *Waiting* – The process is time critical, particularly for students in need of access to study materials, most often just a few days before an assignment or exam is due. As demonstrated in the scenario, the missing item search process could take up to three months before the item would be reviewed for repurchasing.

iii) *Wasteful motion* – As the list of missing items grew, it was simply not practical to search for each item every day. There was no established mechanism to determine how frequent an item should be searched for, as a result, some items got searched for more frequently than necessary. Furthermore, when the search was completed, the printed search list was delivered to the acquisitions team in person for further processing, often with the list just left on "somebody's" desk.

What Does Better Look Like?

The RIE offered a safe space for the working group to come up with creative ideas. These so-called "Blue Sky" ideas encouraged thinking outside the box and away from traditional boundaries. The team came up with the following recommendation to eliminate identified workflow wastes:

"When a client reports an item being missing from the shelves, a library staff member will perform another shelf check with the client. If the item cannot be found, the client will be offered the Library's interlibrary loan service, where a copy of the equivalent item will be obtained from another library at no cost. Item will be marked as missing in the library system and a report containing a list of all missing items will be generated daily. Each missing item on the list will be marked the number of days since missing and collection organisation staff will perform shelf checks periodically. However, if an item has been marked missing for 14 days or more, it will automatically drop off the shelf check list and alert procurement team for repurchase." (See Figure 4.4.)

How Do We Know It's Better?

We know it is better when looking at what workflow wastes were eliminated:

i) *Over-processing* – Instead of manually exporting the list of missing items, a scheduled email containing the report is now made available to collection organisation staff. Macros are applied so that no filtering or modification of the report is required, essentially cutting down manual handling. We have also updated the roster so that the report will only be printed once a day, eliminating any confusion caused.

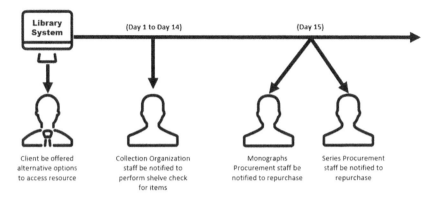

FIGURE 4.4
Missing items workflow after improvement.

ii) *Waiting* – Clients who have reported the item as missing, instead of waiting for the procurement process to be completed, will now be offered the interlibrary loan service, where a copy of the equivalent item will be obtained from another library at no cost to them.

iii) *Wasteful motion* – A script has been written into the missing item list so that it calculates the number of days since the item has been missing. With that number available in the spreadsheet, collection organisation staff will only perform shelf checks on items that land on a certain number of days, for example, every fifth day. This has significantly reduced the number of books needed to be checked every day and reduced the amount of unnecessary walking to and from the book shelves. Furthermore, if the item still cannot be located after 14 days, the item will drop off from the missing item list and reappear onto another report for the procurement team to repurchase. This takes place automatically, cutting out all the unnecessary communication and confusion between the collection organisation and procurement team.

CASE STUDY TWO: LIBRARY WITHOUT PAPERS? A PAPER-LESS DIGITIZATION REQUEST PROCESS

The Library has been constantly reviewing legacy workflows and looking for more economic and environmentally friendlier ways in which to operate. Reducing the use of paper was one initiative. By using less paper in day-to-day work, not only was Macquarie University Library fulfilling its responsibility to protect the natural environment, but actual workflow benefits for clients were also created. Let's examine this from the Library digitisation request management perspective.

What Can Be Better?

"When Library clients want a chapter of a printed book scanned and emailed to them, they will firstly be asked to visit the library in person and fill in a paper request form. They will be asked to provide the book title, call number, chapter title, page number, their student/staff number and contact details on the request form. Client services staff will receive the request form and place them into a paper tray for digitisation staff to collect for processing…." (See Figure 4.5.)

Again, applying what has been learnt about Lean workflow wastes:

i) *Over-production* – A lot of paper request forms were made which may never be used if no request was received.

ii) *Wasteful motion* – There is no way for digitisation staff members to keep track of incoming requests unless they take a stroll and check the request in-tray for paper forms submitted. Therefore, staff had to keep walking to and from the tray location, often to find out there was no work required. Furthermore, making the client visit the library just to place a request is not the best use of their time.

iii) *Waiting* – What if the paper request form went missing? It is not uncommon to see papers go missing and without that piece of paper,

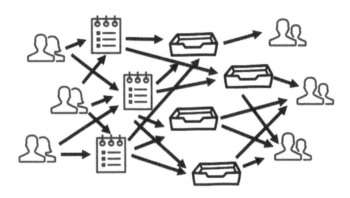

FIGURE 4.5
Illustration of paper request forms management.

the scanning request could not be completed. In that case, the client may be wasting time waiting for no outcome.

How Do We Know It's Better?

"Clients perform a search on the Library website for their desired item. If an electronic version of the item is not available, a digitisation request link will appear next to the item. The online request form will pre-populated with the item title, call number, student/staff number and client contact details. The client will be asked to indicate the required chapter and the request will be queued in a centralised location inside the library system. Digitisation staff log into the Library system and respond to requests as they come along…." (See Figure 4.6.)

While the improved workflow was designed to streamline the digitisation request process for Library clients such as University staff and students, it has yet to be fully implemented due to change in organisational priorities. This has given the Library the opportunity to further test and refine the workflow using internal Library clients (i.e. Library staff who require printed materials to be digitized to support research and teaching practices in the University) as pilots. Through the pilot, further improvement on naming convention for digitized files and better copyright management mechanism was achieved. The enhanced workflow has now been adopted as a regular process for internal digitization requests and has since serviced over 4500 requests.

Several workflow wastes have been addressed by piloting the new process internally:

i) *Over-production* – With the request form being moved online, paper forms were no longer required, and this process officially became a paper-less operation for staff requests.

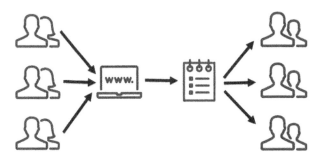

FIGURE 4.6
Illustration of centralized request management using Library systems.

ii) *Wasteful motion* – Digitization staff no longer need to travel back and forth to the paper trays to look for incoming requests as they are now computerized and stored in a central location inside the Library systems.

iii) *Waiting* – As there is now better visibility of incoming requests, digitization staff members' time can be better managed. Furthermore, peak demand can be forecast, and a flexible rostering system can be in place throughout the year. Rosters are regularly reviewed to this end, enabling more efficient processing of requests and reduction in the amount of time the client needs to wait for the request to be fulfilled.

CASE STUDY THREE: ANOTHER MOBILE APP: DO YOU REALLY WANT ONE?

By year 2022, it has been forecasted that there will be approximately 5.5 billion smartphone users around the world (Fullerton, 2017), with each person having at least four connected devices, meaning there will be approximately 24 billion connected smart devices in total (Lant, 2017). This figure shows how important it is for the Library to have a presence in the mobile world. However, would a mobile app be any good for the business?

In 2016, the Library was invited to participate in an early access testing program for a mobile app integrating with our library system. The aim of the app was to streamline the process of retrieving items from shelves. The Library's role was to evaluate if the app would bring any actual benefits to the business operation.

Pre-Mobile App Workflow

"Library staff firstly log in to the library system via a desktop computer to export the list of books to be collected from the shelves. They sort the list based on shelf location and print a paper-copy out for processing. Once all the books are located, the staff member will push the trolley of books back to a desktop computer, scan the item in one by one and then shelve them again to their destination." (See Figure 4.7.)

FIGURE 4.7
Illustration of the lengthy pre-Mobile App workflow.

FIGURE 4.8
Illustration of the "Lean" Mobile App workflow.

Post-Mobile App Workflow

"Library staff open an app on the work mobile phone, where it displays the list of books to be collected from the shelves. As the staff member finds each book, they use the mobile phone's camera as a scanner to scan the book and identify its destination. Books are sent to the respective destinations." (See Figure 4.8.)

How Do We Know It's Better?

In the attempt to compare the two workflows and determine which one was more efficient, a simple time-based comparison test was conducted (Figure 4.9). Library shelvers were asked to use the existing workflow, so called Desktop workflow, for the first two weeks and record the number of items processed as well as the amount of time spent in minutes. Then for the next two weeks, shelvers were asked to adopt the new workflow, so called Mobile App workflow, and record the exact same information. At the end of the period, results were compared.

The result was, in fact, anticipated. The Mobile App workflow took an average of two minutes to complete the end-to-end process while the Desktop workflow took an average of three minutes. A 30% reduction was observed, confirming, as suspected, that the Mobile workflow was more efficient than the Desktop workflow.

It had already been established through workflow mapping that there were fewer steps in the Mobile App workflow and that the steps removed were tedious tasks, such as manipulating Excel spreadsheets and walking to and from a desktop computer. This is another example of eliminating workflow wastes such as motion and over processing.

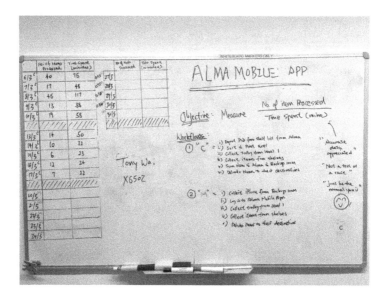

FIGURE 4.9
Data collection during Mobile App testing.

User Feedback

The question remained unanswered: Why only a 30% improvement? If the mobile app was that good, why was it not even faster? Quantitative data could not provide the answer and qualitative data needed to be examined instead.

The method used to collect qualitative data was simple: talk and watch. Time was spent walking through workflows with staff members and asking open-ended questions to understand staff attitudes towards using the mobile app. Observations were made without interaction with staff and insights gained regarding actual staff behavioural patterns when using the mobile app. As a result, many useful insights regarding the mobile app usage was gathered. For example:

i) While the mobile app can be installed on to any mobile devices, it was deemed by the staff member that using the app on a phone would be preferable over tablets as it was easier to manoeuvre.

ii) As the app relies on availability of Wi-Fi connections, some blind spots in the Library building were located, in which the app displayed reduced response time, making the process slower.

iii) It was also noticed that the app occasionally failed to sort the books in correct Call Number orders and hence Library staff had to revisit the same book shelf twice to collect items.

iv) When collecting items with a printed paper list, Library staff were able to use a pen to make notes in cases where books were not found on shelves. With the mobile app, that was no longer possible and a new way of communicating missing books was needed to be established.

Now, with both quantitative and qualitative data in hand, the Library was able to make an informed decision to determine whether the mobile app should be adopted as part of their operations.

CONCLUSION: LESSONS LEARNT

While participating in the workflow improvement activities, several important lessons were learnt. They are:

Who can help make it happen? – Having the right people in the room is important. Rapid Improvement Events can only be "rapid" if the discussions can flow seamlessly with the required expertise available at the event. Furthermore, the team should be given a clear role and authority to make decisions that are within the scope of the RIE.

Establish safe space for creativity – While appreciating the fact that staff of various seniority may participate in the same RIE, it is important to ensure everyone in the room has an equal opportunity to voice their opinion, be creative and avoid group-thinking.

Be open-minded and embrace differences – "Improvement" means "Change" and "Change" means moving out of one's comfort zone. At times when a different opinion from yours is voiced, it is important to take a step back to understand and reflect on how the opinion is formulated. Embrace the differences as they often spark new ideas.

Having staff directly involved in these processes for continuous improvement and seeing their ideas valued and included gives them a sense of ownership and a vested interest in seeing new processes they helped create succeed in practice. The sense of contribution and feeling respected in the workplace has given Library staff the opportunity to develop a true understanding and appreciation that What We Do Matters.

REFERENCES

Bremner, J. 2016. Lean in the library: Building capacity by realigning staff and resources. In: A. Mackenzie & L. Martin (ed.), *Developing Digital Scholarship: Emerging Practices in Academic Libraries*, Facet Publishing, London, UK.

Fullerton, L. 2017. Global mobile device usage is expected to reach more than 5.5bn by 2022. *The Drum*, https://www.thedrum.com/news/2017/07/20/global-mobile-device-usage-expected-reach-more-55bn-users-2022.

Hicks, B.J. 2007. Lean information management: Understanding and eliminating waste. *International Journal of Information Management*, 27(4): 233–249.

Lant, K. 2017. By 2020, there will be 4 devices for every human on earth. *Futurism*, https://futurism.com/by-2020-there-will-be-4-devices-for-every-human-on-earth/.

Macquarie University. 2017. Lean Methodology, https://staff.mq.edu.au/support/business-process-improvements/lean-methodology.

5

Developing a Continuous Improvement Service: From Inception to Reality in 18 Months

Katie Wall and Emma Morris

CONTENTS

The purpose of this chapter is to introduce the Continuous Improvement Service at Sheffield Hallam University and describe its journey, from recognising a need within the institution and harnessing the initial idea, through to the creation of a dedicated Continuous Improvement Team. It focusses on how support was gained from senior leaders, how a foundation of Lean tools and techniques was used to tailor the service to meet the needs of customers, plus the challenges, successes and lessons learned along the way. Written from a personal perspective, the aim is to provide an insight into how existing skills can be utilised to create a Continuous Improvement Service, and to give ideas of how to really bring it to life within an organisation. The idea for this chapter grew from a presentation delivered by Claire Ward and Lauren Wagstaff at the International Institute of Business Analysis conference in 2017.

WHO ARE WE?

Sheffield Hallam University (SHU) is a very large, diverse, complex institution with many customers – students, staff, funders and local and international partners. It is the seventh largest University in the UK with over 31,000 students, 4400 staff members, and a turnover of £266.5 million (based on 2015/16 figures). The origins of the University date back to 1849 when the Sheffield School of Design was founded, transforming over time to become Sheffield Polytechnic in 1969 and then later gaining University status in 1992. Throughout this time the institution has seen many changes in its estate, structure and strategic direction.

Currently SHU offers over 670 courses that are managed across 18 subject departments in four academic faculties, supported by many professional services directorates. The University also has a range of research centres and is in the top five of all UK modern universities for research quality. The University has a large estate split over two campuses and includes brand new, purpose-built facilities as well as listed buildings.

SHU has strong links locally and globally with over 100 partner schools and colleges plus numerous NHS Trusts, and maintains lucrative partnerships in industry offering 19,000 work placements per year. More than half of courses offer integrated practice or work placement opportunities.

Although the organisational and staffing structures of the four faculties are similar, in many ways they operate as autonomous units. Delivery is organised and managed locally – sometimes at faculty or department level and sometimes even down to course level. This presents a challenge in maintaining consistency both within faculties and across the institution as a whole, and it can be difficult for central professional services to interact with faculties in a standard way. Bespoke tailoring of processes and systems is common, which can create inefficiencies and the risk of inconsistent experiences for students, staff and partners.

The Continuous Improvement (CI) Service at SHU currently consists of two people, a CI Manager and a CI Analyst. It is centrally funded as a University resource which means that any faculty, directorate, department, team or individual across the University can draw on its support. The service sits within the Planning Directorate and forms part of the University's Strategic Portfolio and Business Change (SPBC) department. The remit of SPBC is to support corporate/strategic change projects and, in addition to the CI Service, it provides project and programme management and business analysis services. Whilst the majority of staff within SPBC are focussed on corporate change, the CI Service has the flexibility to work more widely across the University at a variety of levels. Working alongside the corporate change team in this way enables the service to retain both a high level view of dependencies and of the potential impact of institutional change, which can then be used to inform improvement activities.

The CI Service has three strands to its offer:

1. *Practical support for process improvement initiatives*:
   Facilitated, one-off workshops that aim to investigate and implement small changes at a local level, plus on-going support for larger initiatives that may span several months and/or have an impact across the institution.
2. *Training and knowledge transfer*:
   Consisting of both formal and bespoke offers, the main output here is delivery of a four-part modular course that combines theory and practical activities to train delegates in the application of various CI tools and techniques.
3. *Institutional culture change*:
   The ambition of the service is to develop a culture of continuous improvement at SHU, with all staff having an element of CI delivery embedded in their roles and at least a basic understanding of CI tools and techniques. The first two strands of the service offer contribute towards this, but there is a long way for the service and the institution to go.

Each of these strands will be explored in more detail later in the chapter.

In the Beginning...

The idea of developing a CI Service dates to late 2014 and originated within our team of Business Analysts (BAs). At this time, each of our BAs was allocated to a specific corporate project and their posts were funded through project budgets. As such, the team fluctuated between 7–10 people, in line with the number and scale of projects running at any one time. Although BAs were allocated to specific pieces of work, it had become custom and practice to support other ad-hoc activity outside of their allocated project when the peaks and troughs of project work allowed. These additional, ad-hoc requests for support were varied and included traditional BA activities such as process mapping, data modelling and requirements gathering, in addition to more general 'improvement' work, for example facilitation, service improvement, problem solving and conflict resolution.

The BA team had always received and responded to these types of requests, but it became clear that demand was increasing. The cause of this was likely due to several combining factors. One being that the University was largely running on aging cross-functional processes which, in many cases, had not been updated in line with historical staff and structural changes. More specifically, a University review of professional services staff in 2011 had led to the implementation of dramatic and widespread change to staff and services across the institution. After a year or more of embedding and working through the changes, staff began to identify problem 'hotspots' and think about how they might improve them. There seemed to be a growing realisation from staff that poor processes could not be fixed by throwing new systems at them and lasting improvements would only be achieved by addressing the underlying root causes. However, despite a growing desire from staff at all levels to improve how they worked, they didn't necessarily have the skills or time to move forward and there was no appropriate central resource that could support them to do this.

Meanwhile, the reputation of our BA team was growing across the University and they were becoming known as a team that could provide practical support or advice flexibly, quickly and without the need to go through the perceived bureaucracy of a 'formal' project. The team increasingly became the natural destination for staff seeking support to resolve their operational problems.

Understanding the Demand

As requests continued to filter into the BA team it became clear there was an opportunity to further develop our formal service offer and also add significant value to the institution. But in order for us to fully articulate that opportunity, we needed to understand the demand. What were staff asking for? What skills did they need? And what support could we offer them?

By analysing the incoming requests, it became clear they were increasingly of a process improvement nature. Typically requests for support would include statements such as: 'This process just isn't working', 'It's not clear why my team is doing this', 'It takes up too much staff time', 'No-one takes responsibility', 'We don't know why students won't engage with this', 'Mistakes are being made but I don't know why'. Staff often felt they had an idea of what the issue was, but were coming to us because they had no idea of how to begin to tackle it.

Through our analysis it became clear that what people were really asking for (without realising it) was a professional approach that used process improvement tools and techniques, and which was also flexible and tailored to their specific needs. They wanted objectivity, neutrality and common sense. They wanted someone who could provide clarity for them and ask the stupid or difficult questions. They wanted a facilitator that could engage and motivate their stakeholders to develop solutions collaboratively. They wanted someone who had experience of problem solving and could inspire confidence. They wanted someone who could understand and translate complex processes and issues. They wanted a structure that enabled them to quickly get to the heart of a problem, and then develop solutions and implement actions efficiently, without the need for a lengthy, time-consuming project.

So, we now understood what potential customers wanted and what skills were needed but could we deliver it? The BA team at that time was a varied mix of professional, formally trained BAs with skills and experience of working on systems and data type projects, as well as BAs that were trained 'on-the-job' and had experience of working on projects that were more people and process orientated. We also had team members that were Lean Six Sigma trained in public sector organisations, and a team manager whose career had been built on process improvement in manufacturing and various other sectors. As a collective, the team was excited and motivated to further develop the service we offered to include process improvement. There was recognition of the value it might bring to the University but also that it would create opportunities for team members to develop their skills and networks outside their assigned projects.

The foundations to develop a fully-fledged CI Service were in place.

Developing the Opportunity

Formal development of the CI Service began in Spring 2015 and it began with a question. It was clear there was an opportunity for us to use the skills in the BA team more widely and we knew there was a demand for those skills within the University – but how could we better define and 'market' what we could offer? We quickly realised that to progress any further in a credible way we needed to gain support from the University's senior leaders and understand how we could better support them.

The starting point was to approach the Head of Service and, after pitching our ideas to her informally, she gave permission for two members of the team to develop and run a small pilot that would offer Continuous Improvement support as a service. This led to the development of a short presentation that served as an introduction to CI methodology and the types of activity we could support. We showcased the 'new offer' through existing networks and contacts, and engineered invitations to leadership and team meetings. A new University strategy had recently been launched which talked about 'putting the student at the heart of everything we do' and we were able to take advantage of this message by showing how CI methodology could help achieve this ambition by designing processes around the needs of the student, and encouraged managers to consider where we could help them add value in their areas. The key aim of this stage of development was to increase awareness about the benefits of CI generally; improve our visibility across the institution, particularly with leaders that had the power to enable change; and strengthen relationships with staff that had previously engaged with us to encourage them to champion the service.

Several pilot CI projects followed and demand snowballed – each piece of work seemed to lead to two or three more as the staff involved in the sessions began to generate their own ideas of how we could help them. We learnt a lot from these initial pieces of work, but the two key requests described in the following case studies, really helped us to drive progress and shape the direction of the CI Service.

CASE STUDY 1: STUDENT SERVICES IMPROVEMENT PROGRAMME

Request Brief

One of the faculties had undertaken work with its Student Services staff to identify key issues that were having a significant impact on the work of the various teams. They needed practical support to investigate and resolve the issues raised, but also wanted to take the opportunity to provide skills development for the staff group.

Our Approach

We designed a programme of three workshops for the staff group which incorporated an introduction to the theory of a particular improvement tool or technique and immediately followed this up with a practical session that enabled staff to apply the theory to their identified problem.

The sessions delivered were:

- A process review using the SIPOC tool to investigate problems in the Disclosure & Barring process
- A customer focussed review using Personas and Customer Journey Mapping tools to examine a student's experience as a course representative
- Root cause analysis using 5-Whys & Fishbone to explore why classes were being cancelled

Outcomes

The sessions received an excellent response from staff involved and the outcomes generated through each prompted the faculty to invest in three graduate interns to lead on the implementation of actions. The Customer Journey workshop was particularly powerful with one attendee describing it as 'eye-opening' and, as we closed the session, commenting 'what are we doing to these students?'. We found that the approach of combining learning with practical application worked very well, as it helped to embed the theory and provided a real understanding of how the techniques can and do work in an HE setting.

CASE STUDY 2: CONTINUOUS IMPROVEMENT TRAINING

Request Brief

After being previously involved in an improvement project led by the CI Service, a senior manager in one of the faculties asked us to develop a one-day training programme that could be delivered to all their professional services staff. The manager was keen for us to deliver an interactive day that included lots of tools and techniques, such as the ones she'd seen us use.

Our Approach

We designed and delivered a one-day course as requested that combined Lean theory with practical activities.

Outcomes

Generally, feedback was that participants had enjoyed the day and learnt a lot from it; the majority of attendees had not come across the methodology or techniques before and were very engaged and enthusiastic. However, the overwhelming message was the session attempted to cover too much content and a full day was much too intense. This, and the rest of the feedback from the pilot course, was invaluable and helped shape our future training offer.

The two pieces of work described in these case studies also delivered the following key lessons for us:

- We needed to provide more cohesive support for larger programmes of work.

  It isn't always enough to provide support on a one-off basis, we needed to be able to commit to providing ongoing support, whether that be through practical facilitation of follow-up work, analysis of outputs, helping to prioritise and plan implementation, or by providing coaching and mentoring over a longer period of time for staff taking actions forward.
- We needed to develop and embed CI 'ambassadors' at key levels of the organisation as they would be crucial to our success.

  Staff involved in these early pieces of work went on to request more work in their own areas and also recommend the service to others.

- We needed to make the 'industry standard' tools work effectively and efficiently for our audience.

  'We haven't got time…' is a message commonly heard and, to maintain staff engagement, we needed to ensure that we got the most out of every session we delivered by tailoring our approach – more on this later in the chapter.
- We needed additional, dedicated resource to cope with demand.

  Success breeds success and it was becoming less viable to continue to meet demand 'off the side of our desks' and alongside project work.

By November 2015, we were in a position to go back to the Head of Service with evidence of the work we had been involved in and the value we were adding. This evidence was very much limited to qualitative information – testimonials and feedback from staff we'd worked with and reports about the types of work we'd completed including improvements recommended or made. The service had not been in operation for long enough to determine any quantifiable, tangible benefits in terms of cost or time savings and we didn't have the capacity or measures to provide any meaningful forecasts. However, based on the qualitative evidence alone, we were able make a compelling case to recruit an additional BA in a fixed-term training position, who would be dedicated 0.5FTE to support the development of the service. In reality, 0.5FTE became 1FTE very quickly and the addition of another BA in July 2016 helped us to further progress the service development.

The additional skills and resource brought into the team meant, not only could we take on more work, but we could also begin to respond to the lessons we had learned and move on to the next stage of development of the service, for example:

- We were able to develop a suite of standard templates to record workshop outputs.

  This enabled us to write up and circulate outputs to stakeholders much more efficiently and provide more proactive, cohesive support to initiatives through follow-up work such as supporting business leads to analyse outputs, determine next steps, develop actions plans and move them forward to implementation.
- We could refine and standardise our approach and make a step change towards formalising the service.

  We began to standardise the journey a customer, or 'business lead', could expect through our service from their initial request,

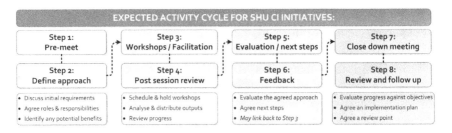

FIGURE 5.1
Customer journey.

the delivery of an agreed approach, right through to implementation and hand-over. Figure 5.1 describes the standard customer journey.

- We could develop systems to track and report on our work more efficiently.

  The first iteration of this was a simple Excel spreadsheet log of incoming work requests with a rudimentary method of categorising the type of initiative and estimating its scale in terms of resource requirements. This enabled us to produce some basic reports and analysis about the work we were undertaking, as well as track and keep in touch with our key stakeholders. The work quickly outgrew Excel and we moved to using a SharePoint site for both logging work and storing files. This gave us two key benefits, firstly we had a secure space where we could share workshop outputs with groups of stakeholders (rather than emailing attachments and updates back and forth) plus we could collectively work on viewing and updating action plans with the added benefit of built-in version control. Secondly, it enabled us to more easily analyse our work. By using consistent categories to log the work, we could use SharePoint reporting tools to create a basic dashboard showing our activity over a month or a quarter. See Figures 5.2 and 5.3 for some examples from the dashboard.

- Finally, we were able to use the feedback we had received about our pilot training to further develop and launch a modular training course.

  We took the content from the pilot, added in some additional tools and techniques, and actively promoted a four-part course designed to lead participants through a continuous improvement cycle, from initial idea to implementation.

By October 2016 we had enough evidence to build a solid Business Case to propose and request funding for a formal CI service. The Business Case

How the work was split across the University:

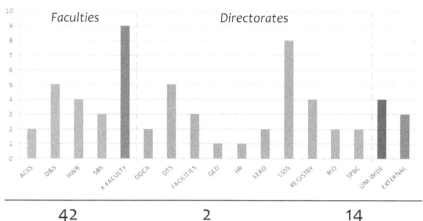

42	2	14
initiatives and activities were closed in the last 12 months	initiatives became formal projects	initiatives and activities were never progressed by the business lead

FIGURE 5.2
Reporting dashboard example 1.

The scale of the work:
- **Small:** 1-2 workshops / less complex process
- **Medium:** 3-4 workshops / more complex process
- **Large:** 5+ workshops / very complex process

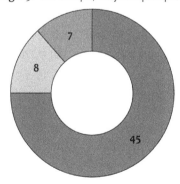

FIGURE 5.3
Reporting dashboard example 2.

included data we had gathered about the scale of demand, i.e. number and size of incoming requests, and, by recording the origin of the requests (i.e. from specific faculties and directorates), we could show the breadth of demand from across the University. We were still not able to demonstrate any tangible benefits but by using case studies of the work we had undertaken, the qualitative information gathered in the form of testimonials and the uptake of the training course, we were able to provide forecasts of the benefits the University could reasonably expect from the service.

In November 2016, exactly 18 months from its inception, the Business Case to formalise the service, and recruit two full-time staff for an 18-month trial period, was approved.

THE SHU CI TEAM IS BORN!

The two BAs working on the service were recruited into CI Manager and CI Analyst roles and began to develop a vision for the service and a roadmap of goals and milestones for the next 18 months. The first step on the road map was to create a clear and marketable description of the three strands of the CI Service offer. This description is true to the service today and has changed little from what was developed through the initial pilot period, it consists of:

1. Practical support: Requests for work range from one-off, problem-solving workshops and bespoke delivery at away days, to longer term, cross-functional activities that span several months and require more intensive support. The main route into the service has always been, and continues to be, word of mouth with around 78% of requests for support coming in this way. The service typically has 30–40 open initiatives 'on the books' at any time (but often many of these are waiting for the business lead to move them forward).
2. Training: The four-part modular course is the main output of this strand, with over 250 staff having now fully or partially completed the course or booked onto future cohorts. The course consists of four half-day sessions over a five-month period and broadly covers the type of content you would expect from Lean Six Sigma yellow belt training. We also deliver bespoke training to groups, one-to-one mentoring, coaching and knowledge sharing through communities of practice.

We recently piloted a Workshop Facilitation Skills course in response to feedback from delegates of the modular course that, although they understand the tools and techniques, they lack the confidence to use them to facilitate group work. The Facilitation Skills course is therefore designed to help delegates understand how to choose an approach to an initiative and build their confidence in the delivery of a problem-solving workshop. The pilot was very well received by attendees and will be rolled out in 2019 as a 'next step' for staff that have completed the modular course.

3. Cultural change: Building on the core offer of practical support and training, the service also aims to build up a network of CI ambassadors, champions and local CI groups across the University. The CI Service will sit at the centre of this network, in a hub and spoke type model as per Figure 5.4.

This model would enable the CI Service to support the formation and work of the local groups and ensure there is a central forum to share best practice and information about improvement work across the University at both a local and institutional level. SHU is still very immature in terms of its engagement and understanding of CI so, although we have supported the development of one local group, it has been difficult to achieve traction in other areas as yet.

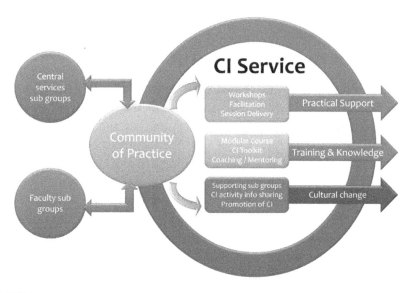

FIGURE 5.4
Future vision.

The development of the formal service offer was followed by a 'soft-launch' through internal communication channels and local networks. As a result of this modest promotion, demand tripled, rising from an average of six requests per month to 18 in the first month and remained at this level throughout the first half of the year. Now demand tends to follow the peaks and troughs of the standard annual lifecycle of University activity, and in quieter times we are able to proactively seek opportunities for the CI Service to add value as well as concentrate on further development of the service.

As a result of a small restructure in 2017, the status of the service changed from an 18-month pilot to become one of the permanent teams within Strategic Portfolio and Business Change. This added commitment to the future of the service enabled us to switch focus from essentially aiming to justify the investment by the end of the 18-month pilot period, to considering how we could develop and achieve more strategic aims for the service over a longer period. Since its inception, the service has continued to develop, learn, adapt and grow and strives to respond to the changing needs of the University and its customer base. The demand for both practical support and training remains high and we are confident we are making small but significant steps towards developing an improvement culture at the University.

SECRETS OF OUR SUCCESS – 'SHU-IFICATION'

'SHU-ification' is a term we coined during the pilot of the CI service and describes how we have made tools and Lean methodology work for us by amending our language, adapting our approaches and getting the most from the tools and techniques we use. We identified early on that the key to staff engagement is selecting an approach that meets the required objectives in an accessible and efficient way, i.e. by using language that our customers can understand and work with, and by trying to make the most of the time we spend working with them. The majority of tools and techniques we use come from Lean Six Sigma methodology but we have also collected various approaches from elsewhere and, when we are introduced to something new, our first thoughts are usually: 'Would this work for us?', 'Can we adapt it to make it work for us?' and 'Where can we try it?'. The following examples demonstrate some of our main

SHU-ifications, the reasoning behind them and how they have benefited the service:

AMENDING THE LANGUAGE

- Continuous Improvement: Even though the majority of our service delivery is based on Lean methodology, we have always referred to the service and its offer as Continuous Improvement. This was a conscious decision made partly because of how the service grew initially from the wide-ranging skill set within the team, rather than through the training or implementation of Lean, but also because we felt the phrase was a better fit for the support our customers were asking for, and that it was a description they could easily understand and trust.
- SHU CI Improvement Framework (Figure 5.5): We wanted to shape our modular training course around an improvement framework similar to the Six Sigma DMAIC framework but felt staff would not engage with the language it used. Therefore we developed a framework that echoed DMAIC but used our own language: Start

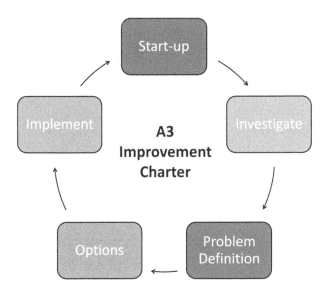

FIGURE 5.5
SHU CI Improvement Framework.

up (Define); Investigate (Measure); Problem Definition (Analyse); Options (Improve); Implement (Control). Again, we felt this was a better reflection of the service we offer and the journey our customers can expect to take.

ADAPTING TOOLS AND TECHNIQUES

- **Kanban:**

  To better manage the increase in demand for the service we introduced a heavily tailored version of a Kanban board and held weekly stand-up meetings to manage and prioritise our workload. The board displays all current initiatives and helps to show at a glance how much work we are actively engaged in over the next 4–8 weeks, who is allocated to what and the stage of the cycle that each initiative is at, e.g. planning, workshops, evaluation, etc.

- **A3 Improvement Charter:**

  We use a document based on an A3 problem-solving template for all the work requests we receive. Using this A3 Improvement Charter at the start of discussions with our customers ensures we take a consistent and efficient approach when defining the objectives of the work. It prompts us to gather all the information we need at the start of an initiative and provides us with an ongoing method for recording and communicating progress throughout the lifecycle of the initiative in a clear and concise way.

- **SIPOC & RACI:**

  One of the tools we use most frequently for process reviews is the SIPOC tool but after using it in the 'traditional' way for workshops during the pilot period, we realised we often needed to complete follow up work to identify roles and responsibilities at a greater level of detail, and also needed a space to capture the many issues that staff naturally raised during the session. We developed a method whereby we work through each high-level process step to capture the specific inputs and outputs of that step, and we replace the Supplier and Customer sections with the RACI (Responsible, Accountable, Consulted, Informed) tool

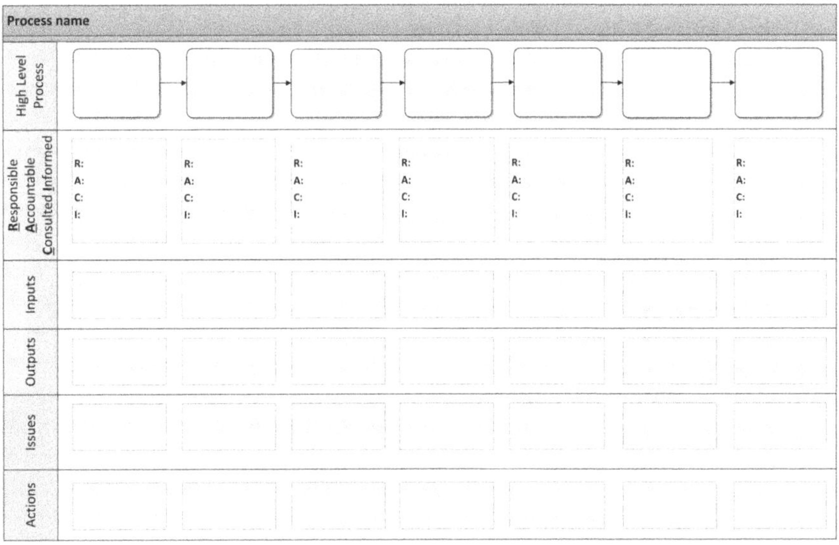

Process name								
High Level Process								
Responsible Accountable Consulted Informed	R: A: C: I:	R: A: C: I:	R: A: C: I:	R: A: C: I:	R: A: C: I:	R: A: C: I:	R: A: C: I:	
Inputs								
Outputs								
Issues								
Actions								

FIGURE 5.6
SIPOC with RACI template.

to give greater insight into the range and roles of stakeholders. Issues and actions are also captured under each process step. We've found this reduces the amount of subsequent investigation work we need to do, has a positive impact on our time as well as our customers, and is a really efficient way of capturing a detailed view of the high level process and determining next steps. See Figure 5.6 for an example of a SIPOC & RACI template.

- **Personas and Customer Journey Mapping:**
  We use a marketing tool called Personas (see Figure 5.7) to encourage staff to create archetypal customer profiles, and then use their creations to talk through a Customer Journey Map. We often struggle to get students to come to feedback sessions so these tools are incredibly useful as a way of encouraging staff to consider processes through the eyes of a student and gather insights into a student's needs and requirements. This approach works really well with cross-functional groups when assessing how a student would experience an end-to-end process as staff are obliged to consider the whole picture objectively, rather than focus on their small part of it, and it can be a really powerful way of ensuring they consider lots of different perspectives.

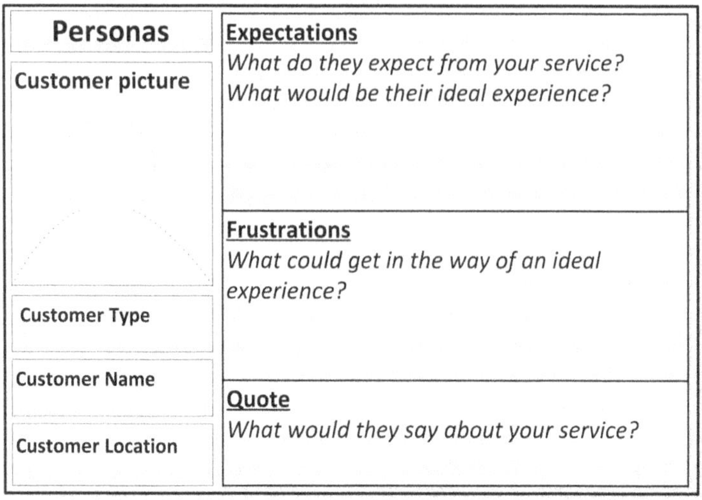

Personas	Expectations
Customer picture	*What do they expect from your service?* *What would be their ideal experience?*
	Frustrations *What could get in the way of an ideal experience?*
Customer Type	
Customer Name	**Quote**
Customer Location	*What would they say about your service?*

FIGURE 5.7
Example of a Personas template.

LESSONS LEARNED

Hopefully our story has provided you with some insight about how you could begin to develop a CI Service in your organisation, or at least given you some ideas of different things you might want to try. The following points highlight the key lessons we have learned through our journey and that we believe have contributed to the success of the service:

1. **Take people on the journey with you.** Show people the value of CI through action, don't just tell them – demonstrate how it can engender change.
2. **Seek out new skills.** There will be lots of talented people around you, both within your immediate team, but also across your institution and beyond. Create opportunities to discuss best practice and learn from others – there is always something new to discover.
3. **Make the tools work for you.** It's not just about using an out-of-the-box approach and sticking to the rules – create your own version of SHU-ification. Mould the techniques, adapt them, combine them and make your own unique, flexible and efficient tool-kit. Listen and learn from your customers, if they are not engaging with you, then you probably need to try a different approach.

4. **Find your Ambassadors and Champions.** When you meet someone who is really on board with what you do, hang on to them, recognise their efforts, encourage them and they will spread the word and open doors to other parts of the organisation. Keep these people engaged by setting up networks, communities of practice, social media groups, or even just catch up for a coffee, whatever it takes to keep the conversation, motivation and ideas alive. You will need to accept that there will be cynics and some people will never fully embrace the methodology – choose your battles and cultivate relationships with those that are enthusiastic and, ideally, influential!

5. **Be clear about your objectives.** Think about what you want your service to be at the start and try to define what you will offer both in the short-term and in the future. Think about the direction you want to head in and what steps you will need to take to get you there.

6. **Finally, make sure your service lives and breathes continuous improvement.** Always be open to change and new ideas, review your own performance and that of the service, ask for feedback where you can. Don't be afraid to fail, but make sure you learn from your mistakes. Take time to look back at how far you've come – celebrate your successes and take pride in the improvements you have helped to make in your organisation.

WHAT'S NEXT FOR THE CI SERVICE AT SHU

Despite the success of the CI Service so far, we can't afford to rest on our laurels and we have a number of priorities as well as challenges over the next 12–18 months:

- We have a new University strategy which is impacting every corner of the institution.

  This brings an opportunity for the CI Service to further strengthen its position and play a role in the implementation of strategic aims. This will help to raise the profile of the service at a senior level and work towards cultivating top-down support to embed a CI culture.

- We want to continue to expand our reach across the University and make more people aware of the value the service can add.

  Up to now, the work and staff we have supported have mainly been non-academic and, although we do have a few vocal academic champions, the academic community is an area we really need to target and to develop relationships with.

- We want to further develop our existing internal training offer and look at how we can encourage more staff to lead their own CI initiatives.

    A new 'Capabilities Framework' has recently been launched for staff and there are many elements of it that we could support through development of additional training programmes. Next on our road-map is a CI skills course for both managers and senior managers which will be designed to provide them with an overview and under-standing of CI, but also equip them with skills to encourage and empower their team members to seek out opportunities for improve-ment and support them to take them forward.

- We want to continue to work with and help develop practitioner networks, not just with other Universities but also with other types of organisations who use Lean in their day-to-day activities.

- We want to develop and implement a framework to evidence the benefits of the service and the work we support.

    This is a constant challenge for us, and we know we are not alone from the conversations we have had with colleagues in similar roles at other institutions. However, it is an important ambition that we must not lose sight of.

Finally, when we take a step back and look at our service, what do we see? We are by no means perfect and it is very easy to focus on the things we have not got quite right, or the things we have not yet achieved. Our service still feels new and fairly vulnerable to being lost amongst the challenges and changes of a large university. Things outside of our control often pop up and 'kill off' initiatives before we get to implementation and it is hard not to be disappointed when that happens. We question ourselves and we wonder what we could have done differently, should we have anticipated the outcome or spotted the risks and dependencies sooner? We need to remember that there will always be obstacles for us to overcome, but patience and hard work will eventually pay off. Ultimately, while ever we still have a passion for what we do, have motivated people around us, and we continue to challenge ourselves and strive every day to make improvements that positively impact our service, our university and our students, then we are sure we will keep moving in the right direction.

Section II

People

6

Identity and Values to Drive Respect for People: A Case Study Based on Embedding Kindness as an Organizational Value

Susanne Clarke, Laura Roper,
Lois Farquharson, and Vianna Renaud

CONTENTS

Kindness isn't only measured by what you do – it's also measured by how you do it

---

INTRODUCTION

At Bournemouth University (BU), we have been bringing to the fore the importance of kindness, and for exceptionally good reason. Popular opinion suggests kindness is good for you and kindness is increasingly recognised as a core skill for professionals in the workplace. Employers tell us that socio-emotional intelligence and 'soft' skills such as kindness are as important as technical skills. By embracing and role modelling kindness as the foundation of our university community we can inspire our students and shape society.

We also believe that kindness and lean are partners in building university culture. After all the two key principles of lean are, 'continuous improvement and respect for people'. This chapter will present our case for kindness and share our experiences in embedding kindness as a workplace value – encouraging everyone to make kindness a key part of their daily life. We start by outlining some of our key concepts, detail how kindness has practically been applied in BU, note two activities readers could experiment with in their context, and conclude.

Key Concepts 1: Benefits of Kindness

David Hamilton (2017), states that there are side effects of kindness: These are presented in Figure 6.1.

We have found that cultivating kindness in the workplace supports culture change and encourages collaboration in ways we had not anticipated. We have been particularly pleased with the number of staff from across the university who have activity engaged with the kindness agenda. This chapter shares our experiences as well as outlines suggested activities that you may wish to try out.

Key Concepts 2: Service Excellence and Kindness

In BU, service excellence is at the core of all our continuous improvement activity and our actions to deliver a great student experience. Service excellence, we believe, goes beyond the transactional norms of customer service in that it promotes the development of communities, where

FIGURE 6.1
Side effects of kindness.

students and staff thrive. Service excellence focuses on the quality of the relationship, where kindness, care and respect are inherent. We strongly believe in building a community of scholars, where academics, students and professional support staff are equal partners.

Key Concepts 3: Lean and Kindness

As a university we have introduced lean and other continuous improvement concepts to support our strategic goal to embed service excellence. We have achieved both quick wins and longer term benefits through using lean and service excellence principles to simplify and improve how we organise work across many departments. It is, however, true to say that we have been more successful in embedding a culture of service excellence in some areas of the university than in others. Kindness has given us another approach to engage the harder to reach corners.

Key Concepts 4: Culture Change is Difficult, Why?

The realities are that promoting lean thinking to minimise waste and drive improvements to the student experience, whilst delivering benefits in target areas, doesn't always lead to culture or behavioural change across the organisation.

Reasons for this are complex and include the fact that many improvement concepts, including lean, originated from the manufacturing and the private sector. A review of current literature and published studies provide us with evidence that core principles of lean are often lost when adapting lean for public service environments (Radnor and Boaden 2008). Further studies highlight what is sometimes referred to as the 'forgotten' lean principle of 'respect for people' (Coetzee et al. 2016) as the potential 'missing link' to support real culture change.

In many ways all of us involved in change and improvement in the higher education sector are still learning and trailblazing approaches to successful change management. This includes how best to adapt lean and an ethos of continuous improvement within our unique environment. Culture change as someone once said is 'what happens in an organisation when no one is looking'; it therefore can't happen simply by telling people what to do. Sharing knowledge to use the tools and techniques is important but fundamentally we need to engage with an embodied relational understanding (Todres and Galvin 2008). By that we mean with our heads (knowledge), hands (practice) and hearts (emotions). By doing so we create a culture where care, kindness and a strong sense of partnership drives everything else that we do (Figure 6.2).

There is not one answer to culture change, and we know it is the hardest thing to change in any organisation. Universities come in all shapes and sizes, some of us work in modern universities and some of us in universities rich in heritage and tradition. Higher education has been around a long time, so why the increased sense of urgency to embark on continuous improvement initiatives and embed new cultures now?

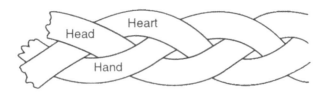

FIGURE 6.2
Applying an embodied relational understanding. (Devis-Rozental 2017, p. 168.)

Key Concepts 5: The Current Higher Education Landscape and Context

Universities are going through an incredible amount of change in the UK, and from our experience change is just as fast paced globally. There is a disconnect between stakeholders such as governments, senior management and policy makers, who work at strategic level and the wider higher education sector staff on the front line, who experience day-to-day operational challenges. Therefore, we must consider the context when looking at the lean principle of 'respect for people'.

One of the biggest issues facing universities in the UK is that of competition. In the UK institutions are caught up in the race to secure as many students as possible (Gov.UK, 2017). Given that typically university budgets are closely tied to student numbers, the sector is seeing an impact with budgets stretched. There is some evidence universities are increasingly being run like big business (Molesworth et al. 2011), with a mantra of 'doing more with less'.

Therefore, it is all the more important to ensure that – amidst this environment of uncertainty and challenge – we do not get tied up with just unthinking routines of continuous improvement; without also incorporating the 'respect for people', in order to provide the necessary environment for collaborative working.

PRACTICAL APPLICATION: EMBEDDING KINDNESS WITHIN BU

At BU an annual Service Excellence Conference is held to celebrate, share and inspire ideas to promote excellence. For the 2017 conference, the Service Excellence team challenged themselves to come up with just one word to describe service excellence to help bring this largely intangible concept to life. The word that felt right was 'kindness'. The Cambridge English dictionary defines kindness as 'friendliness, generosity and consideration', which summed up how BU wanted to explain service excellence and what it means for the university community.

There were many reasons why kindness was right for our university. Student feedback suggested that BU was already known for its friendliness and there were also clear synergies with areas of academic excellence in the university. This included work undertaken over the past two decades by academics at BU, who had developed an approach – of which kindness is at the core – to humanising health care supporting practitioners.

This humanisation framework was developed at Bournemouth University by Todres et al. (2009) who identified the need to engage practitioners to be more compassionate and caring. Originally created for health practitioners, within the context of organisational values this framework can easily be used to embed kindness as an intrinsic driver to service excellence (Devis-Rozental 2018).

The framework consists of eight dimensions which present 'a spectrum of possibilities' (Todres et al. 2009, p. 2). At the end of this chapter we have included an example of the humanising framework with practical examples of how this can be used in teams.

As well as collaborating and adapting ideas from areas of academic specialism within BU, we also looked to external organisations for advice and support including Kindness UK and the Anthony Nolan Trust. A newly formed Kindness Steering Group encouraged staff to collaborate across many kindness-focused projects and where possible to secure funding to take forward research or practice-based ideas. This led to funding for co-creation projects with our students to research and feedback ideas to embed kindness as a key enabler of our new strategic plan.

Following positive conversations and consultation with staff and students, kindness is now included as a strategic enabler for our new corporate plan and underpins the institutional values. A current initiative is being planned to refresh the approach to service excellence with principles underpinned by kindness, care and a positive mind-set.

Respect for people and kindness in the workplace covers a number of different areas including:

- Listening to staff
- Providing an opportunity for two-way conversations and valuing staff feedback
- Recognising and celebrating staff successes
- Encouraging staff to go beyond the boundaries of their role, providing them with the opportunities to grow

Kindness in the workplace focuses on recognising that people are not roles, they are individuals who all work together to make up a dynamic learning community.

Staff and teams have come up with their own ways of embracing kindness; the fact that many across the university want to know more, and are talking about kindness is having a defined impact on our culture. To find out more about staff and students' perceptions of kindness and what this has meant to them, we surveyed a sample of staff and students. The sample included staff who are members of a service improvement community of practice.

We asked what kindness as a concept in the BU community meant to them in a recent survey and we have selected two perspectives to share in this chapter; the first from a current undergraduate student, and the second from a senior member of academic staff:

> Kindness is a maverick concept in the organisation and one that people do not initially understand. They trivialise its benefit as a secondary outcome but really, it is a value that should be at the forefront of any organisational behaviour. It is the collective responsibility to be kind that brings people together and bides them the time to understand each other because the goal isn't individual, it is shared. Having been part of many (of the university's) kindness workshops and initiatives, it is only a matter of time before this value becomes embedded within the culture and will eventually bring tangible outcomes such as improved communication and strong teamwork to the fore. (UG Student).

> I think that I have always had an element of kindness in life and work, but the kindness initiatives have made me reflect more about how I can use kindness in all my interactions with others – whether they are positive or challenging interactions. I find this particularly useful during conversations which are about change or improvement – colleagues sometimes have a hard time with this and taking time to listen, find out their perspective, and what I can do to smooth the change journey is often the start of colleagues accepting change and moving forward. I also feel that my actions as a leader are important in setting the example for others, and therefore if I can do genuine acts of kindness or take a kind approach in situations, others may see the results and follow in their own actions. (Senior Academic).

The analysis of the full survey highlighted for us that staff are making a more conscious effort to make kindness part of their daily life, and importantly staff and students want to be actively involved in kindness initiatives.

PRACTICAL APPLICATION: LOGICAL LEVELS OF EMBEDDING KINDNESS

We described earlier in the chapter the interconnectedness of head, hands and heart, and the need to engage with all of them as inseparable and interrelated to each other. To explain how this idea can be put into

FIGURE 6.3
The foundations of organisational growth. (Adapted from NLP Logical Levels by the authors.)

practice, we have adapted a Model of Logical Levels developed by Robert Dilts (2014).

Focusing on the levels of vision, identity, values and beliefs is where changes in thinking (head) happen and culture change begins (heart), but often when initiating improvement programmes, we begin by focusing on making changes at the level of capabilities, behaviours and environment (hand). This can give people a clear idea of what we want them to do, how and where we want them to do it, but perhaps will not motivate them to identify with, value or believe in why we want the changes to happen. If the culture we want to create becomes part of what those within an organisation understand they are part of, can identify with, value and believe in, great things will happen, and importantly these things will happen when no one is watching (Figure 6.3).

PRACTICAL APPLICATION: BUILDING, VISION, IDENTITY AND VALUES AROUND KINDNESS

In order to successfully embed kindness at BU we started with the University's four core values. These are our desire to:

- Strive for *excellence* in everything we do
- Value and respect diversity and act to ensure that we are *inclusive*

- Be imaginative, innovative and *create* solutions to problems
- Take *responsibility* for the impact of our actions and focus our activity as a learning community on making a positive contribution to society.

By focusing on these core values, we begin to build the foundations of kindness at the University. Kindness, care and respect for people is a core part of our identity and strongly influences our beliefs, values and our motivation. This then sets the scene to successfully deliver at more operational levels, developing a value driven approach to our capabilities, our behaviour and our environment.

Feedback from staff at the University has shown that actions towards embedding kindness within their everyday practice is now viewed as an important part of team development. As one interviewee noted:

> The team I work with appreciate the opportunity to network with the wider BU community at these (kindness) events as networking in an inclusive way can be a challenge for staff in Professional Services. They come away motivated and feeling part of (the University's) vision with many ideas on both personal and professional improvements that they can introduce. (BU Staff Member).

TEAM CASE STUDY: A WALL OF KINDNESS

One example we particularly liked was shared by a line manager who attended a kindness seminar at BU.

The university recognised that the lean principle of 'respect for people' needed to transcend from not just recognising abilities as professionals, but also valuing each other as human beings and valuing kindness. In many areas of the university we already have good practice forums, performance indicators and other recognition of tasks. The kindness wall was implemented to recognise, celebrate and treasure human acts of kindness.

The team discussed the need not to take each other for granted, recognising the small human acts that we do for each other that represent kindness and care. These acts are written up on sticky notes and put on the 'kindness wall' and once a month these are read out at a team meeting.

> … I was going through a particularly challenging day, lots of deadlines and demands, when I got back to my desk I was presented with a cup of tea and a cheese straw, I knew that this took time and effort and the thought behind this made me feel valued and cared for, my day suddenly seemed brighter. A real positive for me was being able to say thank you and post this on the kindness wall.
>
> … Within the team the concept of kindness is in our thoughts, in terms of giving and receiving, we are more aware of the positive impact of kindness and look for opportunities to give, and what is more important these acts are not taken for granted, the team itself has become more cohesive, more positive and we ensure that especially in times of challenge we look after each other. (Team Leader).

Human acts of kindness within the work place and the changes in behaviours this brings does not stop at the workplace door; each team member that learns the value of kindness as a way of life will take it out into society. This is how universities change not just their immediate environment, they change the world.

The next section of this chapter includes activities to use within teams and as ice-breakers for improvement events, which we have found to be exceptionally useful in supporting culture change and embedding kindness at BU.

ACTIVITIES TO EMBED KINDNESS 1: HUMANISING FRAMEWORK ACTIVITY

The humanising framework can be used as a way to reflect on current practice and to identify how kind organisations and teams are.

How to Use It?

Working in small groups use flip chart paper to consider where your organisation/team is currently in each of the dimensions and what actions you can take to improve provision and to practice in a more humanising way (Table 6.1).

TABLE 6.1

Humanisation Framework in Practice (Devis-Rozental 2018)

Forms of Humanisation	Forms of Dehumanisation	Example	Where Is Your Team/Organisation?	Moving Forward
Insiderness: The way we experience life from the inside, our feelings, emotions and even our mood. This allows us to have a sense of self and it is influenced by how we are treated or identified.	**Objectification**: The notion that we have no value as we must fit into a given statistic or system without regard to how we feel and express and what matters to us.	Making people feel valued and respected with our approach.		
Agency: The possibility of making choices, participating and having responsibility for our actions and things that happen around us. It is related to our sense of dignity.	**Passivity**: The lack of control in an environment where we don't have any say and we are merely subjected to what happens. For example, being micro managed without any freedom.	Opportunities to delegate or where others can contribute so that they feel valued.		
Uniqueness: Celebrating that we are all different and drawing on these to make a positive impact.	**Homogenization**: Too much focus on standardisation and having to fit into labels, groups or situations.	Identifying each individual's strengths within a team and how to further develop it.		
Togetherness: We are social beings and part of a variety of communities, so it is also important to find out what we have in common whilst perhaps practising it in a unique manner. Empathy, a sense of belonging, social cognition and effective relationships are all part of this dimension.	**Isolation**: Feeling that we don't belong with others. Situations where we can't find what we have in common with others. When we are isolated we may feel alienated from others.	Working on collaborative projects where everyone can have an input and where their contributions are valued and respected.		

(Continued)

TABLE 6.1 (CONTINUED)

Humanisation Framework in Practice (Devis-Rozental 2018)

Forms of Humanisation	Forms of Dehumanisation	Example	Where Is Your Team/ Organisation?	Moving Forward
Sense-making: The way we see things with clarity. We are story makers of our own experience and that needs to be valued.	**Loss of meaning:** Being seen as a number rather than as a person where our experiences don't matter.	Knowing people within the team by name and paying attention to what they say.		
Personal journey: The sense of continuity within our life journey. To be connected to our past whilst navigating new experiences.	**Loss of personal journey:** When our history, culture or any other area of our identity is not taken into account.	Understanding and celebrating multiculturalism and respecting everyone regardless of their personal journey.		
Sense of place: Knowing and understanding where we belong, but rather than a physical place, it's about the type of belonging that makes us feel good, that gives us comfort or familiarity.	**Dislocation:** When we don't feel we belong and can't find the space where things are familiar and we feel as strangers.	Making people feel welcomed into our environment.		
Embodiment: Being present, having a sense of well-being where our holistic needs are met.	**Reductionist body:** Neglecting to account for our needs or being seen in a holistic way. For example, an over emphasis on our physical appearance or a disability.	Accepting others unconditionally and celebrating their contributions as these are unique to them.		

ACTIVITIES TO EMBED KINDNESS 2: A PHILOSOPHY OF HUMAN KINDNESS, UBUNTU (ICE BREAKER)

Originating in South Africa, Ubuntu acknowledges the value of each individual within a group. It embodies the importance of reconciliation, building bridges and creating unity and is therefore key in developing an environment which has a strong focus on respect for people. Ubuntu focuses on the value of each individual within a team and community and how, by identifying their individual strengths and values, you can create a more efficient and successful team with improved output.

Ubuntu based 'ice breakers' are an effective way to humanise workshops, committees and meetings, acknowledging the individuals present and making them feel welcome and valued. This increases engagement in the content of the meeting making it more focused and effective.

We simply ask people to stand up, walk around the room, and talk to each other and really pay attention to the person they are talking to, to really 'notice' the good in the other person and share what they 'notice', either through writing down the key qualities they notice and handing this back to the person they are talking to or just by telling them. After a couple of minutes ask people to mingle and find someone else to talk to.

We have found the Ubuntu activity to be a great start to a lean improvement workshop; the energy and sense of team it creates lead to lots of ideas for improvement.

CONCLUSION

Kindness is growing in currency. Writing on the approach in BU, Kindness UK said:

> we are delighted that focusing on the values of kindness is now gaining prominence in Higher Education, and Bournemouth University must be congratulated for all that they are doing to embrace and in making kindness a key part of the what they do.

We would like to end this chapter with our favourite quote:

> Be kind whenever possible. It is always possible.

Dalai Lama

REFERENCES

Coetzee, R., Van der Merwe, K., and Van Dyk, L., 2016. Lean implementation strategies: How are the Toyota Way principles applied? *The South African Journal of Industrial Engineers*, 27(3).

Devis-Rozental, C., 2017. Developing Socio-Emotional Intelligence in Early Years Scholars. PhD Thesis. Bournemouth: Bournemouth University.

Devis-Rozental, C., 2018. *Developing Socio-Emotional Intelligence in Higher Education Scholars*. London: Palgrave Macmillan.

Dilts, R., 2014. A Brief History of Logical Levels. Available at: www.nlpu.com/Articles/ LevelsSummary.htm [Accessed 05 September 2018].

Gov.UK, 2017. www.gov.uk. Available at: www.gov.uk/government/statistics/higher-education-student-statistics-2016-2017 [Accessed 13 August 2018].

Hamilton, D., 2017. *The Five Side Effects of Kindness*, 2nd ed. London: Hay House UK Ltd.

Molesworth, M., Scullion, R., and Nixon, E., 2011. *The Marketisation of Higher Education and the Student as Consumer*. London: Routledge.

Radnor, Z., and Boaden, R., 2008. *Lean in Public Services-Panacea or Paradox? Public Money & Management*, 02, 3–7.

Todres, L., and Galvin, K.T., 2008. Embodied interpretation: A novel way of evocatively re-presenting meaning in phenomenological research. *Qualitative Research*, 8(5), 568–583.

Todres, L., Galvin, K.T., and Holloway, I., 2009. The humanization of healthcare: A value framework for qualitative research. *International Journal of Qualitative Studies on Health and Well-Being*, 4(2), 68–77.

7

Inspiring Sustainable Higher Education and Lean through a Lean Ambassadors Network

Tammi Sinha and Claire Lorrain

CONTENTS

The chapter explores the successes, barriers and key requisites for the introduction of a HEI Lean Ambassadors Network using workshops and live projects. We conclude with a summary of successes and key challenges, and summarise the next steps for the launch of LeAN 2.0 in the spirit of continuous improvement and Lean Learning.

INTRODUCTION

This chapter outlines, documents and records the benefits of a Pilot Lean Ambassadors Network, and critically reflects on the first year of running the programme. The Lean Ambassadors Network was launched in October 2016 as part a wider Continuous Improvement Agenda, led by University of Winchester's Continuous Improvement Unit (CIU), with the strategic objective of embedding a culture of improvement at the institution. Lean in higher education has been shown to provide tangible and intangible benefits to students and colleagues in focusing on:

- Respect for people, continuous improvement, and the eradication of waste.
- Three tenets of lean

Lean thinking is a philosophy and methodology built on the Toyota Production System, and significant research has been undertaken in the last ten years to identify impact (Cristina et al, 2012). Lean thinking has evolved from the foundation of continuous improvement and excellence in manufacturing and is embedded in organisations around the globe. The concept of Lean focuses on optimising value within processes. The intention is to provide sustained value to the customer, and create a process that has zero waste.

To achieve this, Lean thinking changes the focus of management from focusing on one component of a process, to reviewing a value stream in a holistic way to improve the flow. The benefits of identifying waste is that it eliminates these wastes from whole value streams, compared to other methods which have a tendency to concentrate on isolated processes. The overarching objective is to create a process that needs less human effort, less space, less capital and with much fewer defects, compared with traditional methods.

CONTINUOUS IMPROVEMENT UNIT

The Continuous Improvement Unit (CIU) is a hub for operational excellence and improvement at the University. Set up as an activity and knowledge repository for improvement, the team has a unique make up

FIGURE 7.1
LeAN 1.0 in action.

of: professional services colleagues; and academics who are seconded into the team on a fractional basis, whilst remaining as academics in their chosen disciplines. The team have a participatory and inclusive approach, with the aims of embedding improvement routines into the culture of the organisation. This is done through workshops, improvement projects, papers for the Senior Management Team and through engaging colleagues and students in improvement initiatives (Figure 7.1).

BACKGROUND AND EVOLUTION OF LEAN IN HIGHER EDUCATION

Many universities are focussing on becoming more effective and efficient (@Efficiency Exchange, @LeanHE) by focusing on streamlining their processes, improving the student (customer) experience, and promoting staff engagement in improvement and change initiatives. University governance and structures are at best complicated and have many processes and layers, involving multiple faculties, and professional departments, which requires co-ordination between vertical and horizontal layers. HEIs can be complex, chaotic and messy organisations, where the creation, transfer and exploration of knowledge make the sector challenging and a joy to work in. The external and internal pressures for change are immense. In the UK, where the University of Winchester is based, there are pressures for change including for the marketisation of higher education, the chaos of Brexit, increasing national measures (Research, Teaching, Knowledge Excellence Framework) and changes in student expectations. This makes a heady mix for change. Within this are opportunities for the sector to further professionalise their services to students and staff, and to embrace disruptive innovation to create an even more dynamic, secure sector. Lean has a significant part to play in this.

The evolution of Lean has seen the principles and approach through manufacturing to service, to the public sector (Thirkell & Ashman, 2014) and more recently to higher education (Sinha & Lorrain, 2017). Over the last 5+ years, attempts have been made to embed the principles and culture of Lean in the higher education sector, with mixed results.

To be more effective, Lean practitioners and Lean educators benefit from being immersed in contemporary research and practice in applying Lean concepts in complex environments. It is interesting to note that ALL sectors think they are 'unique' when embarking on a Lean or Continuous Improvement journey. The principles of Lean are sound and CAN be applied in any environment. Context is of course important, the pilot LeAN tests the HEI context for Lean education, learning Lean AND Lean Learning.

In developing our Lean Ambassadors approach, we examined how Lean Principles were taught within contemporary academic syllabus, across partner HEIs and reviewed how this pedagogical approach could help embed the culture and practice of Lean within HEIs.

THEORETICAL AND EMPIRICAL FOUNDATIONS OF LEAN

Lean has been used by many HEIs, on a global and local level to pursue improvements and savings. This is in response to the changing demands on higher education. However, when reviewing universities' use of Lean and Six Sigma, it was noticeable that Six Sigma had not been as widely adopted, perhaps due to shortage of or reluctance to use key data sets which can be powerful drivers in improvement. The launch of the TEF (Teaching Excellence Framework) in the UK and the importance of the NSS (National Student Survey) in the UK is changing this with more HEIs focusing on the data-rich Six Sigma tools. HEIs focusing on key data sets provides opportunities for Six Sigma to become more widely used. A focus on data helps to develop long lists for opportunities for improvement, and to provide evidence for trends and possible causes for problems.

The foundations of LeAN 1.0 are shown in Figure 7.2.

1. 'Respect for People' (Distributed leadership, Going to the Gemba, Senior Management Team visibility, Values driven improvement objectives, Nurturing talent through experiential learning and mentoring, Recognition of challenges and success and Celebrations).
2. 'Continuous Improvement' (Value stream mapping, Eradication of waste through TIMWOODS analysis, tackling Muri, Mura and Muda, the 5/6S, Visual Management, Problem solving, Cause and effect, Total Productive Maintenance, Poke yoke – error proofing, Dashboards and a focus on Value).
3. 'Strategy, Systems and Standard Work' (Policy deployment/Hoshin Kanri using the A3-X templates, CATWOE and Root Definitions

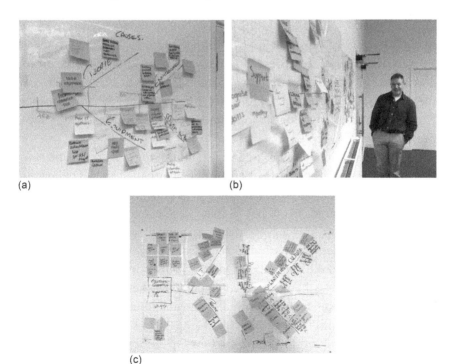

(a)　　　　　　　　　　(b)

(c)

FIGURE 7.2
Foundations for LeAN 1.0.

from Soft Systems Methodology, Process analysis through SIPOC and other approaches, Standard work, Runners Repeaters and Strangers).
4. 'Stability' (Processes, kaizen mindset, Going to the Gemba and High performing teams).
5. 'Lean Ambassadors Network' (Building capability across the University for colleagues and students, Foundations of university values, Respect for people, Continuous improvement and the Eradication of waste).

These foundations were crucial in developing the workshops for LeAN 1.0. Staff and students were invited to participate, with the opportunity to take a Lean online qualification at the conclusion of workshop 3.

EMBEDDING CONTINUOUS IMPROVEMENT AND SERVICE EXCELLENCE WITHIN AN HEI

In the University of Winchester, a two-pronged approach is used to improve University processes, environments and ways of working: the strategic top down and incremental bottom up approach. The top down approach used the European Foundation for Quality Management (EFQM) Business Excellence Model, as the driver for improvement across the nine key areas used in the EFQM model.

The Excellence model is an industry standard, focusing on enablers for improvement which include leadership, people management, policy and strategy and resources, processes and the results. The Excellence model mirrors the balanced scorecard (Kaplan & Norton, 1995) in terms of analysing results from four perspectives: people satisfaction, customer satisfaction, business results and societal results.

The University won the British Quality Foundation Excellence award in 2016, due to the hard work completed by the CIU, faculties and professional services teams involved. The fundamental elements of the model are shown in Figure 7.3.

The incremental, evolutionary bottom up approach to continuous improvement has provided a platform for colleagues and students to voluntarily participate in Lean workshops and projects. Invitations were sent via the staff and student portal, inviting colleagues and students

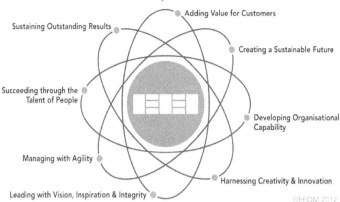

FIGURE 7.3
Fundamentals of the Excellence Model.

to participate in three workshops, providing the foundations of Lean, principles and tools to enable improvement projects to be run.

These workshops started in October/November 2016 and the first wave of workshops were completed in February 2017. Lean Ambassadors were then invited to start improvement projects, supported by the CIU team for coaching and mentoring. Lean big breakfasts and ad hoc mentoring sessions were scheduled to provide a rhythm to coaching and mentoring, with ad hoc meetings arranged in addition.

LeAN 2.0 was launched with the workshops accredited by LCS (Lean Competency System) to become Lean foundations and Lean practitioner professional qualifications. Plans include cycles of workshops to match the rhythm of the academic year (LeAN 2.0) and to hold celebration events every six months to showcase colleague and student projects. To date (September 2018) 70 students and 45 colleagues have participated in the programme, leading to Lean and Continuous Improvement projects and action.

WORKSHOP DEVELOPMENT AND DELIVERY

LeAN 1.0 workshops were developed using Lean principles, Game-storming, Systems theory and Change Management principles. The aim of the workshops was to introduce participants to Lean principles, to enthuse

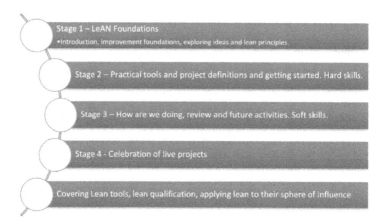

FIGURE 7.4
Initial structure of LeAN 1.0.

them in the opportunities for bringing about positive change in their HEI, and to build capability as an organisation in Lean and Continuous Improvement.

Participants were to be drawn from professional services, students and academics in the HEI. This provided challenges and potential for transformational learning across stakeholders, and a unique opportunity for academics and professional services colleagues to work together on improvement, with the voice of the student as a key partner in the process. The initial structure of the workshops are shown in Figure 7.4.

Workshop 1 – LeAN Foundations

The purpose of the workshop was to introduce colleagues and students to the fundamentals of Lean, to explore Lean ideas and apply Lean principles in a fun and experiential way. The structure was as follows:

- Introduction and Course Overview
- Leaders and Followers
  - A brief introduction to the importance of the 'first followers' in any change initiatives
- An Overview of Continuous Improvement at the University so far
- Appreciative Enquiry exercise
  - Identify what is going well as the basis for thinking about ways to make positive change in the future

- Introduction to Lean and Continuous Improvement
  - Lean principles and their meanings
  - Lean origins
- Finding Opportunities for Improvements
  - Going to the GEMBA – using a Lego game to create a real scenario and looking for improvements
  - Discussion of TIMWOODS, Classic and Service wastes giving University examples
  - Introduction of 5S as an improvement tool and 5S exercises
- Next Steps
  - How participants can use tools in their own sphere of influence
  - 5s challenge
  - The next workshops (Figure 7.5)

Overall the workshop was designed to give participants a high-level understanding of Lean and Continuous Improvement, but also to engage participants through demonstrating how they as Lean Ambassadors could help to make change happen in their own sphere of influence. The focus was on the importance of smaller scale initiatives and really engaging participants in Lean ways for thinking. The use of simulations and games was effective in breaking the ice but also to help participants see the large impact small scale changes can have. The games and simulations we kept simple so only minimal resources were required.

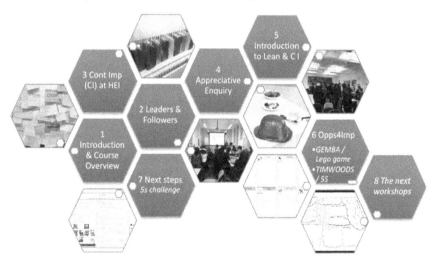

FIGURE 7.5
Structure of Workshop 1 LeAN 1.0.

Workshop 2 – Opportunities for Improvement

The purpose of the workshop was to build on Workshop 1 and to explore further ways of identifying opportunities for improvement. The structure was as follows:

- De-brief from Workshop1
  - 5s challenge – what went well, what were the challenges
- Introduction the University Process Library
- Cause and Effect
  - Fishbone diagram brainstorm exercise around current causes of excellent student and staff feedback
  - Go the Gemba – observe an area of the University in action
  - Add to Fishbone diagram exercise what are the current causes of poor student and staff feedback
  - Creation of 'long-list' of opportunities for improvement
- Further Consideration of 'Long-list' Thinking about Value and Waste
- Prioritising Matrix
  - Using impact and effort matrix to prioritise from the 'long list'
- Next Steps
  - Encourage participants to go and observe own work area and prioritise opportunities for improvement
  - Bring opportunities to next session (Figure 7.6)

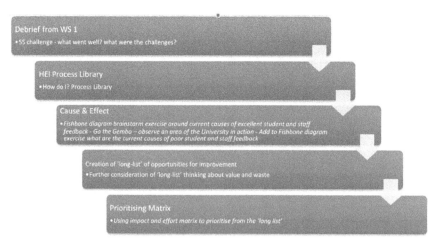

FIGURE 7.6
Structure of Workshop 2 LeAN 2.0.

Overall the aim of the workshop was to equip participants with further skills needed to identify and prioritise opportunities for improvement. There was also however a careful emphasis on participants thinking about their own sphere of influence and the consideration of effort in any improvement initiative. The intention of this was to maximise the chances of success of any initiatives they may later take forward.

Workshop 3 – Let's Get Started

Workshop 3 introduced colleagues and students to the DMAIC (Define Measure Analyse Improve Control) cycle, a cycle commonly used in Lean to guide teams through a problem identification, solving and implementation process. Following a recap of Lean principles, DMAIC was introduced step by step, with a worked example. The workshop ended with opportunities for projects discussed and expectations set.

Structure of Workshop 3

- Recap of Lean principles
  - o Value, value stream, flow, pull, perfection: Respect for people, eradication of waste and continuous improvement.
- Opportunities
  - o Using appreciative inquiry to identify strengths and cause and effect to identify problems.
- Our Approach
- DMAIC
  - o Define: What where why how who when, improvement charter, stakeholders, risk.
  - o Measure: Understanding the current situation. Identify possible causes. Identify waste.
  - o Analyse: Identify true causes of problems and strengths, check data sets.
  - o Improve: Remove causes through redesign, implementation.
  - o Control: Embed the improvements, move to business as usual, use visual management to hold the gains.
- Next Steps
  - o Improvement projects, mentoring and coaching.
  - o Improvement katas (Figure 7.7).

FIGURE 7.7
DMAIC in action.

The participants were led through a worked example, and then provided with the scenario of 'your journey to work/university' using DMAIC to work through problem definition, measuring key aspects, analysing the data, identifying improvements and identifying how these could be implemented and reinforced.

The next steps were for participants to identify projects and work with the CIU as mentors, on small projects, bounded within their sphere of influence.

Workshop Data

Staff – 32 members of staff expressed interest in engaging with LeAN 1.0. A mixture of professional services and academics signed up. Twenty-four colleagues engaged in the first series of workshops (Workshop 1 was run three times to enable colleagues and students to attend). It was voluntary to participate, and colleagues who attended were, on the whole, enthusiastic and positive with the ethos and purpose of LeAN 1.0. Six colleagues attended Workshop 2, and nine attended Workshop 3. The reduction in numbers was disappointing, and feedback indicated the point in the academic calendar was a key issue with timing.

Students – 29 students signed up for the network; this was a promising start, however only ten participated in Workshop 1, one in Workshop 2 and six in Workshop 3 (Figure 7.8) (Table 7.1).

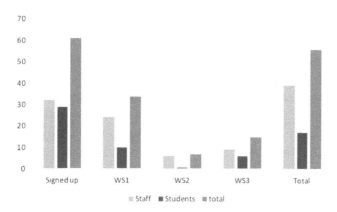

FIGURE 7.8
Engagement data.

TABLE 7.1

Staff and Students Sign Up and Workshop Attendance

	Signed Up	**WS1**	**WS2**	**WS3**
Staff	32	24	6	9
Students	29	10	1	6

56 colleagues and students took part in the LeAN 1.0 pilot, five projects were launched as a result of the pilot.

The data provides evidence of the challenges faced with improvement initiatives in HEIs, the premise of a network of people engaged and passionate about change was received positively, however the mechanics of inviting and persuading people to fully commit and engage to this activity was difficult. Lessons were learnt from the pilot and the second phase of the Lean Ambassadors Network began to take shape. The addition of a professional qualification, linked to employability and the Higher Education Achievement Record, has provided an added benefit for students and colleagues.

REVIEW OF PILOT HEI LEAN AMBASSADORS NETWORK (LEAN 1.0)

The chapter set out to explore the fundamental successes, barriers and key requisites for the introduction of an HEI Lean Ambassadors Network using workshops and live projects.

Successes: The workshops provided the opportunity to build on the success of the BQF Excellence award, and to seek to involve a greater variety of colleagues and students in improvement at the University. The initial workshops were well attended, and the possible causes for this are timing, the appeal was evident, the intended outcomes were to enthuse and energise. Colleagues and students who attended the subsequent workshops and initiated projects were highly motivated and clearly wanted to be involved. In some ways this acted as a natural filter; those who did not participate after the initial workshop indicated that it was difficult to attend the subsequent ones for a variety of reasons. Five projects were initiated as a result of these workshops, and are ongoing at the time of writing.

Barriers: Many lessons have been learned from the pilot launch of LeAN 1.0, these have included:

- Communication of the network, workshops and benefits to participation need to be improved.
- The timings and attention paid to overloading and overburden (muri and mura) may have had a negative effect on participation.
- A clearer indication of the commitment expected and needed to sustain a Lean Ambassadors Network.
- Reinforcement of the opportunity to take a Lean online accredited qualification.
- Clear timetable for workshops and expectations for projects.
- Vocal support from SMT (Senior Management Team) that this initiative supports university values.

Key requisites: For launching a Lean Ambassadors Network in higher education:

Following on from the successes and challenges of the pilot LeAN 1.0, LeAN 2.0 has provided additional opportunities for embedding Lean and Continuous Improvement across the institution. A timetable for launch is being closely aligned to the academic year, bearing in mind the challenges that professional services, academics and students have at different points of the academic cycle.

A Lean for leaders' focus is also helping teams work together using a common language for problem solving, Lean and improvement. Colleagues engaging in the Vice Chancellors Futures Programme participate in sessions providing the core principles of Lean and the DMAIC cycle.

Colleagues will have an element of continuous improvement as part of their annual staff development review/appraisal.

Workshops are now interspersed with 'fieldwork', enabling participants to build up their confidence, capability and experience in applying Lean principles in their sphere of influence, and gaining their Lean foundation and practitioner qualifications.

The chapter explored the successes, barriers and key requisites for the introduction of an HEI Lean Ambassadors Network using workshops and live projects. We concluded with a summary of successes and key challenges and showing the evolution of LeAN 2.0 in the spirit of Continuous Improvement and Lean Learning.

BIBLIOGRAPHY

Cristina, D., & Felicia, S. (2012). Implementing lean in a higher education university. *Universitatii Maritime Constanta Analele, 13*(18), 279.

Hines, P., Holweg, M., & Rich, N. (2004). Learning to evolve: A review of contemporary lean thinking. *International Journal of Operations and Production Management, 24*(10), 994–1011.

Kaplan, R. S., & Norton, D. P. (1995). Putting the balanced scorecard to work. *Performance Measurement, Management, and Appraisal Sourcebook, 66*, 17511.

Thirkell, E., & Ashman, I. (2014). Lean towards learning: Connecting Lean Thinking and human resource management in UK higher education. *The International Journal of Human Resource Management, 25*(21), 2957–2977.

Wiegel, V., & Brouwer-Hadzialic, L. (2015). Lessons from higher education: Adapting lean Six Sigma to account for structural differences in application domains. *International Journal of Six Sigma and Competitive Advantage, 9*(1), 72–85.

8

Improving Performance through Engagement – The Impact of Daily Stand Ups in the University of Strathclyde

John Hogg and Heather Lawrence

CONTENTS

Daily stand ups are an innovative meeting style adopted from the manufacturing sector which has been proven to be immensely powerful in achieving a culture of continuous improvement, resulting in improved communication, productivity, and efficiency savings for organisations. The 'daily stand up' is based around three key pillars:

- **People** – The team owns the meeting. Everyone is expected to contribute and a rota is used to appoint each day's leader.
- **Performance** – Performance measures specific to each team are introduced, so that the team is always aware of how it is performing and how its performance affects the wider organisation.

- **Continuous Improvement** – Recent performance is analysed and opportunities for improvement are identified. Agreement is reached on who is responsible for executing any necessary actions. Successes are shared and celebrated too.

The impact of daily stand ups at Strathclyde are:

- Over 70 per cent of university employees who take part in daily stand ups feel more confident about raising concerns and improvement ideas.
- 70 per cent feel more empowered in their role.
- 100 per cent feel that teamwork and collaboration has increased.

AN INTRODUCTION TO LEAN AND CONTINUOUS IMPROVEMENT IN THE UNIVERSITY OF STRATHCLYDE

An innovative operational excellence initiative is driving transformational change throughout the University of Strathclyde. The Continuous Improvement Directorate's (CID's) work is revolutionising the way the University operates – increasing effectiveness and efficiency across the institution.

Established in 2013, the CID – part of Strathclyde's professional administrative services – is increasing employee engagement by empowering staff to identify and implement improvements. The motivational impact is enabling the delivery of initiatives with evidenced benefits, directly impacting on performance across all strategic themes, particularly operational excellence.

During its first year, the CID led a University-wide project to redesign the Postgraduate Taught (PGT) admissions process, a core business area essential for enhancing Strathclyde's academic profile and increasing income.

The transformational effect of stakeholder engagement in this project resulted in more than 200 staff contributing in participative sessions, with intensive training on a streamlined admissions process to approximately 150 staff. The significant benefits include more than £100,000 in efficiency savings, an 80% reduction in errors and a 15% increase in the international student conversion rate, directly supporting the KPI to increase the PGT population.

The positive impact of this initiative significantly boosted the CID's profile, establishing credibility amongst senior management and staff at all levels across the University. This early support from prominent senior leaders has been vital in the ongoing success of the team, who have continued to be the biggest advocates for the work of the CID.

Over the last five years, the CID has delivered an impressive portfolio of improvements that have not only focused on increasing income and reducing costs, but on establishing a culture of continuous improvement.

Evidencing Continuous Improvement

A unique focus of the CID has been to quantifiably demonstrate the impact of improvements. Having a clear evidence base not only clearly communicates whether each improvement initiative has delivered the intended results, but it also demonstrates value for money and return on investment. The CID received funding from the Leadership Foundation's Innovation and Transformation Fund in order to research and develop a transferable methodology for benefits management realisation appropriate for the higher education sector. The CID published two guides with the most recent *'A Guide to Evidencing the Benefits of Change in Higher Education'*[*], published in January 2017[†]. The guide provides the sector with a practical resource to support the national reporting of efficiencies and value for money.

The guide has transformed how improvement initiatives are managed within Strathclyde, resulting in £450,000 of annual recurring efficiency savings, 27,000 hours of staffing capacity released each year, contributing to an increase of over £15 million to University revenues to date.

The significance of the methodology has been recognised by the Office for Students[‡], the British Universities Finance Directors Group and Universities Scotland – and is being recommended as the standard practice for how institutions can demonstrate greater efficiencies to enhance sector-wide reporting.

DAILY STAND UPS – AN OVERVIEW

Daily stand ups are an innovative meeting style adopted from the manufacturing sector which has been proven to be immensely powerful in achieving a culture of continuous improvement, resulting in improved

---

[*] https://evidencingbenefits.strath.ac.uk/
[†] Original Guide to Evidencing the Benefits of Business Process Improvement in Higher Education was published in July 2015
[‡] Formerly the Higher Education Funding Council for England

FIGURE 8.1
Photograph illustrating a daily stand up.

communication, productivity and efficiency savings for organisations. In 2013, the CID was the first university within the UK to widely adopt this innovative approach (Figure 8.1).

Daily stand ups have revolutionised the way staff communicate and have enhanced working practices to include the opportunity for continuous improvement to take place. Supported by a visual management board, the daily stand up is a place where teams meet daily for a maximum of 15 minutes to plan activities, review performance and agree actions on how to deliver improvements. Every member of a daily stand up is encouraged to make a contribution, to assess team performance directly aligned to strategic priorities and constructively challenge others to identify opportunities for improvement and share successes on a daily basis.

The format of the 'daily stand up' is based around three key pillars with a focused agenda that discusses:

1. **People:** The team owns the meeting. Everyone is expected to contribute and a rota is used to appoint a weekly leader. There is a standard agenda that ensures a consistent format to discussions. There is a clear resource planner and an opportunity to raise any health and safety risks relevant to the team's working environment.
2. **Performance:** Performance measures specific to each team are introduced, so that the team are always aware of how they are performing and how their performance affects the wider organisation, contributing towards the achievement of strategic key performance indicators.

3. **Continuous Improvement:** Opportunities for improvement are identified, with an agreement reached on who is responsible for executing any necessary actions. Any lessons learned are shared across the team, with successes shared and celebrated.

Any 3Cs?

In the short 15-minute daily stand up, the emphasis of discussions is primarily focused on motivating team members on how they can deliver improved performance. The stimulus for the continuous improvement discussion in a daily stand up is triggered by the question 'Are there any 3Cs?'

What Is a 3C?

- Concern – What is the problem or opportunity for improvement?
- Cause – Why is it a problem or an improvement opportunity?
- Countermeasure – How can the problem be solved or the improvement implemented?

When a 3C is raised, the 'concern' is briefly discussed and recorded on the daily stand up visual management board. A 3C review meeting, usually held every two weeks, provides the opportunity for more discussion on the progress of 3Cs and where they can be 'closed', when a solution has been successfully implemented. These meetings also allow more time to identify possible causes and suitable countermeasures for more challenging 3Cs.

IMPACT OF DAILY STAND UPS

The greatest impact resulting from daily stand ups is the number of improvements made by staff within their own business area. Since the introduction of the first daily stand up at the University of Strathclyde, over 4,000 improvements have been implemented which have directly resulted in staff capacity and efficiency savings for the University. These are improvements generated by staff at all levels of the organisation that have a direct impact on the effective and efficient operation of the University.

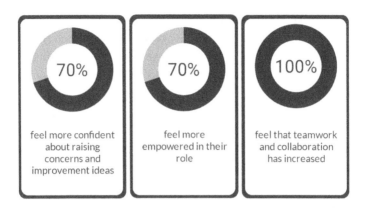

FIGURE 8.2
Average results from the anonymous baseline survey completed by University of Strathclyde teams attending a daily stand up.

Prior to introducing a new daily stand up, an anonymous baseline survey is carried out with the team to understand how they feel about the current approach to communication within the team, how empowered they feel in their role and how confident staff feel about suggesting and implementing improvements. The survey is then repeated two months following implementation to allow a reasonable period for the daily stand up to become embedded within the team.

On average, the results from the survey (see Figure 8.2) demonstrate that:

- Over 70 per cent of university employees who take part in daily stand ups feel more confident about raising concerns and improvement ideas.
- 70 per cent feel more empowered in their role.
- 100 per cent feel that teamwork and collaboration has increased.

Driving Daily Improvements – The Theory of Marginal Gains

The concept of marginal gains (Harrell, 2015) posits that a number of small incremental improvements to a process can lead to a more significant improvement overall. This is certainly the ideology behind the continuous improvement segment of the daily stand up. The team are encouraged to raise 'concerns' that may be currently impacting the work they do, or if they have ideas on how to improve the current ways of working – no matter how small or large. These are then taken forward by members of the team who are tasked with identifying the 'cause' and a suitable 'countermeasure'. This effectively removes the leader/follower relationship and creates a leader/leader relationship; producing leaders at every level. It encourages the team to be pro-active, empowered and improvement-focused.

The feedback from teams that the CID has worked with highlights the transformational impact that the introduction of a daily stand up has had and demonstrates the tangible benefits that can be gained from incremental continuous improvement activity:

> Our daily [daily stand up] meetings give me an understanding of what colleagues are working on and what we all hope to achieve that day. I can put forward ideas at the meetings and realise that they can be achieved. One good idea can inspire others to improve it and this has led to savings in time and resources, and more efficient processes within the team. (Strathclyde daily stand up attendee.)

In one business area, Student Lifecycle Services, a number of improvement ideas were raised via the daily stand ups which were all related to the student registration process. Each daily stand up could have addressed these individually, however, as a Department, they wanted to tackle them in a joined-up way to maximise the impact of their improvements and take a more holistic approach to creating a better student experience.

Registration marks an important phase at the start of a student's journey at Strathclyde, and to create a positive impression from the outset, this process must be as effective and efficient as possible. The project, supported by the CID, implemented a number of improvements which resulted in an 83% reduction in the average waiting time for international students and 1,800 students benefitting from the introduction of the early card collection scheme. These benefits directly contributed to achieving the strategic objective to deliver an outstanding student experience.

DAILY STAND UPS AND HIGH PERFORMING TEAMS

The CID sought to work in a way that tapped into the talents of every member of staff within the institution, generating positive employee engagement leading to a long-term culture of continuous improvement.

Working on a number of cross-university initiatives with staff at all levels demonstrated that when they were provided with the mechanisms to be creative, share collective knowledge and had the opportunity to communicate in a more transparent way, it had a huge impact on all aspects of their work and to the overall team.

The daily stand up provides a key opportunity for managers to work more proactively with their teams by focusing on improvements and performance that align to the delivery of the University strategy. It helps to create a culture that that empowers staff to generate improvements by identifying the most suitable solutions as a team.

Performance measures help to identify a baseline for continuous improvement and connect the specific work of the team to the high-level key performance indicators, demonstrating how each area supports the University in achieving these. By discussing performance regularly, every individual is aware of how the team is performing against its objectives. This results in targeted progress towards achieving the University's strategic goals and an understanding amongst all staff of how their own contribution can be used as a proactive visual to help achieve objectives. Any deviation from the typical performance can be detected early and rectified if necessary. It helps to build a picture of what good looks like and assess the impact improvements are making.

The power of engaging staff by being transparent with performance data and information should not be underestimated. At Strathclyde, our staff want to know what they are doing, why they are doing it and have the opportunities to shape how the University achieves its ambition. This results in staff who are far more invested in the strategy and direction of the University and motivated to improve.

CONCLUSION

The University of Strathclyde has taken an innovative approach in the higher education sector to introduce regular face to face communication, reinventing the concept of the daily team briefing as a 'daily stand up'. This approach is one of the key foundations in helping to embed and sustain a culture of continuous improvement across the University.

With over 50 daily stand ups in operation* with hundreds of staff participating, this innovative approach is revolutionising the way in which teams not only communicate with each other, but how the organisation communicates as a whole. This approach has been powerful in establishing a continuous improvement culture.

The CID philosophy is that continuous improvement is never ending. The introduction of daily stand ups has provided a practical mechanism to positively change the institutional culture to one of continuous improvement and collaboration ensuring that the University's collective mind-set is focused on the future.

A daily stand up is an extremely effective way of empowering and engaging staff through encouraging the team to take ownership and responsibility for making improvements. Importantly, it also provides a forum to record the outcomes of improvements and celebrate the successes.

The focus on driving improved performance and demonstrating tangible benefits can be gained from incremental improvement activity and engaging talent at all levels of the organisation. Daily stand ups are a catalyst for bigger improvement opportunities and sustainment of change.

---

* As at mid-2018

9

Lean Transformation Management among Employees in Universiti Putra Malaysia

Siti Raba'ah Hamzah and Dalina Kamarudin

CONTENTS

INTRODUCTION

The Malaysian government has been affected by the increasingly challenging world environment, notably due to falling oil prices as well as the rising and falling of currencies. Every year funds allocated by the Malaysian government for public universities are declining, where basic management for public funding is targeted at a ratio of 70:30, and therefore the government will only finance 70% of the budget for the entire university's management (Malaysian Education Development Plan, 2015–2025). To ensure that this new policy does not affect the operations and quality of the university's services, the Universiti Putra Malaysia (UPM) management has implemented controls over the size of staffing, in 2018 with a ratio of academic and non-academic staff to 1:1.75 (UPM's Strategic Plan, 2014–2020).

In 2015, the government has limited the number of civil servants to 1.7 million and no new posts for all ministries and public agencies. In addition, the review of the employment scheme has been initiated by the Malaysia Public Service Department (Service Circular No. 01/2016) to ensure that the existing positions do not overlap in terms of their duties and functions which in 2016, resulted in the rationalization of service schemes being implemented where there are service schemes that have been improved, revamped and abolished.

For the 2017 financial year, UPM's budget was the third largest public university being reduced by government spending, which is a reduction of 29.68%. This involved a reduction of financial allocation of RM130.39 million. This reduction in expenditure by the government was made to ensure that funds donated to public universities should be used to carry out projects that only impact the effectiveness of the country. In that regard, management transformation needs to be implemented by optimizing the use of human resources such as staff, finance, infrastructure and equipment without the need to increase public spending and it requires a more efficient and effective governance for any change. The government has outlined several strategies for enhancing public service delivery and reducing bureaucratic red tape and improving the delivery process to make public services more robust and efficient.

Based on the Malaysia Guidelines for Developing a Transformation Plan (2013), good governance focuses on two key factors, namely: the achievement of efficient and effective performance or value for money, and compliance with laws and regulations. In this regard, implementing lean transformation management is expected to enhance the governance in UPM as well as to increase stakeholder confidence in the implementation itself, decisions and actions made as a result.

BACKGROUND OF THE STUDY

Universiti Putra Malaysia (UPM) is one of the leading institutions of higher learning in Malaysia and is in Serdang, next to Malaysia's administrative capital city, Putrajaya. As a world renowned centre of learning and research, UPM has attracted students and staff from all around the world, making it a well-respected global entity.

UPM started as the School of Agriculture in 1931 and was established as a university in 1971. UPM has made a huge contribution to society and Malaysia in the development of research, teaching, learning, generating innovation and technology. In 2006 it was recognized as a Research University and was granted autonomy from the Ministry of Education Malaysia to take control of the institutional governance, academic management, wealth creation and human resource planning. To date, there are 5,889 staff, with 1,777 academic and 4,112 non-academic staff, to serve a total of 24,874 students – comprising 14,063 undergraduate and 10,811 postgraduates students, with more than 4,000 of those international students.

UPM knows that higher education services, that have been and are being developed, need to be: sustainable, ensuring environmental harmony; relevant to future needs; be able to advance knowledge; and be able to develop human capital, for national progress. Therefore, the goals of: developing good governance, cultivating excellence, preserving and conserving the environment, utilizing diversity, implementing innovative management, and producing high-impact higher education service initiatives sustainability are critical to enable UPM to continue to be able to contribute to the development of global human capital.

This vision, to contribute to the development of global human capital, is highly relevant and significant to UPM's mission to become a university of international repute. UPM plans to significantly develop its direction to increase excellence at an international level. In order to achieve the international repute, UPM seeks to possess the characteristics of: quality leadership, governance and well-ordered administration. The leadership at UPM is stable, its governance is well-structured and its administration is effective and efficient. In pursuing and ensuring quality leadership, governance and administration the university has employed a Quality

Management System (QMS) and is dedicated to Continual Quality Improvement (CQI).

To ensure that quality leadership, governance and administration at UPM can be maintained at the best level, UPM needs to improve its human resource management since the payment of staff emoluments is the highest expenditure made by the university each year. Furthermore, improvements of work processes need to be made to ensure staff can carry out university activities and operations without adversely affecting the interests of customers especially students. Therefore, one approach that UPM wants to implement is to practice lean thinking.

Lean thinking (albeit not referred to as such at the time) was introduced in the early 1930s. It was founded by the world's largest automobile manufacturer, Toyota Motor Corporation from Japan. In Japan, lean thinking has been spearheaded by the Toyota Production System (TPS) which sets out how Toyota Motor Corporation operates based on the principles and philosophy introduced by the company leaders. Among the principles introduced are Jidoka (automation with human touch), Just-in-Time and Kanban. The TPS approach began to gain Western attention when the term 'lean' which meant eliminating wastage was introduced (Womack & Jones, 2003).

Although lean's approach comes from the car production industry, it has been adopted in the public sector, including institutions of higher learning. A study by Radnor & Walley (2008) states that the public sector in Western countries such as hospitals, universities, government agencies and local authorities have adopted the lean approach as one of the mechanisms to achieve substantial cost savings and improve service quality. Lean implementation in the public sector has reduced the timeframe in producing services and outputs, reducing work processes, staff are able to do 50% additional work, cost savings and increased customer satisfaction as they receive faster and more accurate services.

The history of lean implementation at UPM was initiated in 2013 and is a continuation of the organization's successful quality management implementation program. UPM sees lean management as an alternative method of management for organizations to face challenges, such as managing the University in the context of resource constraints such as finance. In addition, UPM sees lean management as an approach to innovation to encourage organizations to improve their work system and new ways of working: '*think differently; do more with less*'.

Therefore, the steps taken by UPM to introducing lean management are best suited to the current challenges. Lean management, which prioritizes the importance of value towards the customers in delivering a service and eliminating wastes, is highly relevant to public universities. Lean thinking at UPM is based on a lean management implementation model developed from the St Andrews Model (Robinson & Yorkstone, 2014). Based on these models, lean governance includes the following principles: structure, roadmap designation, thought-provoking, providing competent staff to implement projects, lean transformation strategies, determining functions and services of the University, determining customer needs, and monitoring and managing risks.

Several sections at UPM were selected for the early implementation of lean management transformation namely the Registrar's Office, Academic Division, School of Graduate Studies, Development and Asset Management Office, Bursar Office, Information and Communications Development Center, Sultan Abdul Samad Library, International Center, Faculty Education Studies, Student Affairs Division, Internal Audit Division, Deputy Vice Chancellor Office (Research and Innovation), University Colleges and Health Centers. All 14 sections involved have undergone lean and medium management awareness courses or have carried out lean management transformation at their respective sections. There are nine steps in implementing the lean management transformation, which are: identifying the process of improvement, planning, training, process mapping, improvement, process re-mapping, new process execution, monitoring and standardization of improved processes. Thus, the high commitment from all parties within the organization is critical to ensure the successful implementation of lean transformation management.

LEAN MANAGEMENT

Lean thinking is a management approach that prioritizes customer needs whether internal and external customers. According to Womack & Jones (2003) it is a systematic approach that focuses on continuous improvement, simplifies work processes, optimizes costs and eliminates wastage through the best process-based workflow to make services more efficient which meets the customer demand. In addition to meeting the customer demand the staff will also be more satisfied with the work performed. There are two key philosophies in lean management using the Toyota Production System (TPS) approach, i.e. continuous improvement or Kaizen and respect for the individual. Continuous improvement or Kaizen focuses on challenging everything in the work process to ensure constant changes towards optimisation can be implemented. Continuous improvement or Kaizen can create a learning atmosphere by consistently appreciating the change. Staff involvement in the improvement of their work creates an environment of respect for individuals. Only through the practice of respecting individuals alone can the environment that encourages continuous improvement be developed. In lean management, the chief is committed to developing and inculcating the trust and understanding among all members of the team, departments, divisions and organizations and together help the staff overcome the challenges and obstacles faced by them in achieving common goals.

The initial stage of implementing lean management is to identify and create a continuous flow in a work process by eliminating wastage, known in Japanese as *muda*. When the continuous flow has been established the completion time of a process has been shortened and the effect of the best product or service quality with minimum cost can be generated. According to Womack and Jones (2003) there are eight wastages that need to be eliminated in the process of work, i.e. excess production, waiting time, transportation, excessive processing, inventories, movements, disabilities and unused staff creativity.

Lean management involves steady activity over a long period of time and emphasizes the principle of continuous improvement to ensure that those involved with the lean management transformation will continue to move forward through innovation creation and improve customer service. The principle of the plan-do-check-action cycle can be used as a means of implementing continuous improvements in the work. In addition, the Malaysian Standard for International Organization for Standardization (MS ISO 9001: 2008) quality system management is one of the systems used to improve service quality and to adopt a plan-do-check-action cycle practice. Hence, UPM has the advantage of implementing lean management because it has held MS ISO 9001: 2008 certification since 2011. The scope of this certification involves all major university processes including teaching and learning, research and innovation, professional services and support.

CONTEXT OF THE STUDY

To enhance the readiness and awareness of the importance of implementing lean's management among UPM staff, the UPM Registrar's Office organized a lean management awareness course at UPM commencing in 2013. This course was aimed at raising staff awareness and readiness before actual changes occur to prevent staff from rejecting the changes. According to Holt et al. (2007) when there is a willingness to change within the organization there will be four beliefs: 1) members in the organization believe that the change can be implemented, 2) the change can benefit the organization, 3) organizational leaders are committed to implementing changes and 4) changes are beneficial to every member in the organization.

There are three phases in the implementation of lean at UPM, namely: 1) awareness phase of lean implementation, 2) the application phase of lean thinking in the work practice and 3) lean transformation management phase. A high commitment from UPM staff is necessary because the transformation of lean management requires changes to the work process, the way of thinking in performing work and changes in work culture. Thus, it was concluded that a study should be carried out to see whether there is a relationship between the organizational commitment and the conscious change of the lean transformation management.

READINESS TO CHANGE

Change is continuous, yet often changes are opposed by the system and the individual, as change challenges the status quo (Peterson & Baker, 2011). When implementing change in the organization, readiness is a 'mind-set' that exists among every employee when implementing organizational changes. Readiness includes the elements of trust, attitude and intentions of a worker on the need and ability to implement changes in an organization (Vakola, 2014; Armenakis & Fredenberger, 1997).

A study conducted by Vakola (2014) show that employees who are confident with their individual abilities and can control stress such as facing changes are likely to see positive changes, and these groups are willing to implement changes in the organization. Employees with a positive outlook on change in the organization would be willing to change because they believe that the change would impact positively on them and the organization. There are four beliefs when there is a willingness to change within the organization; that is when members in the organization believe that changes can be made, the changes can benefit the organization, organizational leaders are committed to implementing changes and changes that benefit individuals (Holt et al., 2007). Enhancing organizational readiness should be undertaken before actual changes occur and organizational leaders should be prepared to deal with it. Some of the strategies that influence individuals to be prepared for change are oral or written communication, active participation and internal information from an organization management group. Organizations should be prepared to make changes to achieve the goal of continuous improvement. Organizational leadership plays an important role in gaining commitment and willingness to change to improve organizational performance. This supports the statement from Kotter (1995) that leadership is the key foundation in making changes in the organization. The leadership process requires interpersonal communication between its head and subordinates.

Active participation contributes positively towards the organization's launching a change process. Willingness to change involves both the individual's desire to change and the individual's ability to carry out the change successfully, in order to enable individuals to participate in the process of change in the organization actively (Cunningham et al., 2002). Cultural factors in the organization can also affect readiness to change where there is a positive and strong relationship between the willingness to change with the work culture within the organization.

Positive changes in the organization can have a positive impact in improving the quality of work in which the quality of work is the desire to maintain standards and increase productivity to be more advanced. Quality is seen from two aspects, namely external and internal aspects, where it needs to meet the needs of the organization as well as customer and user satisfaction. Therefore, in order to achieve that quality, an organization should be bold in dealing with the change so that the governance system can relate to today's changing environment. Overall, the leadership element is a key factor in implementing change (Kotles & Schlesinger, 2008) and contributing factors in maintaining the implementation strategy of change within the organization.

Accordingly, a study was conducted to assess the readiness of UPM staff in preparing the implement of lean transformation management at UPM.

RESEARCH METHODOLOGY

This research study attempts to examine the descriptive analysis and the level of the readiness to change by applying self-administered survey questionnaire. Measurement Scales Survey questionnaire has been developed based on what kind of information needed in this study. Tenth items applied based on Hanpachern's original Scale with slight alterations (1977).

Participants

The population for this study consists of UPM staff who are directly involved with lean Management transformation. A total of 451 staff from 14 sections who have undergone lean awareness courses were selected for the implementation of the lean management system, consisting of representatives from management, professional (non-academic), executive roles.

Validity of the sample for this study relies on the ability to estimate sample size suitability in order to obtain the data needed to give an enlightened and representative view on population characteristics. The actual determined sample size for this study also refers to the Krejcie and Morgan tables, (1970) formula as a step to determined sample of this study which is around 212 people. All respondents are UPM staff has been involved with the transformation of lean management at UPM.

Procedures

The data for this study were gathered via a survey questionnaire. Researchers contacted the respondent for their willingness to take part in the study including their supervisor at work place. The survey was administered to the participants through personal visits. They were asked to complete the questionnaire that was distributed directly among them. Verbal consent was acquired from the respondents and they were assured that the information given would be kept confidential or anonymized. It takes about 5 weeks to collecting the data in 14 sections in UPM from December 2015 until February 2016.

RESULTS

Distribution of Respondents

Table 9.1 shows the respondents distribution according to the 14 sections at UPM. Namely the Registrar's Offices consist of 11.8%, Faculty of Educational Studies consist of 10.4%, Development and Asset Management Office consist of 1.9%, Sultan Abdul Samad Library consist of 6.7%, Bursar Office with 9.4%, Student Affairs Division consist of 7.5%, Internal Audit Division has 2.4%, University Health Center consist of 11.8%, Academic Division consist of 7.1%, Deputy Vice-Chancellor (Research & Innovation Center consist of 7.5%, Residential Colleges consist of 7.5%, Information and Communication Development Center consist of 6.1%, The International Center consist of 2.8% and Graduate School consist of 7.1%. The total number of staff involved is 212 people.

TABLE 9.1

Respondent Distribution

Section in UPM	Frequency	Percentage (%)
Registrar's Offices	25	11.8
Faculty of Educational Studies	22	10.4
Development and Asset Management Office	4	1.9
Sultan Abdul Samad Library	14	6.7
Bursar Office	20	9.4
Student Affairs Division	16	7.5
Internal Audit Division	5	2.4
University Health Center	25	11.8
Academic Division	15	7.1
Deputy Vice-Chancellor (Research & Innovation) Office	16	7.5
Residential Colleges	16	7.5
Information and Communication Development Center	13	6.1
International Center	6	2.8
Graduate School	15	7.1

Demographics of Respondents

Table 9.2 shows the number of respondents, 76 males (35.8%) and 136 females (64.2%). The respondents whose age are between 21 to 30 consist of 53 people (25%), between 31 to 40 consist of 112 people (52.8%), between 41 to 50 consist of 24 people (11.3%), and between 51 to 60 consist of 23 people (10.8%). A total of 123 people (58%) are from the Executives group, 43 people (20.3%) are from the Management group while the remaining 46 people (21.7%) are Professional (non-academic) group. For the service period of less than 10 years, there are a total of 130 people (61.3%), while between 11 to 20 years of service consist of 54 people (25.5%), followed by 19 people (9%) who has between 20 to 30 years of service and those who have 30 years of service consist of 9 people (4.2%).

Level of Readiness to Change towards Lean Transformation Management among Employees

Table 9.3 displays the descriptive characteristics of the items readiness to change and showed the highest level, 4.00 and above on a five-point Likert scale. Descriptive results also indicated respondents used all response

TABLE 9.2

Respondent Demographic Analysis

Profile	Frequency (n = 212)	Percentage (%)
Gender		
Male	76	35.8
Female	136	64.2
Age (Year)		
21–30	53	25
31–40	112	52.8
41–50	24	11.3
51–60	23	10.8
Executives group	123	58
Management group	43	20.3
Professional (non-academic) group	46	21.7
Years of Service		
0–10 Years	130	61.3
11–20 Years	54	25.5
21–30 Years	19	9
>30 Years	9	4.2

TABLE 9.3

Level of Readiness to Change Towards Lean Transformation Among Employees

Item	Min	SD
Support lean transformation efforts	4.29	.46
Learn new things	4.22	.45
Do things in a new or creative way	4.20	.42
Change the way I work because of lean transformation	4.15	.37
Be a part of lean transformation strategic plan	4.15	.35
Promote ideas about implementing lean transformation to improve work process	4.13	.37
Solve organizational problems by using lean approaches	4.12	.36
Change the way I work even if it appears to be working	4.12	.38
Be a apart of lean transformation project	4.06	.37
Work more because of lean transformation management	4.05	.25

options available. Standard deviations ranged from .25 to .46. As shown in Table 9.3, the level of readiness to change was high ($M = 4.03$, $SD = .52$).

Findings

The general purpose of this study was to find out the readiness to change towards lean transformation among employee in Universiti Putra Malaysia. The study demonstrates that employees were characterized by higher level of readiness to change towards lean transformation through supporting lean transformation efforts, learning new things, doing things in a new or creative way, being a part of lean transformation strategic plan, changing the way their work even if it appears to be working and changing the way their work because of lean transformation. They were also wanted to be a part of the lean transformation project and to promote ideas around implementing lean transformation to improve work process and solve organizational problems by using lean approaches. They were also more positively inclined to work because of lean transformation.

UPM MOVE FORWARD WITH LEAN HIGHER EDUCATION

Achievements in UPM were not engineered by one person. The successes of the university are because it has a cohesive team of energetic, talented people working together compatibly. Within the university there are two main job functions: on the one hand the academic staff that excel in conducting research, commercialising their products and innovations, and on the other hand professional services with support staff undertaking administrative work. This duality has the possibility of causing conflict, which automatically makes it harder to implement a lean culture in the whole organization. When we additionally consider that UPM consists of 17 faculties the challenge is clear: however, it is often the case that that faculties work together to achieve the goals of the whole organization.

Academic institutions such as UPM have three missions including teaching, research and public service (Pucciarelli & Kaplan, 2016) and are not immune to changes. Furthermore, the future of academic system will be doubtless more complicated, challenging and uncertain. Based on the findings of this study, lean should at the very least be part of the discussion when planning and develop such strategy for the university's future. Employees of university, both academic and support staff, might not respond to the current changes in a rapid time because of the inherent resistance in university organizational culture. Therefore, the lean transformation for these staff should be done incrementally through training, motivating and persuading the current administrators.

To date, UPM has taken a lead among public universities in Malaysia in applying lean transformation management in the university; with two pillars fundamentals of lean which are continuous improvement and respects for people. For the continuous improvement, best practice was creating a culture that constantly examines work processes and strives to improve using the lean principles and practices such as plan-do-check-act cycle. The second pillar of respect for people involves engaging employees who know the processes, with lean training and lean leaders to identify opportunities, broken processes and bring about improvements.

Within the four-year experience in lean transformation management, the UPM Registrar and the committee members of lean team in UPM has published a book on Lean Management in a Public University Framework: Lean@UA in 2017. This book guides employees in public universities on how to become more efficient and productive in the use of their assets, personnel and resources through the lean management best practices. UPM has also been recognized by the Malaysian Productivity Corporation (MPC) with the special award Creanova Lean in 2017. Creanova Lean is an annual event organized by the MPC as a platform to share experiences and results from the implementation of lean projects, and in recognition of lean projects that have been successfully implemented by government agencies and private companies throughout the country.

UPM believes that lean management transformation is a powerful strategy supported by strong principles and good practice that will create a new university culture to; meet the expectations of people served, free up wasted resources for reinvestment, support positive values and engage all university employees to 'own the process' and ultimately transform the university into a true learning organization.

BIBLIOGRAPHY

Armenakis, A. A., & Fredenberger, W. B. 1997. Organizational change readiness practices of business turnaround change agents, *Knowledge and Process Management*, vol. 4, no. 3, pp. 143–152.

Cunningham, C. E., Woodward, C. A., Shannon, H. S., MacIntosh, J., Lendrum, B., Rosenbloom, D., & Brown, J. 2002. Readiness for organizational change: A longitudinal study of workplace, psychological and behavioural correlates, *Journal of Occupational and Organizational Psychology*, vol. 75, no. 4, pp. 377–392.

Hanpachern, C. 1997, *The Extension of the Theories of Margin: A Framework for Assessing Readiness for Change (Organizational Culture)*, Fort Collins, Colorado State University.

Holt, D. T., Armenakis, A. A., Feild, H. S., & Harris, S. G. 2007. Readiness for organizational change: The systematic development of a scale, *The Journal of Applied Behavioral Science*, vol. 43, no. 2, pp. 232–255.

Kotter, J. P. 1995. Leading change: Why transformation efforts fail, *Harvard Business Review*, vol. 73, pp. 59–67.

Kotter, J. P. & Schlesinger, L. A. 2008. Choosing strategies for change.*Harvard Business Review*. Available at: https://hbr.org/2008/07/choosing-strategies-for-change.

Krejcie, R. V., & Morgan, D. W. 1970. Determining sample size for research activities, *Educational and Psychological Measurement*, vol. 30, no. 3, pp. 607–610.

Peterson, S. M., & Baker, A. C. 2011. Readiness to change in communities, organizations, and individuals, in *The Early Childhood Educator Professional Development Grant: Research and Practice*, Emerald Group Publishing Limited, pp. 33–59.

Pucciarelli, F., & Kaplan, A. 2016. Competition and strategy in higher education: Managing complexity and uncertainty, *Business Horizons*, vol. 59, no. 3, pp. 311–320.

Radnor, Z., & Walley, P. 2008. Learning to walk before we try to run. Adopting lean for the public sector, *Public Money and Management*, vol. 28, no. 2, pp. 13–20.

Robinson, M., & Yorkstones, S. 2014. Becoming a lean university: The case of the University of St. Andrews, *Leadership and Governance in Higher Education*, vol. 1, pp. 42–69.

Vakola, M. 2014. What's in there for me? Individual readiness to change and the perceived impact of organizational change, *Leadership and Organization Development Journal*, vol. 35, no. 3, pp. 195–209.

Womack, J. P., & Jones, D. T. 2003. *Lean Thinking: Banish Waste and Create Wealth in Your Corporation*, New York, Free Press.

Yorkstone, S. 2013. Lean goes back to school, *Lean Management Journal*, vol 8, no. 3, pp. 24–27.

Section III

Projects

10

Applying Lean in Projects; from Visualisations to Process Engineering – It's Covered!

Laura Hallett

CONTENTS

This chapter explores the application of Lean concepts to manage projects, providing practical advice and guidance for project implementation and delivery. Guidance spans a range of techniques from how to use visual agendas to maximising participation in workshops to running a successful retrospective to remove unnecessary waste. The chapter presents a range of tools to use to manage projects within your own organisation. Alongside the techniques, you will be presented with a case study demonstrating how this has been used on a project with Higher Education, providing you with a 'tried and tested' approach.

A CONTEXT FOR LEAN

We are at the start of the fourth industrial revolution. The jobs of the future are impossible to define and hard to conceptualise. Big data, machine learning and artificial intelligence have delivered advances which seemed inconceivable five years ago and the role of the 'human' is being challenged and redefined. Higher Education continues to change. Social, economic and political factors are impacting both the role of the University and how it is perceived in the world.

Unprecedented change across the world impacts upon all business sectors. It has never been more important to adapt quickly to accommodate and respond to the uncertainty. One constant within the current business environment is that humans (people) continue to make the decisions leading the strategic direction of organisations. And despite the excitement of machine learning enabling some business processes to be conducted effectively, efficiently and economically by robotics, the emotional and interpersonal skills of people are unlikely to be replicated or replaced by machines.

SETTING THE SCENE FOR THE PROJECT

The three P's make me tick: people, processes and perfectionism. Accepting perfectionism can offer more problems than it solves, I have settled on excellence. Lean places these three themes at its centre, valuing the skillset of people. The first thing you should do as a project manager, project sponsor or project stakeholder is to think about the people involved in your project. The next is to develop an understanding of your processes from the standpoint of what are you changing and why are you changing it. Finally, and in your specific context, you should determine how you will deliver excellence, factoring in what value you will add, what waste you will remove and which individual's under-utilised talents you will help rediscover.

When Setting Your Project Scene, Get Visual

Complete this scene of the current context drawing on a Strengths, Weaknesses, Opportunities and Threats (SWOT), a stakeholder Persona Analysis, a Political, Economic, Social, Technological, Legal and Environmental (PESTLE) analysis and, most importantly, a summary of your customers' aims and views (Figure 10.1).

WHY CHOOSE LEAN TECHNIQUES TO MANAGE YOUR PROJECT

The world is fast paced, it is changing rapidly, it is uncertain and it requires us to be agile and creative in how we operate. Lean techniques work in this environment. The foci on people, adding value, visualisations and eliminating wastes are transferable to managing all projects. Many organisations struggle with appropriate project governance and transparency. There is a lack of project management skills in many

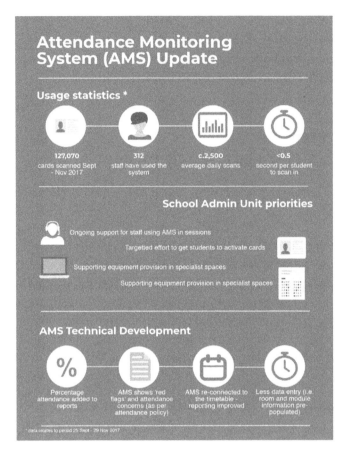

FIGURE 10.1
Setting the scene. Example shown designed in Piktochart. It was used to set the Project Scene prior to a new version release.

organisations and gaps in basic knowledge amongst project stakeholders. Within such a context, and working with an ever present need to respect our own time and that of others, Lean project management works.

COMPLIMENTARY TECHNIQUES TO USE ALONGSIDE LEAN

Tailoring is a critical element of the Prince 2 doctrine of project management. It is the element of Prince 2 I value the most and a project characteristic I take into every project. No organisation is the same. No two sponsors are the same. Our personalities impact how we like to digest information and respond to risks and there will never be enough time or resources to deliver the perfect product. There will always be the influence of politics (both the small and the capitalised 'p'). This requires the project manager to tailor their approach and draw on all tools, techniques and styles of project management to get the best from their people, in their organisation whilst managing the internal and external factors as best as possible. Draw on Agile, Kanban, Waterfall, Prince 2 and Continuous Improvement. Do not become a purest and don't be afraid to try something new. With a world changing around us, we have to change ourselves or we risk being left behind.

USING VISUAL PROPS TO MAXIMISE ENGAGEMENT

An Introduction to Visual Management

We each have different learning styles and preferences. Individuals can learn to adapt their preferences with time. When we listen to others, we can get distracted and our concentration sometimes wains. As a general rule of thumb, we remember things in groups of three, need these repeating to be remembered and actively listen when we are engaged. Project content is not always exciting. You don't always care what the issue facing your colleagues within the admissions team are if you have delivered your output. However, you're a member of the project team and you're all responsible for the collective delivery of the project. What's the solution? How do you get all stakeholders to engage for most of the time? You make it interesting, you make things different, you get creative: you use visuals.

Through using visual tools and techniques you can engage teams quicker as you catch and maintain their attention. Visual representation of concepts, ideas, agendas and retrospectives are better to 'write-up' and easier to digest. In recognising time is precious, using visual tools makes better use of everyone's time. As a sector, we are still committed to long written reports, verbose debates of alternative options and overly complex audits to evidence decision making. Longstanding conventions mean that these are essential components of the HE research arena. However, I would argue for project delivery, refinement and retrospectives, the additional time they take to complete nearly always outweigh the value they add.

Using visual tools and techniques does not require qualifications in art and design. There are hundreds of templates and methods available on project blogs and teaching resource websites alongside curation platforms such as Pinterest and Padlet. Use the internet to help develop your creative, visual tools and understand your stakeholders. What works for one group may need adapting for others. My approach has developed over the years, and it keeps changing. In the following sections I highlight my current favourites alongside my trusted tried and tested visualisations which I have been using for years.

Using Visual Agendas to Maximise Participation in the Project Workshops – Accommodation Project

We have all attended a meeting which involved one or two prominent voices hijacking the agenda. Using a visual agenda alongside a 'car park' is a successful way to mitigate this risk. With the 'car park' function you manage the session and keep attendees focused. You can work collaboratively with the project team to develop your visual agenda for project workshops if you need to increase engagement. A visual agenda requires your participants to stand up and engage in the meeting rather than sitting comfortably behind their paper agenda. This minimises distractions and increases participation.

Visual agendas should feature the following key points (Figure 10.2):

- The high-level aim of the workshop.
- The objectives – Try to stick to three and make them tangible.
- A structured plan of attack with timings and lead facilitators (allow more time rather than less).
- The rules of engagement for the workshop.
- A roles and responsibilities section that explain who's doing what.
- A 'What Next' section with timings and owners for the actions.

Explanation of and Deployment of the 'Car Park'

Figure 10.2 is the version Christina and I used to launch our Project Management Training Framework. This isn't a rigid template, get creative and design it in the way it works best for you. If you start to use it as often as I do, changing how you present it will keep it fresh and directly

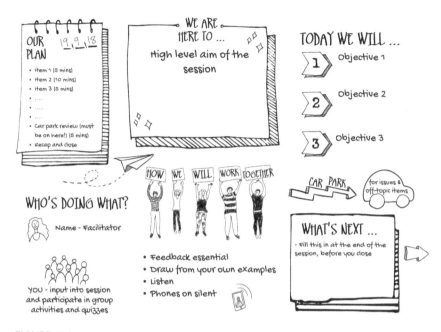

FIGURE 10.2
Visual agenda. Example created in Canva, designed by Christina Nichols (York St John University) and Laura Hallett.

applicable to the project. There are a number of versions you can use, online (Figure 10.3).

Use a car park alongside a visual agenda but ensure participants understand what it is for. It is designed to help you, the facilitator, manage the session and ensure the objectives are met. When you find individuals are slipping away from the aim and objectives of the session, give them a post-it to write their point on and then ask them to park it on the car park. Ensure you review the car park as part of the session (it will need to be in your structured plan of attack) and make sure owners are assigned to the car parked items which guarantees follow-up. Don't be afraid of making the owner of the parked item the person who parked it.

Visual Tools That Increased Engagement with the Project – Preparing for the Implementation of the EU General Data Protection Regulation (GDPR)

Engaging colleagues in regulatory and statutory projects is hard work. Even the most conscientious seize up when data protection or legal requirements are mentioned. Trying to engage staff in dry topics requires

FIGURE 10.3
Car park. Example created in Canva used for Project Management Training Programme, designed by Christina Nichols (York St John University) and Laura Hallett.

creative thinking, word play and a fresh (and visual way) of capturing the imagination and attention of people. This was the approach I took in managing a GDPR Project, recently.

A Data Breach Policy is not a thrilling read but faced with UK Information Commissioner Office fines of up to £17 million (or 4% global turnover) I needed a creative way to educate all staff on the key components of the policy (see Table 10.1). This involved creating a simulation of the Data Breach (i.e. inadvertently sharing an individual's personal data with someone whom you do not have a legal right to share the data with). A simulation activity is incredibly impactful on projects where you need a group of stakeholders to understand a process, policy or experience. Creating a visual simulation which guides stakeholders through a process or policy is engaging and informative. It also increases the likelihood of the topic sticking. I have used similar techniques on projects where business areas do not see why their processes and systems are confusing and burdensome for their customers.

Reporting and Monitoring within a Project Using Visual Templates – Setting Up an International Pathway College

In the fast-paced world of work, we have become overly reliant on the written form. Email and instant messaging in the workplace threatens to replace the human contact we have. Academia celebrates written prose,

TABLE 10.1

Simulation Exercise

Invented Scenario	Data Breach Simulation		
	• Card 1. Suzie arrives into the office flustered having attended a conference in London yesterday. She's unable to locate her laptop which she took to the conference with her. • Card 2. Suzie doesn't have encryption on her laptop but she does have a password set to log-in. Suzie is worried because she was working on graduation preparations for November's ceremony, this was using an Excel sheet of data downloaded from SITS. • Card 3. Suzie had stored the Excel sheet of data on her 'My Documents' on the laptop, not on a network drive. Suzie is also worried that she may also have some other SITS downloads within her 'Downloads' folder, which contain personal data. • Card 4. Suzie realises that the data on her laptop also relates to graduation guests – including some high profile VIPs.		
What the group are given and what you ask them to do	1. Group to be given first card of a scenario, then to ask the following:	• What are your priorities? • What is your role and what do you need to do? • What do others have to do, identify who the others are? • What action do I need to take?	
	2. Group to be given second card of a scenario, then to ask the following:	• What are your priorities? • What is your role and what do you need to do? • What do others have to do, identify who the others are? • What action do I need to take?	
	3. Repeat above per card numbers…	• What are your priorities? • What is your role and what do you need to do? • What do others have to do, identify who the others are? • What action do I need to take?	
Group feedback, discussion and next steps	1. Five minutes per group on what decisions they made and why 2. We cross check decisions against the ICO checklists 3. We make a note of any changes needed to policy 4. facilitators note on flipcharts any learnings which need to factor into policy changes or wider communications).		

Simulation designed by Laura Hallett and used in the GDPR Project.

analytical debate and thorough evidence-based discussion. A detailed bibliography is celebrated within an academic journal. One unfortunate consequence of this is that the writing norms and requirements for Higher Education management often replicate those necessary for academic

TABLE 10.2

Project Progress Report Template

Project Name:	Project Name		
Date range:	from DD/MM/YY to DD/ MM/YY	Created by	Name of author
RAG:	**Time (red)**	**Quality (amber)**	**Budget (green)**
Progress since last update	How does what has happened compare against the plan		
Actions for the next period	List what is to be done in the coming period		
New issues, risks and blockers	List management and mitigation against the issues and risks, also detail any blockers that are impeding your progress		
Update on issues, risks and blockers raised in last update	What's happened to what you raised last time		

Example created by Laura Hallett and used on various projects during career as a Project Manager.

journals and publication. This results in a proliferation of extensive papers to be read alongside the email traffic and reading required of the day-job.

Project progress updates do not need to fall foul to this trap! Progress updates can be done visually, reporting by exception in a succinct manner. As a firm believer of project teams needing to meet to discuss their project at key points, the progress update becomes the prompt to accompany the discussion. The development of an International Pathway College at the University of York was a complex programme involving a number of stakeholders leading different elements of the programme of activity. It was essential to use visual progress updates to manage this programme, utilising the time at the Project Board to focus on key decisions and risk mitigation escalated.

Table 10.2 showcases the progress report approach used on this project. I have subsequently tailored this to use on a range of other projects at alternative organisations.

CONDUCTING PROCESS REENGINEERING IN CHALLENGING CLIMATES

An Introduction to Process Mapping

Process mapping is the technique of mapping the sequence of actions which get you from the start to the end of an activity. Everything in life is a process and all transactional processes can be mapped. 'Why would I map a process?', may people often sigh. There are three main reasons:

- You have identified a problem with the process and you want to improve it.
- You need to explain how a process should be completed in an easy way so that different stakeholders will understand.
- A change is being introduced which requires you to change your processes.

Each of the reasons relate to working more. This should be borne in mind when process mapping. When mapping out your process you will identify unnecessary actions, duplications or actions that are unclear. Through identifying these and discussing them with the business area, you will remove actions. That is why every process mapping exercise involves completing the current way of operating, the 'as-is'. And the future state, the 'to-be'.

HOW-TO BUSINESS PROCESS REVIEW, A CASE STUDY WITH 'TOP TIPS'

I used these 'top tips' last year for the curriculum approval activities at York St John University. It had been recognised that a business process review was needed to address the dissatisfaction with the process and streamline key processes, such as marketing and recruitment for new programmes. Using my top tips, I identified the (Figure 10.4):

- High level process we would interrogate: The process of approving a programme to run at the University.
- Start, end and middle points of the process: From the idea to develop a new programme through to the programme starting (and all curriculum approval and recruitment steps in between).
- Stakeholders involved: Almost every stakeholder in the University was involved, alongside a number of externals (e.g. External Examiners).
- Manual parts of the process: A number of key process steps were in the heads of the experts in Business Areas and nowhere else.

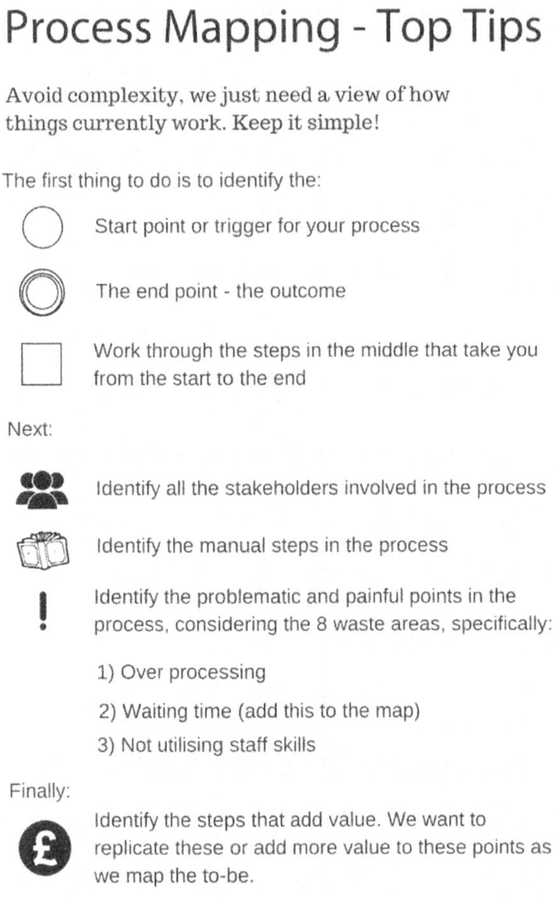

Process Mapping - Top Tips

Avoid complexity, we just need a view of how
things currently work. Keep it simple!

The first thing to do is to identify the:

○ Start point or trigger for your process

◎ The end point - the outcome

☐ Work through the steps in the middle that take you
from the start to the end

Next:

Identify all the stakeholders involved in the process

Identify the manual steps in the process

! Identify the problematic and painful points in the
process, considering the 8 waste areas, specifically:

1) Over processing

2) Waiting time (add this to the map)

3) Not utilising staff skills

Finally:

 Identify the steps that add value. We want to
replicate these or add more value to these points as
we map the to-be.

FIGURE 10.4
Top tips for process mapping.

- Problematic and painful points: From gathering feedback from the
  key stakeholders involved, I designed a mood board consisting of the
  key works which detailed the pain points; we then targeted these in
  building the 'to-be' process.
- Added value points which needed replicating: From the feedback
  gathered, I identified the added value points which we targeted when
  redesigning the 'to-be' process.

The business process review consisted of four workshops through which
we redesigned the process, agreed new timeframes for the process, agreed

new communication points and roles for managing communications, removed waste and pain points from the process and removed the perceived bureaucracy. The end process was made into a screencast for stakeholders to watch, and we redesigned the Quality Gateway with the novice user in mind as the key audience.

The key to successfully managing this business process review was to manage the workshops well through using a visual agenda and a car park. It was essential to do a lot of research and planning in advance of the sessions. I showcased the process to the team of experts from a novice's perspective, enabling the team to see how complex the process was. I had to manage the individuals present and monitor the time in the workshops really carefully to ensure we made best use of the time available. Derby and Larsen (2006) provide a range of excellent approaches to plan such sessions. Finally, I scheduled in a review of the changes for the business areas to conduct after one year of operations – this is an essential part of any process review.

REFLECTIONS: INTRODUCING BUSINESS PROCESS MAPPING INTO DAY-TO-DAY WORK

I practice what I preach; therefore, I apply business process mapping into my day-to-day work as well as in how I lead and manage my team. It is important to reflect on how we can improve our own daily processes, for example, email management, running one-to-ones with staff members and leading meaningful team meetings. Continually reflecting on our own processes in the workplace and improving them in light of the tops tips for process mapping ensures we are working in the smartest, simplest and most organised way. Three reflections I suggest you consider applying to improve your effectiveness and efficiency at work are:

- Inbox Zero for email management
- Agile stand-ups for weekly team meeting
- A standing agenda in one-to-ones designed to encourage exception reporting and 360 feedback (for you and your staff member) (Figure 10.5).

FIGURE 10.5
Standing agenda for one-to-ones.

ADDING VALUE

An Introduction to the Value Adding Principle in Lean

When managing a project using Lean, the project is set up to maximise value and minimise waste (Ballard and Howell, 2003). I applied Lean Project Management to the Accommodation System Replacement Project I managed during 2013–2016. During the analysis and design phase of the project (prior to the Business Case sign-off), I mapped every current business process alongside the Business Analysis and Business Owner. Once mapped, I identified the value added activities and the waste within the process before mapping the 'to-be' processes for the new system. This resulted in the project delivering a new system to manage accommodation alongside a range of changes to the core accommodation functions. Post-project, we had enhanced the applicant and student experience and seen efficiencies in the time it took staff to complete a number of processes.

RUNNING PROJECT TEAM MEETINGS
THROUGH SCRUMS AND STAND-UPS

With its routes firmly in the Agile development arena, stand-ups (and scrums) have a firm place at the table of all effective and collaborative workplaces. Narayan (2015) observes the culture necessary for Agile development, noting one focused on collaboration and skills development is needed in place of control and capability management. This culture needs to be present to adopt scrums and stand-ups within your workplace and the projects you manage.

I use a stand-up in place of a project team meeting for the London Campus Project I am managing. This group meet every three weeks and the stand-up consists of each workstream lead providing a three-minute, by exception, update on: (1) progress made; (2) plans for the next three weeks; (3) any issues, risks or blockers which is impeding or may impede progress. The stand-up keeps colleagues focused on the important points, encourages collective ownership for things that impede progress and removes the risk that project team members become passive during the meeting.

To successfully run a project team stand-up you must keep to time. I set an alarm which sounds if the three minutes are exceeded, stopping colleagues once they have reached their allocated time. You must also coach colleagues and develop their confidence to understand that a short update is positive and that exception reporting is most effective. This can be a challenge as some individuals have worked in environments where talking more and providing comprehensive lists of progress is seen as preferential to a short, succinct update on the salient points. You must also facilitate the stand-up, ensuring there is structure and that the things impeding progress are managed, mitigated or removed to enable colleagues to continue to progress, post-meeting.

Stand-ups and scrums can be applied to a number of meetings that take place in the workplace. As referred to earlier, I use a weekly stand-up meeting in place of a regular team meeting. The objective of this is to provide all members of the team with an overview of the high-level activities their colleagues are undertaking. This helps to promote a collaborative workplace alongside ensuring single failure points are minimised. The stand-up also enables individuals to assess their workloads and planned activities in light of the amount of reactive work they are subjected to each week. This is useful for me as team leader as I can then assess the workplans for my areas over the coming six-week period in light of the previous progress made. The stand-up also provides a quick and efficient way for any risks, issues or blockers to be escalated, monitored and managed. The standing update for the weekly stand-up is: (1) progress made last week; (2) plans for this week; (3) any issues, risks or blockers to escalate.

RUNNING SUCCESSFUL PROJECT RETROSPECTIVES

Darby and Larsen (2006) provide the toolkit and building blocks necessary for running a successful project retrospective. Defining the project retrospective as:

> A special meeting where the team gathers after completing an increment of work to inspect and adapt their methods and teamwork. Retrospectives enable whole-team learning, act as catalysts for change, and generate action. Retrospectives go beyond checklist project audits or perfunctory project closeouts. And, in contrast to traditional post-mortems or project reviews, retrospectives focus not only on the development process, but on the team and the team issues. And team issues are as challenging as technical issues – if not more so.

I have drawn on the advice presented by Darby and Larsen in detailing my own guide to running a successful project retrospective, see Table 10.3.

Figure 10.6 details the output of the retrospective I ran post-implementation of a new Voice Over IP Telephone System. As well as drawing on visual tools in the retrospective, use visuals to detail your findings and agreed actions.

TABLE 10.3

Guide to Running Retrospectives

Objective:	Through looking back on what happened you learn and improve things in the next phases.
How:	1. Agree the period of time to determine what you are reviewing.
	2. Agree who will lead/facilitate (and apply the top tips).
	3. Plan the session, consider: group dynamics; managing time;
Using Darby and Larson (2006) you should:	resources needed; activities to make it successful.
	a. set the scene; what are you reviewing and what do those attending want to get out of the session/how are they feeling (this is like an ice-breaker but is relevant to the task, project or event being reviewed)
	b. gather data; get the participants to provide information for you to analyse to make decisions on what you need to repeat, do differently or stop doing next time you approach the task, next project phase or re-run the event
	c. generate insights; get the participants to talk about the data/information and discuss/analyse it with a view to providing an evaluation
	d. decide what to do; what can you do to address the insights gathered
	e. close; ensure every participant knows what they need to do post-attending to put the steps in place to improve
	4. Ensure participants know they are expected to engage with the retrospective but recognise different styles of learning, personality type preferences and the group dynamics.
	5. Take action on the back of retrospectives or you will lose engagement from the team and credibility.
Who:	Everyone involved in the event being reviewed should be included in the retrospective.
When:	Assess this based on the level of project activity, if a lot of work is happening on a project, regular retrospectives will be useful. If there isn't much action on the project, there won't be much to review.
Where:	Try to find a collaborative space where you can get the attendees to work both independently and collaboratively.
Warning:	Retrospectives will review positive and negative parts of a project. It's essential to do this if you want to improve. However, individuals will get sensitive if blame is associated with things that have gone badly. Stick to facts and the information available not to individuals and their actions of failure or success. This should keep the retrospective constructive.

Example forms part of the Project Management Framework at York St John University. The framework was co-designed and delivered with Christina Nichols at York St John University.

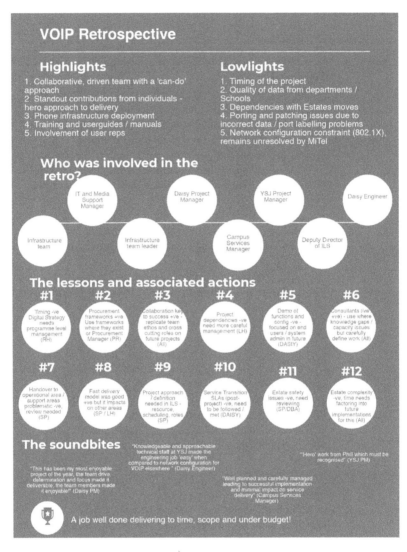

FIGURE 10.6

'Retrospective output' example designed by Laura Hallett using Piktochart.

REVIEWING LESSONS LEARNT AND CHANGING PROJECT MANAGEMENT

I apply retrospectives to my own work as a project manager. Retrospectives highlight areas of good practice alongside the improvements needed to manage the project more effectively. As the project manager you have a responsibility for responding to this feedback and adjusting your approach accordingly. Alongside the retrospective, it is important to develop strong working relationships with your project stakeholders and seek their feedback on the project at regular points. This should form part of your own refinement of your practice as a project manager.

Another key element of successful project management is to capture lessons learnt and change practice as a result. The simplest method for capturing lessons is to create an online form (for example both Google and Office 365 have good options) to capture the information. You must then set aside time each week, fortnight or month to review the lessons and change practice to minimise the likelihood of the same thing happening again. Capturing the lessons in a structured way allows you to categorise the lessons and publish the register to the project team to show you are engaged and change things on the back of their feedback. It also allows you to develop lessons learnt for programme teams, improving the learning across different projects within the organisation.

ONGOING REFLECTION AND REFINEMENT WITHIN PROJECTS

Successfully managing projects requires ongoing reflection and refinement. The project parameters will change as issues arise and risk mitigations have to be applied. Timeframes are regularly adjusted as the scope and acceptable quality standards are redefined. You have to continually assess whether the project is on track to deliver the benefits associated with the change/new product whilst maximising opportunities to add value and minimise waste. Add into the mix the need to continually engage with the project team to ensure they are collaborating and delivering against the plans, and you find you are never standing still. Reflection and refinement within projects maximises the likelihood of success. It also increases buy-in and engagement from the project stakeholders as it shows your commitment. Incorporating value added principles, stand-ups, retrospectives and lessons learnt into your standard project management approach, alongside your day-to-day work, will deliver benefits.

EMBEDDING CONTINUOUS IMPROVEMENT INTO BUSINESS AREAS

An Introduction to Continuous Improvement

Angelis and Fernandes (2012) note, 'Innovation is a key source of competitiveness in the knowledge economy, and continuous improvement (CI) is a key element of such corporate pursuit.' With its history firmly rooted in the manufacturing industry, Continuous Improvement (CI) is now found in all sectors. In fact, it is difficult to find a modern organisational strategy that does not reference CI, or its key characteristics.

In simple terms, CI is about incremental change, empowering front-line staff responsible for the change to make the change, utilising the talents and skills of all members of the team to complete the improvement, and, reflecting and refining the change, post-implementation. An organisation which successfully embraces CI will have a culture that empowers and trusts its staff, provides freedom to its staff, offers the space to be innovative and will not be afraid to take risks.

In my current and previous roles, I have worked hard to provide a supportive, open and encouraging environment in which my team are able to continuously improve. CI is about people and behaviours, and it's rarely possible to satisfy everyone, at all times, along the journey. The aim is always to empower the enthusiasts, marginalise sceptics and engage those that sit in the gulf in-between. In cultures that see an unsuccessful change as failure, CI will fail. CI requires an environment in which an unsuccessful change is not seen as a failure but as another opportunity to improve. All changes bring with them a risk of not being successful when first adopted, and you have to be brave enough to accept this to truly embrace a CI organisation.

CI AND PROJECT MANAGEMENT: THEY DO WORK TOGETHER!

Let's try to apply CI to project management. Having previously covered the need for review and refinement in projects, we know that incremental change is part of managing a project. We have also discussed the need to listen to the feedback of the project group to learn lessons and improve how we manage projects. Project teams are made up of multi-disciplinary stakeholders. Therefore, a large range of skills and talents are available and these people are regularly reflecting and refining what they do in light of the project parameters changing. You can see from this that applying CI to how you manage your project is simple.

Whilst managing the GDPR Project, I applied CI to the governance in place for the project. Having been asked to act as Project Manager on the project post inception, the governance and reporting lines had already been determined. After two project team meetings, it became apparent that the meetings were not making the best use of staff time nor was there sufficient time to discuss issues that had arisen. A simple amendment to the frequency of the meetings, combined with three, weekly stand-up meetings with myself and the workstream leads responsible for the key work areas, saw a positive change. Detailed progress reporting could be managed at the stand-ups, allowing time for the team to discuss the important business in the core team meetings. Attendance at the meetings also improved as a result of the change.

This example shows a simple, small change which had a positive impact. When applying CI to how you manage your project, focus on incremental change that delivers small-scale positive impacts. This should not deter you from empowering your project team to seek to adopt CI in all areas of the project. An incremental, beneficial change is a step in the right direction and sometimes your project team peers will see things you haven't noticed are in need of improving.

CI – All in a Day's Work!

We all know how exciting it is when a new colleague joins the team. They are keen to learn and enquire as to why we do the things the way we do. A new colleague started within my team just over a month ago and the CI seen since their arrival has been transformative. We expanded our one-to-one training drop-ins to bookable events others can sign-up to, and this simple change has enabled the team to work more efficiently. Using analytics in a more sophisticated way is enabling us to monitor the demand for courses and supply courses accordingly. Asking colleagues in the team who aren't familiar with the technology to prepare a training workshop upskills and trains the team as well as removing single knowledge points. Fantastic improvements achieved, via incremental tweaks and changes to the ways we had previously worked.

Encouraging all members of the team to think in this way from day 1 (to day 1001) is critical within the changing world in which we work. When the Strategic Projects and Change Team formed in January 2018, I made it my priority to spend time to get to know the members who were joining me from other areas of the organisation. Focusing on the values we each had, detailing my expectations of the team and deciding together what our brand for the team would be, provided the building blocks for success. Actively seeking feedback, listening, observing and changing in response to these factors ensures you stay on top of what you do.

It's essential to always have one eye on the future and prepare yourself and your team for the changing workplace and the new technologies we need to embrace. Finding the time to do this can be challenging but through incremental improvements and changes to the day-to-day business as usual, you will find the time to add value to your skills development and growth.

'LEANING' FORWARD

Reflections for Adopting Lean, Post-Project

Once a project has delivered the change or the product becomes operational, the work of the senior business owner really starts. All projects involve some level of snagging to deal with the changes which are unsatisfactory and hone and develop the business processes in light of the change or new product. During this post-project phase there are a number of Lean concepts it is worth repeating as well as some to shelve.

Techniques to Repeat

The Optional Module Project (2012–2014) changed the tool and processes associated with student module choice, allocation and satisfaction. Over the two-year cycle, I piloted implementation with two departments before widening the rollout to 20 (from 27) departments across the University. During the post-project phase, the business areas found the following tools detailed within the chapter were invaluable:

- Visual agendas and the use of visualisations.
- Retrospectives – These were used to engage with students to seek their feedback on the changes to the choice and allocation methods, alongside measuring their satisfaction.

- Exception reporting – This was used to detail the benefits realisation associated with the project over the 6–18 month period post-implementation.
- Lessons learnt – Capturing the lessons learnt during each cycle the tool operated helps the users to detail the support and technical considerations that need to be considered annually as the tool is used.
- CI – As you would expect this supported and reinforced points 1–4!

Ideas to Shelve

It is perhaps no surprise that the tools which were not valuable post-project phase are those which required a detailed understanding of how to successfully adapt and tailor the tool to successfully embed its success. The following tools were applied post-project with limited value-added:

- Visual scene setting – The business owners did not feel confident in applying this tool post-project despite seeing the value of the technique within the project.
- Introducing the stand-up or scrum to the community of practice colleagues maintained to keep the discussions alive around the project – In the absence of a neutral facilitator or scrum master at these sessions, this format was seen to be challenging for all colleagues and disrupted the group dynamics.
- Business process mapping – The business owners recognised the value of this activity but drew on the Project Team to facilitate these sessions. This recognises the need to upskill staff in how to conduct effective process reengineering alongside the benefit of having a neutral facilitator to ask the more challenging questions associated with minimising waste.

This chapter provides a number of tools and examples on how to apply Lean concepts when managing projects. With a focus on people, adding value, visualisations and eliminating wastes, it is easy to transfer the principles of Lean to project management. Throughout the chapter we have explored how many of these concepts can be applied to your day-to-day work and business operations.

THANKS AND CREDITS

Templates and figures detailed within this chapter have been developed over the past six years of working as a Project Manager at University of York and York St John University. The development of these templates has been informed by tailoring the standard practices of Prince 2, Agile and the Association of Project Management (APM) Book of Knowledge alongside drawing on the expertise and experience of the colleagues I have been fortunate to work with at those institutions, particularly Hannah Smith, Kathryn Woodroof and Christina Nichols.

Thanks to all who've reviewed the chapter, particularly Rob Hickey.

BIBLIOGRAPHY

Angelis, J., and Fernandes, B. (2012). Innovative lean: Work practices and product and process improvements. *International Journal of Lean Six Sigma*, Vol. 3, no. 1, pp. 74–84.

Ballard, G., and Howell, G. (2003). Lean project management. *Building Research and Information*, Vol. 31, no. 2, pp. 119–133. USA: Spon Press, Taylor & Francis Group.

Derby, E., and Larsen, D. (2006). *Agile Retrospectives: Making Good Teams Great.* Washingon, DC: The Pragmatic Bookshelf.

Nayaran, S. (2015). *Agile IT Organization Design: For Digital Transformation and Continuous Delivery*, pp. 36–43. New York: Addison-Wesley.

11

BOSCARD: A Scoping Tool for Lean Continuous Improvement Projects

Mark Robinson

CONTENTS

INTRODUCTION

This chapter focusses on BOSCARD*, a scoping tool which, as used by the Lean Team at the University of St Andrews, is:

- A collaborative and empowering facilitator-led tool for defining the parameters of a Lean process improvement project (Lean Project)
- A consultative approach to securing group agreement on problem definition
- A means of creating structure out of what can be an unstructured discussion

After introducing the University and its Lean initiative, the chapter begins with a brief overview of the importance of scoping a process improvement

---

* The origins of BOSCARD are unclear. It is believed to have originated with consulting company Cap Gemini in the 1980s, see https://www.projectsmart.co.uk/boscard.php

project. It then briefly looks at Quad of Aims and SIPOC, scoping tools previously used by the Lean Team.

BOSCARD is then discussed in depth with each section explained and potential questions for eliciting relevant information provided. The in-house development of BOSCARD, 'BOSCARD+' is then discussed as are each of its elements. Advice on how to facilitate a scoping meeting using BOSCARD and BOSCARD+ is provided.

THE UNIVERSITY AND LEAN

Founded in the 15th century, St Andrews is Scotland's first university and the third oldest in the English-speaking world. Teaching began in the community of St Andrews in 1410, and the University was formally constituted by the issue of a papal bull in 1413.

The University is a relatively small and highly international community of almost 10,000 students, with just under half from outside of the UK. It has, over the past dozen years, improved its standing to consistently feature in the top five universities in the UK.

St Andrews was one of the two early adopters of Lean in higher education in the UK*. In 2006 the then Finance Director (now the CEO) agreed that a Lean approach to ensuring a better use of resources would suit the University's ethos of focusing on people and the contribution they make to institutional success.

The Lean Team had three main goals:

1. **Culture Change** – to create a drive and appetite for continuous improvement
2. **Effectiveness** – to ensure that all institutional processes meet existing and emerging needs
3. **Efficiency** – to maximise the use of all resources in the delivery of high-quality services

These goals were met primarily through staff training, and delivery of Lean Projects, a core activity of which is the facilitation of rapid improvement events, the 'Redesign' or fifth step of the eight-step Lean project model

---

* For an overview of Lean at the University of St Andrews see Yorkstone, S. 2016. Lean universities. In: *The Routledge Companion to Lean Management*, T. Netland, and D. J. Powell (Eds.), New York: Taylor & Francis (Routledge).

TABLE 11.1

The St Andrews Eight-Step Lean Project Model

Step	Activity
1 Request	An area of work is identified
2 Scoping	Clear goals and the time frame are established, the project team members are identified and the required resources are identified
3 Training	The project team are introduced to Lean thinking and techniques
4 Planning	The project goal, approach, timetable and data requirements are reviewed and agreed by the project team
5 Redesign	The project team meets for a focused period of time, with the authority to create a new process and complete the required actions. The result is a documented new process and an action plan for further work
6 Implementation	Items on the action plan are completed by the project team
7 Review	The project team meets regularly to ensure items in the action plan have been completed, and to identify and remove any barriers to implementation
8 Feedback	The project is completed and closed and feedback is taken on the Lean process as a whole

developed iteratively by the Lean Team. The Lean Team delivered significant success in many areas in the University and this success saw the Lean Team invited to support other universities (and other organisations in e.g. public, legal and third sectors) in their Lean activities, both in the UK and globally.

The model, steps and high-level activity at each are seen in Table 11.1.

WHAT HAPPENS AT SCOPING?

A Scoping meeting is held to determine whether or not an idea for a Lean Project merits the investment of resources required to redesign a process. The meeting is not held with the intention of solving a process problem there and then.

To determine the way forward, it is essential to answer a number of questions including:

1. Why do we want to do this piece of work?
2. Where does the process we are talking about start and finish?
3. What do we hope to achieve?
4. Who do we need to involve?
5. How long will it take?
6. When are we going to do it?

Answering these and other important questions typically requires the right people in a room for the right amount of time. The who, when and where of the Scoping meeting is established at the Request step. It is at the next step, Scoping, where the six questions just mentioned, and many more, are considered.

Typically, a Scoping meeting will last three to four hours and should take place two to six weeks prior to the Redesign event. A Scoping meeting cannot be rushed; there is, as informed by experience, no cutting of corners. And time is needed to pull together the material and people required for a successful Redesign event.

Failure to ask the right questions and evaluate the answers will lead to a poorly scoped Redesign event. A poorly scoped Redesign event will not deliver good results – without clarity of where the process concerned starts and finishes, it is not likely that the right people will be in the room for Redesign, and without the right people the current state process will not be sufficiently understood, and without the right understanding it will be difficult to deliver an optimal new process. And, a lot of staff time and money could have been better spent.

The tools used to scope a Lean project need not be complex. Scoping tools used at the University prior to BOSCARD were one or other, and occasionally both, of Quad of Aims and SIPOC. Answers to questions not posed by the headings of Quad of Aims and SIPOC were still recorded but often in not as a useful manner as provided by BOSCARD.

QUAD OF AIMS

Completing a Quad of Aims is a simple way to establish the bounds of a Lean project. The four quad headings are drawn on e.g. a white board, and the facilitator engages with those in the room to record relevant information under the headings of Purpose, Stakeholders and Benefits, Deliverables, and Measurables.

- **Purpose** – A clear and concise statement of what the Lean event is aiming to achieve.
- **Stakeholders and Benefits** – A list of stakeholders and the benefits they can expect to see on implementation of the new significantly improved process. Stakeholders can include the university itself,

TABLE 11.2

Example Quad of Aims

Purpose	Stakeholders and Benefits
To ensure the provision of quality food for our customers, food that is local, seasonal and sustainable and that delivers value for money	Stakeholders: Students, staff, visitors, suppliers Benefits: Consistently fresh, healthy, sustainable food Value for money Help local economy Long term contracts Better supplier relationships Reduced carbon footprint Enhanced reputation
Deliverables	**Measurables**
Set of seasonal recipes and menus with costings List of local suppliers and offerings Feedback procedure for students and other consumers Documented process Training plan Communication plan On demand reporting	By start of next academic year: Seasonal recipes and menus with costings in place Suppliers contracted Feedback procedure in place Process documented and followed Training completed Communication plan enacted On demand reports meet needs

process owners and operators, suppliers and customers. Benefits typically concern e.g. new process in place and delivery of output right first-time, on-time, etc.

- **Deliverables** – Typically quantitative, and occasionally qualitative, outcomes of the work to be undertaken.
- **Measurables** – How meeting the Deliverables can be determined.

A Quad of Aims for a project to improve student residence menu planning could be as seen in Table 11.2.

SIPOC

As with Quad of Aims, the facilitator engages with those in the room to record relevant information under appropriate headings.

SIPOC focusses on documenting a process by determining the process Suppliers, the Inputs those suppliers provide, the Process by which those inputs are transformed into Outputs, and the Customers of those outputs.

- **Suppliers** – Can be internal or external to the organisation performing the process, and they must provide at least one process input.
- **Inputs** – Can be services, materials or information.
- **Process** – A high level map, typically six to nine steps, that shows the key activities that transform the inputs into the outputs.
- **Outputs** – Goods or services that satisfy customer expectations, and meet or exceed their requirements.
- **Customers** – The people who receive the outputs, and those who put requirements on the outputs, but do not receive the output. They can be internal or external to the organisation performing the process.

As well as clearly identifying suppliers, inputs, etc., a SIPOC helps to determine the boundary of the process to be improved, establishes the right metrics and highlights improvement priorities, and places the focus on the process customer.

A SIPOC for a Lean project to improve a library process from book order to book in the right place on the right shelf could be (Table 11.3):

TABLE 11.3

Example SIPOC

Suppliers	Inputs	Outputs	Customers
Students	Book order	Books on shelves	Students
Academics	requests		Academics
Professional staff			Professional staff
			Other registered users
Publishers	Books		Inter-library loan users
Vendors			
Donors			Students
			Academics
			Professional staff
			Other registered users
			Inter-library loan users
		Electronic catalogue	Anyone else

Process
1. Book ordered
2. Book purchased
3. Book arrives
4. Book catalogued in system
5. Book covered, security strip applied, etc.
6. Book shelved in 'New Books' shelves
7. Book shelved in main library

BOSCARD

BOSCARD is an acronym that typically stands for:

- Background
- Objective
- Scope
- Constraints
- Assumptions
- Risks
- Deliverables

BOSCARD is used by the Lean Team at the University of St Andrews during Scoping, the second step of an eight-step Lean project approach, known as the 'St Andrews Model'. The model was based on the eight broad stages experienced and then identified by the Lean Team during its early Lean project work.

BOSCARD serves a number of purposes including:

- It is a collaborative and empowering facilitator-led tool for defining the parameters of and whether to proceed with an idea for a Lean project.
- It enables a consultative approach to securing group agreement on problem definition.
- It provides a means of creating structure out of what can be an unstructured discussion.
- It is a simple tool with which to quickly gather and deliver all important project information from and to stakeholders.
- It provides terms of reference for a new Lean project.
- It helps creates structure out of what can often be unstructured discussions.
- It provides opportunities for all participants and ideas to be heard, useful where one or more participants or ideas may dominate.
- It prevents participants jumping to conclusions and making sub-optimal decisions.
- It provides a reference point for during and after a Lean project.

Making the most of BOSCARD in the higher education environment has necessitated some minor changes to how BOSCARD is typically used in other sectors, particularly manufacturing. Changes have been made to the definition

TABLE 11.4

Information Sought Per BOSCARD Category in HE

Category	Information sought	Note
Background	Rationale for the event (And relevant information not included elsewhere)	This category tended to be a catch-all for information that did not clearly fall into other categories. Over time this issue led to development of BOSCARD+
Objective	High level purpose of the event An aspirational and inspirational statement	This is not a SMART objective typical of a BOSCARD in other industry sectors. Following the eight-step model, at this stage the process is not fully understood therefore it is difficult if not impossible to create a SMART objective
Scope	Process start and end points What is within scope What is out of scope	We must know the process start and end, otherwise we will not know e.g. the size of the event or who to involve
Constraints	Factors that may impede or prevent the event from going ahead or implementation of its outcomes	Helps identify matters of concern to stakeholders Negative statements
Assumptions	All factors considered to be true and that will lead to a successful event and outcome	A means of addressing constraints Positive statements
Risks	Risks of doing nothing to improve the current process and of implementing a sub-optimal new process	Helps identify matters of concern to stakeholders Sends a clear signal the status quo cannot remain and the most efficacious new process is to be implemented
Deliverables	Key outcomes to achieve the objective	Not arbitrary performance targets, the current process is not yet understood and potential improvements have not yet been raised or considered

of some terms, and, iteratively, additional terms have been added. The latter eventually led to the development of BOSCARD+. Changes to terms are noted where relevant. BOSCARD+ is discussed later in this chapter. One way to think of BOSCARD and BOSCARD+ is as checklists where appropriately working through each category will mean arrival at the right outcome.*

Briefly, the information sought for each category is set out in Table 11.4.

---

* For a discussion of the value of checklists, see Gawande, A. 2010. *The Checklist Manifesto: How to Get Things Right*. London: Profile Books Ltd.

While there are no specific questions to ask to elicit the information required, open ended questions are best. The 5 Whys is an ideal tool to use. As is the 5Ws and 1H* i.e. when, where, what, who and how. Following a set of prearranged questions as in an interview format may stifle the free flow of the conversation and channel the group to an outcome that reflects the questioner's aims and understanding rather than those of the group. Questions that may help generate discussion are set out in Table 11.5.

USING BOSCARD AT A SCOPING MEETING

While much of what follows is applicable whether creating a Quad of Aims, a SIPOC or a BOSCARD, the focus is on the latter.

The most successful Scoping meetings are those where:

- A skilled facilitator familiar with Lean and BOSCARD leads the meeting.
- The room is ready for the meeting before the participants arrive i.e. the facilitator has written the BOSCARD headings on e.g. whiteboards or flipcharts, spaced out so that whatever is written beneath those headings can be seen by all. (The meeting should be low tech, but interactive. Watching a screen while someone populates a document is not conducive to full engagement).
- Meeting ground rules, if required, have been agreed on and are on display.
- The right people are in the room i.e. key process owners and operators, and customer representation.
- Participants understand that the meeting is not an imposition and that their attendance and full participation is required.
- Those involved in the process to be improved are actively involved in the creation of the project scoping document. Open and honest discussion will enable a sharing of information that some may previously have been holding quite closely.

---

* Also known as the KIPLING Checklist, as memorialized in 1902 by Rudyard Kipling in his poem 'The Elephant's Child', which opens with: 'I keep six honest serving-men (They taught me all I knew); Their names are What and Why and When And How and Where and Who'.

TABLE 11.5

Prompt Questions Per BOSCARD Category

Category	Possible Questions
Background	Why do we need to improve the process?
	What is happening now?
	How did we get to where we are now?
	Have we tried to improve the process before?
	If so, when, why, etc. and what was the outcome?
	What is the customer feedback?
	Who is the process owner?
	What might an improved process look like?
	What might the perfect process look like?
	What is the name of this process?
Objective	What, at a high level, do we want to achieve?
	What is the one-liner that would motivate people about this project?
	Will our objective make sense to others?
	Is our objective inspirational and aspirational?
Scope	Where does the process start?
	Where does the process end?
	What is in scope?
	What is out of scope?
	Why are some elements out of scope?
Constraints	Will we get buy-in from stakeholders?
	Do we have capacity to implement the new process?
	Will the current culture have a positive impact?
	Will we have the necessary funds if any are required?
	Are there any compliance issues to be accommodated or overcome?
	Will our IT systems be able handle any IT outcomes?
	Do we have the authority to implement the new process we create?
	Can we and will we do this?
Assumptions	Will we get buy-in from stakeholders?
	Do we have capacity to implement the new process?
	Will the current culture have a positive impact?
	Will we have the necessary funds if any are required?
	Are there any compliance issues to be accommodated or overcome?
	Will our IT systems be able to handle any IT outcomes?
	Do we have the authority to implement the new process we create?
	Can we and will we do this?
Risks	Will the new process deliver the expected gains?
	Will we alienate staff or stakeholders?
	Is there a financial or legal risk?
	Will the customer's experience improve?
	How may changing this process impact on our reputation?
	What is likely to happen if we do nothing?
	What is likely to happen if we do the wrong thing?
Deliverables	Do we need a documented process with clear roles and responsibilities?
	Do we need to implement the new process on time and on budget?
	Do we need a plan to communicate project outcomes?
	Do we need a plan for training staff in the new process?
	Will we need an action list for anything still to do?

- The right amount of uninterruptable time has been set aside, and this is typically half a day.
- The room and environment encourage positive contribution from all.
- The facilitator does not translate into their own words what participants say. A shared understanding is essential.
- What is written down makes sense, at the time of writing and later. It is unproductive to find out at e.g. Redesign, that what was written down at Scoping is some weeks later, no longer understood. Disconnected words, random numbers, abbreviations and jargon are not helpful. Concise sentences are best.
- Judgement is suspended. Scoping is about engagement and information gathering. Record ideas for improvement, they will be considered during Redesign. At this time, 'No idea is a bad idea'.

At the beginning of the meeting, start with Background, it is usually the category participants know most about and it may also be an uncontentious area for some people. Participants are often keen to start with why the as yet undefined process is not working. Beginning with 'Background' can help the flow of ideas for other categories. Participants in their enthusiasm to improve the process may also leap to immediately suggesting potential solutions. Note these under Deliverables.

Working through the BOSCARD categories in order from B through to D is not recommended. To do so is unduly constraining and can led to frustration if participants want to contribute something before the discussion arrives at the relevant category. And, inevitably, many thoughts, if remembered, should they not be captured immediately in what is typically a fluid and very interactive environment, could have their meaning and relevance lost.

In practice, 'Objective' may be the last category completed. It may not be until near the end of the meeting that the participants fully understand what is possible and achievable.

There is an ebb and flow to the discussion as participants offer information and ask questions of each other or of the facilitator. The facilitator's role is to write the comments made under the appropriate heading while testing the validity of those statements by drawing on the expertise of all participants. Questions are likewise fed to the group to discuss and arrive at a decision as to their validity and that of any answers. While a collective agreement of BOSCARD contents is desirable, in some very rare circumstances, this may not be forthcoming. At a bare minimum, at least an understanding why a particular course of action has been decided is required.

Even if some comments have been revised in light of later input, once it is apparent that no additional information is forthcoming, collectively, with the participants, review everything that has been written down. Keep re-working until a shared understanding is reached.

At conclusion of the meeting distribute what has been written down to participants for review and comment. How this is done will depend on how neat the facilitators handwriting is, how orderly the comments were noted, and the technology used. A word document or similar works well. This provides a readily accessible and understandable permanent record, the creation of which gives the opportunity for a significant increase of legibility and a general tidy-up should some re-ordering of comments be required. Photographs of the original material will help should there be the need to revisit this.

BOSCARD+

In practice, a significant amount of information was recorded under Background. The category effectively became a catch-all for information that did not readily belong elsewhere. In an effort to make it easier to make sense of this information, additional categories were developed. Some of these additional categories came from those in Quad of Aims and SIPOC. Others, such as 'Actions' and 'Later' were included when it became evident during Scoping meetings that they would be useful.

These additions to BOSCARD led to the development of BOSCARD+. Arranged in the order shown, the pluses spell out the acronym SPLIT BAR (Table 11.6).

As with BOSCARD, there are no specific questions to ask to elicit the information required, and again, while not an exhaustive list, Table 11.7 may be helpful.

The Lean Team at the University of St Andrews has been using BOSCARD and BOSCARD+ for a number of years, both when working within the University and when supporting other universities and organisations. The development of BOSCARD+, and the unique nature of all organisations, mean there is no one way to use BOSCARD. There is variation in the categories used and in the order they are presented. For an example of a BOSCARD, based on the work at St Andrews and which takes account of the needs of the creating institution, I refer you to Chris Shannon's chapter

TABLE 11.6

BOSCARD+ to SPLIT BAR

Category	Explanation	Note
Stakeholders	Any individual or group interacting with the process	Can be internal or external to the institution Ensure students are included in student facing processes
Process	A high-level map of the six to nine key process steps	An easy interactive and visual way to determine 'Scope' in BOSCARD Ensures all team members and the facilitator have a common understanding of key process steps
Later	Unrelated or peripheral matters for later consideration	A 'Parking Lot' so that nothing of value is overlooked
Information (Documentation and Data)	Available or required Includes policies, procedures, reports, volumes, timings, floor plans and financial statements	Documentation such as policies, procedures, reports are usually readily available Data other than volumes and by time period, may not be readily available
Team	Process operators and other key personnel Core staff and on-call team members	Typically, 6–12 staff from all areas within process scope. A task matrix can help identify those required Consider team dynamics, expertise and personalities. Varied perspectives and resource to implement the new process is essential
Benefits	Expected positive outcomes of implementing the new process	Tangible and intangible benefits, quantitative and qualitative
Actions	Preparatory tasks for the event	Tasks must be completed on time e.g. gathering data and interviewing stakeholders
Reporting	How to communicate event activities and outcomes	Linked to 'Deliverables' in BOSCARD

number 19 'Lessons from implementing lean at the Veterinary Teaching Hospital'.

Regardless of the approach to BOSCARD, at a bare minimum however, the key categories are Objective, Scope and Deliverables. When written

TABLE 11.7

SPLIT BAR Possible Prompt Questions

Category	Possible Questions
Stakeholders	What groups are affected by the process?
	Who are the suppliers?
	What is supplied?
	Where do suppliers affect the process flow?
	How do they affect the process flow?
	Who are the process customers?
	What do customers need or consume?
	How do we engage with suppliers and customers?
	Who else is affected by the process?
Process	Where does the process start?
	Where does the process end?
	What are the high-level steps in-between process start and end points?
	What is the name of the process?
Later	Is this something the relevance of which we're not sure of at the moment?
	Is this something we need to note for action elsewhere?
Information (Documentation and Data)	What documentation and data will or may be useful?
	What documentation and data do we have?
	What documentation and data do we need to collect?
	How can we access the documentation and data we need?
	What does the data tell us?
	What does, or may, the data need to show (volumes, peaks and troughs, frequencies, turn-around time, etc.)?
Team	Who is the overall sponsor?
	Who is the process owner?
	Which, if any, senior managers need to be part of the event team?
	Who are the key process operators?
	Are there staff related to the process who will be needed on an on-call basis?
	Do any other key stakeholders need to be present for the event?
	If so, all or part of the event?
Benefits	Do we expect customer service to improve?
	If so, by how much?
	Do we expect any time savings?
	If so, how much?
	Do we expect any cost savings?
	What are the potential cost savings?
	Will our reputation be enhanced?
	What, if any, are the dis-benefits?
Actions	Do we need to do anything before the next steps, especially Redesign?
	Who will be responsible for carrying out and managing these tasks?
Reporting	Do we need a communication plan?
	What format should it take?
	Who do we need to inform?

on a flipchart or otherwise displayed in the Redesign venue, Objective, Scope and Deliverables become a readily accessible road map that helps keep the Redesign team focussed on the task on hand – the creation of a dramatically improved process.

BIBLIOGRAPHY

Doran, G. T. 1981. There's a SMART Way to Write Management's Goals and Objectives. *Management Review* 70(11): 35–36.

Gawande, A. 2010. *The Checklist Manifesto: How to Get Things Right*. London: Profile Books Ltd.

George, M. L., Rowlands, D., Price, M., and Maxey, J. 2005. *The Lean Six Sigma Toolbook*. New York: McGraw-Hill.

Haughey, D. 2015. BOSCARD (Terms of Reference). https://www.projectsmart.co.uk/boscard.php (accessed September 17, 2018).

Kipling, R. 2008. *Just So Stories*. London: Puffin Books.

Robinson, M., and Yorkstone, S. 2014. Becoming a Lean University: The Case of the University of St Andrews. *Leadership and Governance in Higher Education* 1: 41–72.

University of St Andrews. 2018. Becoming Lean A Pocket Guide. http://standrewslean.com/lean-resources/becoming-lean/ (accessed September 17, 2018).

Yorkstone, S. 2016. Lean universities. In: *The Routledge Companion to Lean Management*, T. Netland, and D. J. Powell (Eds.), New York: Taylor & Francis (Routledge).

12

Six Sigma as a Method for Improving University Processes: The Case of the Academic Assessment Process

Justyna Maciąg

CONTENTS

INTRODUCTION

The process of implementing the Lean Management concept in higher education institutions more and more draws from the Six Sigma methodology, thus creating approaches based on Lean Six Sigma.

The aim of this chapter is to show how the DMAIC model, which is at the heart of the Six Sigma method, can be used to improve the process of lecturer assessment. Six Sigma originates from the manufacturing sector and Statistical Process Control. This chapter focuses first of all on methodological aspects, at the expense of deliberately omitted implementation issues.

It is based on the results of an analysis of the literature on this particular subject, the author's own research conducted within the frame of the "Miniature 1" project financed from an National Science Centre, Poland grant (The Conditions for the Maturity of the Lean Management Culture in Higher Education Institutions in the period from 25 September 2017 to 25 September 2018, nr DEC. –2017/01/X/ HS/00619) as well as her experience gained during the execution of various improvement projects.

Six Sigma – Approaches to Defining Six Sigma as a Concept

The objective of Six Sigma is to improve processes by reducing their changeability by using statistical methods based on measuring standard deviations (the key concept is that of the Six Sigma level) (Antony 2004). The key notion in this concept is the Sigma Level. The Sigma Level is a measure of a quality level; it indicates how many times a standard deviation (marked as sigma) of a given quality is included in a half of the tolerance range (Hamrol 2007). The Six Sigma Level means that there are fewer than 3.4 defects per one million occurrences of a given quality, or the success indicator equals 99.9997%. Therefore, the basic advantage resulting from the use of Six Sigma is a clearly defined level of quality and tolerance ranges for the examined process parameters (Snee 2010), which makes it possible to supervise the course of the process, as well as to find and eliminate the causes of defects and errors (Bandyopadhyay and Lichtman 2007).

Over time Six Sigma has changed from a statistical measuring technique into a philosophy of management based on an appropriate organizational culture and managers' commitment (Tjahjono et al. 2010, Bandyopadhyay and Lichtman 2007). Six Sigma as a concept was introduced for the first time by Motorola. Broadly speaking, Six Sigma can be defined as (Majorana and Morelli 2012):

- A measuring system (basic indicators for a service process) can include the following:
  - o DPMO – an indicator of defects per one million opportunities = 3.4.
  - o C_p a process capability indicator which shows the relation between the tolerance assumed for the process and determined by the lower specification limit (LSL) and the upper specification limit (USL) and the total changeability of the process (6σ). The higher the value of the C_p indicator, the more capable the process is.
  - o DPO (defect per opportunities) – the probability of a defect in a service process – the ratio of the number of defects to the total number of opportunities.
- Continuous improvement (according to the DMAIC model: *Define, Measure, Analyse, Improve, Control*).
- A cultural change in an organization (the awareness that everything can be measured; emphasis on the approach in which first we measure, and then we talk and act).

The DMAIC model is in the core of the Six Sigma methodology (Figure 12.1).

The detailed description of each stage presented in Figure 12.1 can be elaborated in practice.

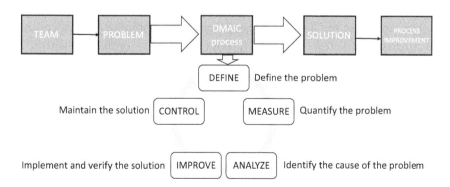

FIGURE 12.1
The DMAIC model.

This model has a universal character. Based on the PDCA cycle (Plan, Do, Check, Act) it shows how it is possible to move in a systematized manner from identifying and defining a problem in an organization to solving it and controlling the effectiveness and efficiency of the applied solutions.

In the DEFINE phase, a problem is identified and described in relation to an organization's priorities; a team responsible for solving the problem is established; individual scopes of responsibility are determined and relevant resources necessary for the successful completion of the project are allocated. This phase also includes the identification of the process in which the problem occurs (its customers and course – frequently on the basis of the SIPOC diagram) as well as the identification of indicators critical for the quality of the process. In this context, it is also possible to use the so-called seven traditional and seven new quality tools.

The MEASURE phase comprises actions related to the identification, measurement and description of the analysed process, as well as the determination of the scale of the problems and their precise sources. For this purpose, it is possible to use the statistical tools of process changeability analysis, risk analysis, e.g. FMEA.

In the ANALYSE phase, comprehensive analyses of collected data are carried out with the use of various statistical tools (changeability source analysis, capability analysis, stability analysis, measuring system analysis, dependency and correlation analysis, etc.) as well as other tools such as root cause analysis or the Pareto method.

The IMPROVE phase includes generating solutions to the problem, assessing the best alternatives, selecting the best solution and preparing an implementation plan.

The last phase of CONTROL is related to developing a plan of control of the implemented solution. It covers actions connected with the establishment of control points, principles and plans of monitoring, standardization, reviews of control and monitoring results, the scopes of implementing necessary changes. Before implementation, the proposed solution may undergo various tests (Vanzant-Stern 2012, Shankar 2009).

Every DMAIC phase uses many methods and tools originating from the fields of quality management, statistical process control, change management or project management.

SIX SIGMA – THE BARRIERS AND BENEFITS OF USING SIX SIGMA IN A UNIVERSITY

Six Sigma is becoming a more and more popular method of solving problems in HEI. This is indicated by the increasing number of its practical applications. There are proposals to combine this concept with TQM with a view to improving administration processes in universities (Campatelli et al. 2011), assessing educational processes, particularly in terms of receiving feedback (Yu and Ueng 2012), assessing the quality of didactic courses (Lu et al. 2017, Bargerstock and Richards 2015), developing curricula in order to reduce work time spent on material preparation and to improve teaching outcomes (Yeung 2013). It is emphasized that the implementation of Six Sigma requires team work and commitment on the part of both academics and students (Kukreja et al. 2009). A prerequisite for Six Sigma is the construction of an appropriate, and sometimes costly, measuring system in a school (Antony 2004); it is also emphasized that this process is time-consuming, which may collide with lecturers' didactic and research obligations (Kukreja et al. 2009).

Researches on Lean Six Sigma conducted in higher education institutions concern the following issues: the examination of leaders' qualities and competences which are the most necessary in the implementation of Lean Six Sigma in universities (Anthony 2013, Anthony 2015, Lu et al. 2017); it is noted that the implementation of the concept requires complete integration of the sphere of administrative internal services with the academic sphere (Yorkstone 2013). Furthermore, the complete adaptation of the LSS concept in universities is impossible without an appropriate organizational culture and leadership (Jones 2013). Various researches indicate that the efficient application of Six Sigma and Lean Six Sigma requires profound changes in a university's organizational, technical and social systems, which may constitute a considerable challenge. The following example presents opportunities and limitations of using Six Sigma and DMAIC in improving the didactic course assessment process.

A CASE STUDY – IMPROVING THE PROCESS OF LECTURER ASSESSMENT IN THE UNIVERSITY

The project was carried out by the author within the framework of the Green Belt certification procedure. The analysis covered the process of students' assessing the quality of didactic courses. The particular phases of the execution of the project are presented in accordance with the DMAIC methodology presented previously.

The DEFINE Phase

Within the scope of this phase, the following actions were performed:

1. Defining and describing the problem
2. Establishing the objective, expected effects and rationale of the project; defining expected risks
3. Conducting an analysis of the project's costs and benefits
4. Determining the scope of the project and appointing the project team
5. Preparing a Gantt chart
6. Presenting the characteristics of the process of the assessment of lecturers (AOL)
7. Defining the customers of the process
8. Preparing SIPOC and determining indicators critical to quality (CTQ)

A Description of the Problem

Ensuring the quality of education is a requirement imposed on the university by its stakeholders, i.e. students, the state, employers, students' parents and other entities. In Poland, students' assessment of didactic courses is a requirement resulting from the applicable legal regulations. The result of an assessment constitutes an element of a periodic employee assessment. It should be taken into consideration in recruitment processes and in the event of extending or terminating a contract of employment. According to the legal regulations, an assessment conducted by a student has to take place after the completion of a teaching cycle, i.e. every semester. In the university, such assessments are carried out by means of anonymous electronic questionnaires filled in by students in the IT student affairs management system. The questionnaire consists of five general university-related questions, faculty-related questions as well as a place for a student's comments. Answers given to the five general university-related questions constitute a basis for calculating a result which is an element in a periodic employee assessment. The questionnaire is filled in on a voluntary basis, which does not ensure the representative character or reliability of research results (a low number of respondents); furthermore, there is a possibility of presenting individual comments, which unfortunately results in a situation in which many students, feeling anonymous, voice emotional opinions (the effect of an Internet forum). The questionnaire generates protests and negative emotions in teachers. Because of its format (answers based on a 1–5 scale), characteristic features (voluntary character, low attendance, emotional opinions, etc.), it is not regarded as a good tool aimed at improving the quality of didactic courses or teaching methods. The AOL process generates additional administrative costs.

PROBLEM: The lack of credibility and reliability of the results of the AOL process, which hinders the improvement of the quality of didactic processes and teaching methods.

The Objective, Expected Effects and Rationale of the Project (Related Risks)

The objective of the project is to evaluate the process of the assessment of lecturers (AOL) and to formulate proposals of changes in its execution. Within the framework of the project, the following tasks were carried out:

- Conducting an analysis of the results of the AOL process
- Conducting an analysis of students' attendance in the AOL process.
- Drafting proposals of changes in the AOL process with a view to improving the credibility and reliability of its results.
- Developing a change implementation plan

The project's effects are the following: the formulation of guidelines for the preparation of a new lecturer assessment questionnaire and recommendations on how to increase the attendance of students in the AOL process.

Justification for the project: The defectiveness of the existing process of the assessment of lecturers (AOL) generates the following risks to which the university is exposed:

- The risk of non-compliance with the legal regulations applicable to higher education institutions
- The risk of the improper planning of capital expenditures on improving the competencies of the teaching staff, which may result in impairing the quality of education
- The risk of litigation brought by employees against the university and students (the labour law, infringement of personal interests)
- The risk of charges of mismanagement – wasting funds on the maintenance and execution of the AOL process, which fails to generate credible and reliable assessments results

An Analysis of the Project's Costs and Benefits

Project-related benefits were divided into direct ones and indirect ones. The direct benefits include the following:

- A proposal of a new research tool (a questionnaire used in the assessment of lecturers by students) and
- a proposal of actions to be undertaken in order to increase students' attendance in the process, which will consequently result in
- obtaining credible results of the assessment of lecturers which will constitute a basis for their periodic assessment and the development of competencies improvement plans.

The indirect benefits of the execution of the project are as follows:

- A higher level of students' satisfaction with the quality of didactic courses.
- An increase in employees' satisfaction and trust in assessment results; opportunities for lecturers to improve their teaching methods.
- The accomplishment of the university's mission and objectives in the field of teaching.
- Low project execution costs.

The direct costs of executing the project comprise the cost of work time of the project executor and the people who have prepared preliminary databases.

The Scope of the Project and the Project Team

The objective scope of the project comprised the process of the assessment of lecturers by students, AOL.

The subjective scope: a selected faculty (the research was limited to just one faculty because of a large quantity of data processed within the scope of the project; for example, the data applicable to the summer semester 2016/2017 for the whole university included 59,193 records).

The time frame: the analysed data concerned the summer semester in the academic year 2016/2017.

The key stakeholders within the university's management: Vice President for Teaching Affairs and the managers of the administrative units reporting to the Vice President.

The customers, recipients of the effects of the project: University President, Vice President for Personnel and Financial Affairs, and their Department, deans, managers of other administrative units, employees conducting didactic courses, students in the year 2016/2017.

A Gantt Chart

A Gantt chart was used in the process of scheduling the execution of the project (Figure 12.2).

A Description of the Process of the Assessment of Lecturers by Students

The objective of the process of the assessment of lecturers by students is to provide credible and reliable information on the quality of didactic courses and students' satisfaction. Such information is necessary for the planning of teaching quality improvement activities such as training courses and other methods or means of supporting university teachers. The process has a seasonal character (January–February, June–July). The university organizational unit responsible for the execution of the project is the Teaching Quality Section.

Activity	Planned start	Planned duration	Real start	Real duration	Percentage of completion	1	2	3	4	5	6	7	8	9	10	11	12	13	14
											Days off							Days off	
1	Preparing a general assumption of a project	1	1	0	0	0%														
2	Preparing a data base	2	2	0	0	0%														
3	Preparing a framework for a project	4	2	0	0	0%														
4	Development of the define phase	8	3	0	0	0%														
5	Development of the measure phase	15	5	0	0	0%														
6	Development of the analyse phase	22	5	0	0	0%														
7	Development of the improve phase	29	3	0	0	0%														
8	Development of the control phase	32	2	0	0	0%														
9	Review of a project	36	5	0	0	0%														
10	Final corrects	43	1	0	0	0%														
11	Submission of the project to the Vice-Rector	44	1	0	0	0%														

FIGURE 12.2

A Gantt chart.

The Customers of the Process

At the next stage, the requirements and expectations of the stakeholders of the process were analysed (Table 12.1).

TABLE 12.1

The Requirements and Expectations of the Customers and Stakeholders of the Process

Customers of the Process	Expectations
Dean, direct superior	Credible and reliable results of students' assessments which are accepted and not undermined by employees. It is a basis for making decisions related to the personnel, promotions, attendance in training courses, etc. Determining the directions of improving the quality of the teaching personnel in the faculty; improving the quality of teaching. A high position in university rankings with respect to particular teaching subjects. Prestige and trust. Low costs. Reducing the risk of litigation brought by employees. Personnel management based on reliable data. Employees' greater commitment to improving the quality of didactic courses.
Representative for teaching quality	Fulfilling the legal requirements, acquiring accreditation for particular teaching subjects; determining guidelines for improving the University's Teaching Quality Assurance System, including the didactic processes and the teaching personnel.
University authorities, vice president for didactic affairs	Improving the quality of teaching in the university, the university's position in the rankings of higher education institutions, students' satisfaction and loyalty, students' high attendance in the AOL process.
Teaching Quality Section (TQS)	Reliable reports on the process, the effectiveness of the AOL process measured by a high attendance indicator, low costs of the AOL process.
Ars Docenti (the unit dealing with the professional development of lecturers)	Reliable information allowing the unit to prepare training plans and programmes for the university's teaching staff.
Student	A sense of exerting influence on the shaping of teaching quality, a reliable tool for conveying information on the quality of the teaching staff's work, the easiness of filling in the questionnaire, a reduced frequency of the AOL process, feedback on assessment results.
Lecturer	A reliable work assessment tool, a possibility of determining the directions of improvement processes, deriving satisfaction from work, respect, a proper presentation and legibility of assessment results, high attendance of students. A sense of justice with respect to awards granted to the best teachers on the basis of AOL results.

SIPOC and Indicators Critical to Quality (CTQ)

A SIPOC diagram was used to draw up a map of the process and to order, elaborated previously, actions influencing the values of CTQ indicators (Figure 12.3).

Critical to Quality is a key measurable characteristic of a product or process which is important for a customer (external or/and internal). Its performance standards or specification limits must be set and monitored to meet customer requirements. In this project, two CTQ indicators were established: CTQ (Y1) value of the assessment of lectures given by students (AOL) and CTQ (Y2) attendance indicator (the attendance of students in the AOL process).

The MEASURE Phase

In the Measure phase, analyses were carried out for CTQ (Y1) and CTQ (Y2). The statistical analyses were conducted with the use of the MINITAB 17 software.

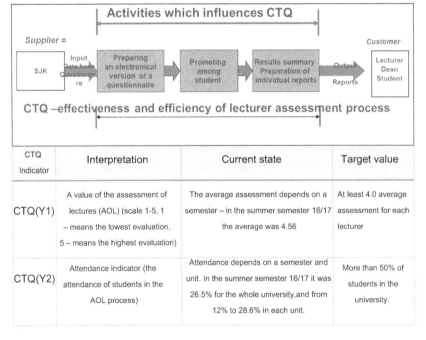

CTQ Indicator	Interpretation	Current state	Target value
CTQ(Y1)	A value of the assessment of lectures (AOL) (scale 1-5, 1 – means the lowest evaluation, 5 – means the highest evaluation)	The average assessment depends on a semester – in the summer semester 16/17 the average was 4.56	At least 4.0 average assessment for each lecturer
CTQ(Y2)	Attendance indicator (the attendance of students in the AOL process)	Attendance depends on a semester and unit. In the summer semester 16/17 it was 26.5% for the whole university,and from 12% to 28.6% in each unit.	More than 50% of students in the university.

FIGURE 12.3
SIPOC & CTQ.

Unfortunately, the method adopted in the university for collecting data concerning the AOL process and students' attendance in it prevented the author from performing many statistical analyses. For the purpose of the project, special tables were prepared on the basis of the existing databases (the databases were transformed many times in order to acquire data in the required sections). From the point of view of the conducted statistical analyses, a very important task was to specify the type of data to undergo analysis (attribute data, continuous data). The type of data determines the scope of the used statistical tools.

For CTQ (Y1) Assessment of lecturers (AOL) the following actions were taken:

1. A plan and a table concerning the collection of data on the values of students' assessment were drawn up.
2. A variability analysis was performed with respect to the particular questions included in the lecturer assessment questionnaire and a variability analysis with respect to AOL.

In Table 12.2 the types of data and a way of collecting were presented.

The collection of data was followed by statistical analyses. In view of the fact that the dependent variable Y1 and the independent variables X1, X2, X3 are attribute data, an analysis of the variability of Y1 was performed with reference to every question Q1, Q2, Q3, Q4, Q5 included in the questionnaire. The following graph presents the results of the analysis (Figure 12.4).

The analysis was carried out on the basis of 5872 assessments completed by students for this question (Sample N). The analysis results show that the distribution of data does not have a normal character. It was assumed that the minimum assessment LB (lower bound) equalled 3.0, while the target assessment – 4.0. The average assessment is 4.2, which is higher than the established target. This value is strongly influenced by the extreme (the highest and the lowest) assessments. Attention should be paid to the high value of the standard deviation (1.14). For every question, the variability distribution was very much similar. On the basis of the obtained analysis results, the following conclusions were reached:

- The distribution of the AOL values does not have a normal character (this may be the result of the specific character of the AOL process; in its case, the target is not normal distribution, but the highest assessments of didactic courses).

TABLE 12.2

A Data Collection Table for CTQ (Y1) Assessment of Lecturers (AOL)

CTQ	Assessment of lecturers (AOL)
Y1	AOL value
Measure type	At the output, process measure
Data type	Attribute
Operational definition	A student's subjective assessment on a 1–5 scale Assessment scale: 1 = definitely not, 2 = rather not, 3 = hard to say, 4 = rather yes, 5 = definitely yes
Measuring procedure	Assessments are made by students at the end of each semester, by means of an electronic questionnaire. The student assesses their lecturer and subject. An assessment is not obligatory
Measuring system	The student assesses their lecturer, answering the following five questions: Q1 Did you manage to broaden your knowledge of the subject thanks to the lecturer? Q2 What is your assessment of the lecturer's ability to impart knowledge? Q3 Was the lecturer ready to provide additional explanations in class or during their consultation hours? Q4 Was the lecturer prepared for their classes and lectures? Q5 Did the lecturer meet the adopted criteria for passing their course?
Measuring unit	Assessments provided for the particular questions; after transformation, the average assessment of the particular questions with respect to a subject
Sampling	An analysis of a selected database (a selected faculty, the summer semester 16/17), 5884 records (one record is one student's assessment with respect to a particular subject). The number of assessed courses: 1040
Sample size	2015/2016 summer semester, 53,467 records, the whole university 2015/2016 winter semester, 42,975 records, the whole university 2016/2017 summer semester, 59,193 records, the whole university 2016/2017 winter semester, 70,794 records, the whole university
X	X 1 teacher's scholarly degree/title (attribute data) X 2 type of course (lecture, other – class, discussion seminar, lab and others) (attribute data) X 3 teacher's gender (W/M) (attribute data)

ID of questionnaire (separate ID for each student's assessment)	Gender of lecturer (man, woman)	Title/degree (PhD, prof.)	Kind of course	Q1	Q2	Q3	Q4	Q5
				Student's assessment of each course				
21005	W	Prof.	Lecture	4	5	3	5	4
21006	M	PhD	Class	4	5	3	5	5
21007	M	Prof.	Lecture	5	5	5	5	5
...	...	....	....	....	....	....	....	....

(Data collection table (a fragment))

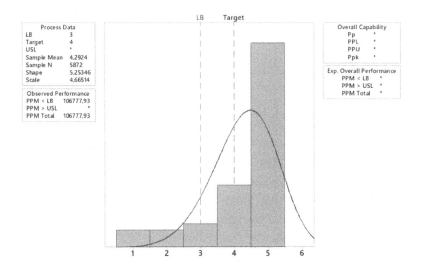

FIGURE 12.4

A process capability report for Q1 calculation based on the Weibull distribution model (Q1 Did you manage to broaden your knowledge of the subject thanks to the lecturer?).

- The AOL process is defective – The measuring tool (the assessment questionnaire with the 1–5 scale) is biased in favour of extreme assessments; it is possible to notice a large number of observations around the maximum values (which is 5).
- The average assessment for each question is higher than the established target. Its value is strongly influenced by the extreme assessments. Attention should be paid to the high value of the standard deviation.

The variability analysis results show that assessment are strongly diversified; the standard established for CTQ (Y1) is not maintained, i.e. not all lecturers receive the assessment of at least 4 in every question. It can be assumed that the assessments of didactic courses have an emotional character (the effect of an Internet forum). Students assess courses when they are delighted or very angry. The distribution of assessments may be influenced also by students' attendance in the AOL process. The attendance analysis results are presented in the following.

During the MEASURE phase the following analyses were performed for CTQ (Y2) Attendance:

1. A plan and a table for the collection of data on students' attendance in the AOL process were prepared.

2. An attendance analysis and an attendance variability analysis were carried out.

In Table 12.3 the types of data and a way of collecting were presented.

The collection of data was followed by statistical analyses. In view of the fact that the dependent variable Y2 is continuous and the independent variables X5, X6 are attribute data, an analysis was performed with the use of an individual value plot graph and a pie chart, as well as an analysis of the variability of Y2. The following graphs present the results of the analysis (Figures 12.5 and 12.6).

The individual value plot graph shows that questionnaires are filled in the most often by up to ten people, irrespective of the size of a group or the type of course. The pie chart shows that 55.9% of questionnaires related to a particular type of course are filled in by up to four people; the most often questionnaires are completed by one or two persons of a whole group participating in a course in a given subject. Figure 12.4 presents the summary report for CTQ (Y2) attendance (Figure 12.7).

The graph shows that attendance distribution is not normal. On average, courses are assessed by fewer than six students, the most often by four students. The mean is 5.6 students, the minimum is one student, the maximum is 82 students.

The conducted research shows that the measurement of attendance is difficult because the manner of data collection does not allow the determination of attendance indicators for particular courses and teachers (the number of students who participated in the AOL process to the overall number of students taking a given course/students of a given lecturer). The analysis of the other data sources shows that in the summer semester 2016/2017 86% of all courses and 89% of all lecturers were assessed. It means that 11% of the lecturers were not assessed, which constitutes a threat of non-compliance with the legal regulations. The low attendance indicator causes the low reliability of the AOL process results, and these results are strongly influenced by emotional factors and the Internet forum effect.

TABLE 12.3

The Data Collection Table for CTQ (Y2) Attendance

CTQ	Attendance
Y2	Number of students who assessed a given subject
Measure type	At the output, process measure
Data type	Continuous
Operational definition	A value from 0 (nobody assessed) to the number of students who had formally participated in a given course
Measuring procedure	Attendance is calculated on the basis of an analysis of AOL databases (the number of students who assessed a particular subject is calculated)
Measuring system	On the basis of databases
Measuring unit	Participation in the AOL process (making an assessment)
Sampling	An analysis of a selected database (a selected faculty, the summer semester 16/17), 5884 records (one record is one student's assessment with respect to a particular subject)
Sample size	2015/2016 summer semester, 53,467 records, the whole university 2015/2016 winter semester, 42,975 records, the whole university 2016/2017 summer semester, 59,193 records, the whole university 2016/2017 winter semester, 70,794 records, the whole university
X	X 5 Semester (2016/2017 summer semester, 2016/2017 winter semester), X 6 the organizational unit offering the subject

The data collection table (an example)

Variable	Z_ID	N	N*	Mean	SE Mean	StDev	Minimum	Q1	Median	Q3	Maximum
mean	337487	8	0	3,925	0,574	1,625	1,000	2,300	4,900	5,000	5,000
	337489	8	0	4,9500	0,0500	0,1414	4,6000	5,0000	5,0000	5,0000	5,0000
	337490	7	0	5,0000	0,000000	0,000000	5,0000	5,0000	5,0000	5,0000	5,0000
	337492	4	0	4,700	0,173	0,346	4,400	4,400	4,700	5,000	5,000
	337494	3	0	4,800	0,200	0,346	4,400	4,400	5,000	5,000	5,000
	337495	11	0	4,7818	0,0989	0,3281	4,0000	4,6000	5,0000	5,0000	5,0000
	337496	4	0	4,000	0,583	1,166	2,800	2,900	4,100	5,000	5,000
	337497	3	0	4,667	0,333	0,577	4,000	4,000	5,000	5,000	5,000
	337498	3	0	5,0000	0,000000	0,000000	5,0000	5,0000	5,0000	5,0000	5,0000
	337499	1	0	5,0000	*	*	5,0000	*	5,0000	*	5,0000
	337500	8	0	4,9250	0,0526	0,1488	4,6000	4,8500	5,0000	5,0000	5,0000
	337502	2	0	5,0000	0,000000	0,000000	5,0000	*	5,0000	*	5,0000
	337507	1	0	5,0000	*	*	5,0000	*	5,0000	*	5,0000
	337508	3	0	5,0000	0,000000	0,000000	5,0000	5,0000	5,0000	5,0000	5,0000
	337523	7	0	4,800	0,145	0,383	4,000	4,600	5,000	5,000	5,000
	337524	3	0	4,533	0,240	0,416	4,200	4,200	4,400	5,000	5,000
	337525	2	0	4,800	0,200	0,283	4,600	*	4,800	*	5,000
	337542	17	0	3,379	0,269	1,109	1,250	2,800	3,200	4,400	5,000
	337543	6	0	3,600	0,584	1,431	1,000	2,650	3,900	4,700	5,000
	337544	14	0	4,457	0,291	1,088	2,000	4,550	5,000	5,000	5,000

The table includes the descriptive statistics data obtained by way of transforming the data from students' assessments – the distribution of the average assessment with respect to the assessed course – 2016/2017 summer semester (Z-ID – course number, N – number of students making assessments, Mean – average assessment of the course)

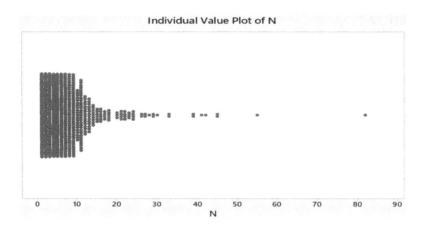

FIGURE 12.5
An analysis of students' attendance in the AOL process (plot).

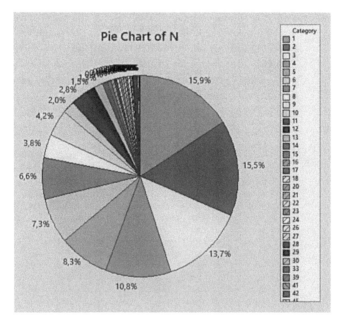

FIGURE 12.6
An analysis of students' attendance in the AOL process (pie).

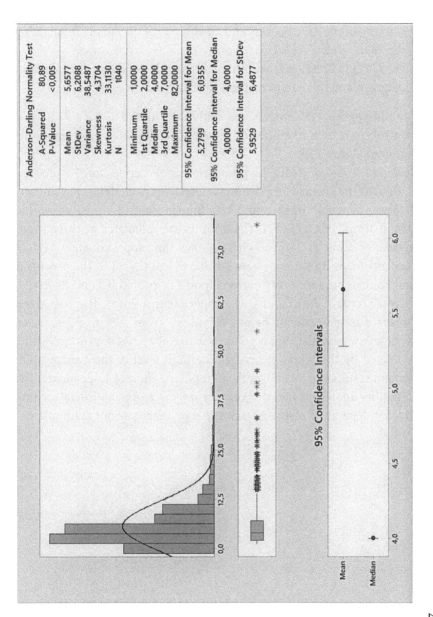

FIGURE 12.7
A summary report for CTQ (Y2).

The ANALYSE Phase

In the Analyse phase, the following analyses were performed for CTQ:

- For CTQ (Y1) Assessment of lecturer (AOL), an analysis of the stability of the AOL process and an analysis of the factors influencing the AOL process were carried out.
- For CTQ (Y2) Attendance, an analysis with the use of the Ishikawa diagram and the Pareto method were carried out.

The stability of the AOL process was analysed with the use of a P chart. It is a control chart used to monitor the proportion of nonconforming units in a sample (Figure 12.8).

The center line represents the proportion of defectives for the process. Minitab used the average proportion of defectives from data, , to estimate. LCL (lower control limit) and UCL (upper control limit) show the acceptable limits of CTQ (Y1). These limits are calculated as three times standard deviation (+, –) The chart shows that approximately 14% of assessments made by students have a value of less than 4.0. The process is beyond control because every extreme point is located beyond its limits, LCL (lower control limit) and UCL (upper control limit). The dispersion of the share of assessments below 4.0 ranges from 22% to 9.5%. Thus, an average assessment is not a good measure of the AOL process, which is confirmed by the research results. The high level of the average AOL assessment results first of all from a high polarization of assessments. The AOL stability analysis shows that one permanent and established teaching standard independent of lecturers or types of courses is not maintained.

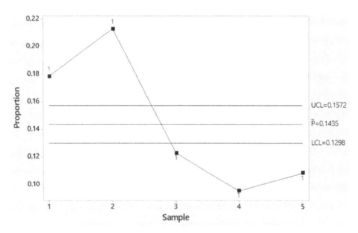

FIGURE 12.8

An analysis of the stability of the AOL process (P chart).

The next step was an analysis of factors influencing the AOL process with the use of a Chi-square test. The correlations analysis results showed the following:

- A lecturer's degree/title did not influence the AOL process.
- Type of a course conducted by a teacher did not influence the average value of the AOL – the average assessment of courses is slightly higher (4.469) than the average assessment of the other forms of didactic courses (4.431).
- A teacher's gender influences the average AOL – the average assessment of the quality of courses conducted by women is higher (4.510) than the average AOL of courses conducted by men (4.376).

In order to analyse the reasons for students' low attendance in the AOL process, a research was carried out among students attending full-time and part-time study programmes with the use of the Ishikawa diagram and the Pareto method (Figure 12.9).

The analysis of the factors influencing students' attendance was based on the Pareto method (the factors were arranged according to the frequency of their indications by students). On this basis, a group of factors which in 80% of cases contribute to the low attendance of students at the AOL process was distinguished. The analysis showed that students did not complete questionnaires because they could not see the results of their assessments and did not receive any feedback about the AOL process. Another important element was the fear of losing anonymity. Table 12.4 presents the results of the Pareto analysis, categorizing the factors indicated by students (this categorization covers only those factors which in 80% of cases contribute to the low attendance of students at the AOL process).

The IMPROVE Phase

In this phase of the project execution process, the author proposed solutions aimed at improving the reliability of the results of the AOL process as well as students' attendance in the process. It was emphasized that it was necessary:

- To change the procedure of conducting the AOL process
- To change the format of the questionnaire
- To develop a mobile version of the questionnaire
- To make additional computers available to students for the purpose of the AOL process

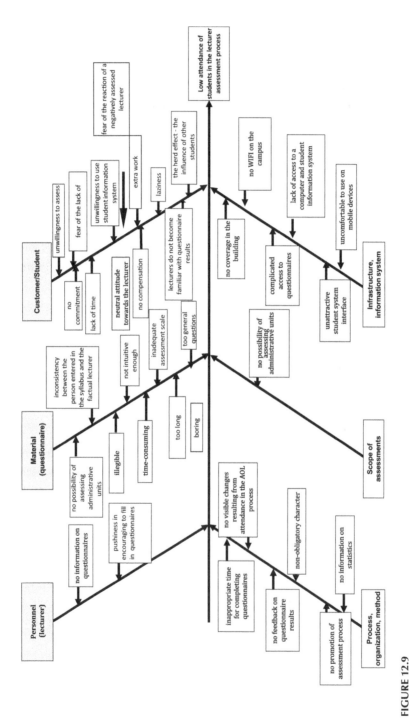

FIGURE 12.9
Fishbone diagram.

TABLE 12.4

Analysis Results – A List of Factors which in 80% of Cases Contribute to Students' Low Attendance

Group of reasons	Causes
Research effects	no visible changes resulting from attendance in the AOL process
	no feedback on questionnaire results
Questionnaire	an inadequate assessment scale
	the questionnaire is unclear (no clear assessment criteria)
	too long
AOL process organization	fear of the lack of anonymity
	voluntary participation in the AOL process
	no promotion of the AOL process and no emphasis put on its importance
	no information on the questionnaire on the part of teachers
	inappropriate time for completing questionnaires
	no compensation
Student	no time for completing the questionnaire
	no commitment
	a neutral attitude towards the lecturer
	laziness
Infrastructure	complicated access to the questionnaire in the student information system
	the unattractive student information system interface

Table 12.5 presents a list of improvement-oriented activities to be undertaken in the university.

The following guidelines for the preparation of a new AOL process were also formulated:

- Before every assessment process, it is necessary to prepare a list of teachers to undergo assessment together with a list of students who attended particular teachers' courses.
- The AOL process should be preceded by a promotional campaign (targeted at teachers, students, the university authorities, the administration personnel). Forms of promotion: posters, emails, information on Facebook and other social media, information presented on monitors located on the premises of a particular faculty. Such information includes the date of an assessment, instructions for participants, the results of previous assessments, the date of publishing new assessment results.

TABLE 12.5

A List of (Selected) Improvement-Oriented Activities

Research Results	Improvement-Oriented Activities	Tasks	Person Responsible	Commencement Date	Completion Date	Impact on Y
No visible changes resulting from attendance in the AOL process	A broader promotion of the results of activities undertaken in consequence of the questionnaire research	1. To change the procedure of conducting the AOL process 2. To change the format of the questionnaire 3. To develop a mobile version of the questionnaire	TQS	April 2018	June 2018	Improving students' attendance in the AOL process, improving the reliability of students' assessments, eliminating the Internet forum effect
No feedback on questionnaire results	The regular presentation of general information and questionnaire research statistics (teachers' overall average assessments, trends, attendance, etc.)		TQS			Improving students' attendance in the AOL process
Fear of the lack of anonymity	Information on the manners of ensuring students' anonymity		TQS			Improving students' attendance in the AOL process
⋮	⋮	⋮	⋮	⋮	⋮	⋮

- During the course of the AOL process, the attendance indicator is monitored on a continuous basis in order to achieve at least 50% with respect to every teacher.
- After the AOL process, general statistics (e.g. attendance, the average assessment of teachers with respect to particular criteria, guidelines and scopes of improvement-related activities together with an implementation schedule) should be published. The promotional campaign should be targeted at teachers, students, the university authorities, the administration personnel. Forms of promotion: posters, emails, information on Facebook and other social media, information presented on monitors located on the premises of a particular faculty.

A new format of the assessment questionnaire was also proposed. The questions in the questionnaire should be replaced with statements of a more objective character (they should not cover aspects which do not depend directly on the teacher, e.g. the availability of books in the library or the number of ECTS points assigned to the subject). The assessment scale should be broadened (e.g. 1–7 or 1–10). The questionnaire should be accompanied by a note containing students' particulars such as the year and form of studies, etc. The questionnaire research should be broadened with other aspects connected with administrative services, the library, the infrastructure, the organization of courses, etc. All these measures would increase students' sense of agency and their involvement in the university's matters. It would additionally support the activities of the students' self-government. Assessment results should be published together with a description of undertaken activities and their effectiveness.

The use of a mobile application in the AOL process would allow students to carry out an assessment at any time, e.g. while coming back home or standing in a queue, etc.

During the course of the AOL process students can be provided with additional computers to fill in the questionnaire, e.g. in the faculty library or next to the reception desk (this would allow the students who are concerned about their anonymity to fill in the questionnaire on a university computer; furthermore, students would be able to fill in the questionnaire during breaks between classes).

The CONTROL Phase

During the course of the AOL process, it is recommended to control reliability and attendance. The attendance indicator should be monitored on a continuous basis in order to achieve at least 50% with respect to every teacher. In the event of a low attendance, additional measures could be taken (e.g. reminder notes sent by email or other social media, information disseminated by faculty employees, etc.).

The measuring system should undergo periodic tests of the variability and capability of the process based on the Ishikawa diagram and the Pareto method with a view to looking for further opportunities for improvement.

Another proposal is to introduce new data collection tables which will allow the monitoring of the assessment process and student attendance with respect to a particular teacher or organizational unit. They will also make it possible to examine relations between student assessment results and other variables such as X_1 gender, X_2 degree, X_3 seniority, X_4 overtime, X_5 didactic training courses, X_6 other personnel related data.

Summing up, a successful execution of the project should bring about the following effects:

- Changing the questionnaire format in order to improve the objectivity of the AOL process (minimizing the emotional character of assessment and the Internet forum effect). Increasing the reliability of the AOL process.
- Increasing attendance (by ongoing control aimed at ensuring the attendance indicator at the level of at least 50%).
- Increasing students' involvement in the AOL process.
- Changing the data collection sections (which will allow a fuller analysis and a capture of factors influencing the AOL process).
- Increasing teachers' acceptance of assessment results (the AOL process becomes a tool for improving the quality of didactic courses and teaching methods).
- Reducing the risk of making improper decisions related to the personnel and employee training.

SUMMARY – HOW TO MODIFY SIX SIGMA IN A UNIVERSITY CONTEXT TO INCREASE EFFECTIVENESS

Preparing for the implementation of the project, the author came across many obstacles which resulted in some modifications in the application of Six Sigma in the university.

Firstly, the processes carried out in universities are very much unique, strongly bureaucratic, frequently periodic, determined by legal requirements; the needs of the university and its stakeholders are of secondary importance. This causes a situation in which the application of various statistical tools to analyse these processes is strongly limited. This results also from the character of collected data (mainly attribute data) and their poor metering (data are collected mainly for the purposes of reporting and national statistics). Furthermore, data are collected in various sections as well as paper and electronic databases which are frequently mutually incompatible. The execution of a Six Sigma project makes it possible to indicate many gaps in this area and to change the university's approach to data collection so that data become useful in process improvement activities.

Another problem which may appear during the phase of testing the proposed changes is that trial tests or process simulations often cannot be conducted in universities, which obviously increases risks inherent in implementing changes in a living and functioning organization. In view of the long process execution cycles in HE, the implementation of changes in successive cycles can be considerably stretched in time.

The methodologies of Six Sigma and DMAIC certainly require some simplification in institutions of higher education. Nevertheless, the presented project results indicate that they can be very useful in determining the causes of problems and solving problems occurring in numerous processes performed in universities. It happens frequently that such problems and their causes are known, but there is no systematized and practical knowledge of these issues. And in accordance with the principles of Lean and the PDCA method, it is only facts and data that should constitute a basis for making decisions.

LITERATURE

Antony, J. 2004. Some pros and cons of six sigma: An academic perspective. *The TQM Magazine.* Vol. 16, No. 4:303–306.

Antony, J. 2015. Challenges in the deployment of LSS in the higher education sector: Viewpoints from leading academics and practitioners. *International Journal of Productivity and Performance Management.* Vol. 64, No. 6:893–899.

Bandyopadhyay, J.K. and R. Lichtman. 2007. Six Sigma approach to quality and productivity improvement in an institution for higher education in the United States. *International Journal of Management.* Vol. 24, No. 4:802.

Bargerstock, A.S. and S.R. Richards. 2015. Case study: The application of DMAIC to academic assessment in higher education. *Quality Approaches in Higher Education.* Vol. 6, No. 2:31–40.

Campatelli, G., P. Citti, and A. Meneghin. 2011. Development of a simplified approach based on the EFQM model and Six Sigma for the implementation of TQM principles in a university administration. *Total Quality Management and Business Excellence.* Vol. 22, No. 7:691–704.

Hamrol, A. 2007. Zarządzanie jakością z przykładami [Quality Management with Examples]. PWN.

Jones, O. 2013. How can Higher Education institutions develop and sustain process improvement capability: An action research proposal. Enhancing Process Efficiency and Effectiveness in Higher Education Using Lean Six Sigma. In: Proceedings of First International Conference on Lean Six Sigma for Higher Education. pp. 51–62.

Kukreja, A., J.M. Ricks, and J.A. Meyer. 2009. Using Six Sigma for performance improvement in business curriculum: A case study. *Performance Improvement.* Vol. 48, No. 2:9–25.

Lu, J., C. Laux, and J. Antony. 2017. Lean Six Sigma leadership in higher education institutions. *International Journal of Productivity and Performance Management.* Vol. 66, No. 5:638–650.

Majorana, F. and A. Morelli. 2012. *Lean Banking.* [Wydawnictwo M].

Shankar, R. 2009. *Process Improvement Using Six Sigma: A DMAIC Guide.* ASQ Quality Press: Milwaukee, WI.

Snee, R.D. 2010. Lean Six Sigma – Getting better all the time. *International Journal of Lean Six Sigma.* Vol. 1, No. 1:9–29.

Tjahjono, B., P. Ball, V.I. Vitanov, C. Scorzafave, J. Nogueira, J. Calleja, M. Minguet, L. Narasimha, A. Rivas, A. Srivastava, S. Srivastava, and A. Yadav. 2010. Six Sigma: A literature review. *International Journal of Lean Six Sigma.* Vol. 1, No. 3:216–233.

Vanzant-Stern, T. 2012. *Lean Six Sigma: International Standards and Global Guidelines.* Fultus Corporation.

Yeung, S.M. 2013. Applying Six Sigma into curriculum design for creating value – Fulfilling accreditation requirements with learning outcomes measured. Enhancing process efficiency and effectiveness in higher education using lean Six Sigma. In: Proceedings of First International Conference on Lean Six Sigma for Higher Education. pp. 101–122.

Yorkstone, S. 2013. Leaning Universities Old and New: A comparative case study on the implementation of Lean Thinking in Universities Ancient and Modern, from the perspective of a practitioner. Enhancing Process Efficiency and Effectiveness in Higher Education Using Lean Six Sigma. In: Proceedings of First International Conference on Lean Six Sigma for Higher Education. pp. 40–51.

Yu, K.-T. and R.-G. Ueng. 2012. Enhancing teaching effectiveness by using the Six-Sigma DMAIC model. *Assessment and Evaluation in Higher Education.* Vol. 37, No. 8:949–961.

13

Lean Training to Lean Projects

Marion Malcolm

CONTENTS

The Business Improvement Team at the University of Aberdeen offer a lean training portfolio to help staff understand and apply lean methodology to improve their work areas and contribute to the university achieving its strategic aims. The training portfolio started in autumn 2015 as a result of the Business Improvement team becoming more experienced in its lean journey and reaching the conclusion that training should naturally be part of its portfolio in addition to other lean activities. In addition, there had been periods of churn within the university and larger organisational change had taken longer than expected. Therefore a new approach was needed to ensure that lean remained an appropriate change methodology to enable smaller scale change.

BACKGROUND

The University of Aberdeen is one of the four ancient universities in Scotland (founded in 1495). It has approximately 3,300 staff and 14,500 students and offers bachelor, masters and PhD study across a wide range of subjects. Approximately 30% of the student population is international and the university operates over in Aberdeen and overseas.

The Business Improvement (BI) team was established in early 2013 with the head of the team being recruited externally, who brought significant lean practitioner experience in a variety of sectors. Other team members (BI specialists) were seconded from existing university posts and had very little lean knowledge but they did have a lot of experience of university systems and processes, had many internal networks, and most importantly had a hunger for positive change within the institution. The BI Specialists worked in various areas and had positive and negative experiences of processes and systems and wanted to make improvements for the benefit of the university, staff and students. Lean practitioner skills and expertise for the seconded staff were developed in-house, through external training and through networking with higher education and local authority partners. In addition a BI coordinator was appointed to support the team with its workload.

WHY DID ABERDEEN START A LEAN TRAINING PORTFOLIO?

The University of Aberdeen launched an integrated applications programme in early 2013 and an individual BI specialist was allocated to individual module development to support process mapping, requirements gathering etc for the modules. In addition team members facilitated kaizen blitzes (also called a rapid improvement event) where a significant area of work is improved over a short period of time and other projects involving multiple areas of the university, e.g. post graduate taught conversion activities. Through hard won experience between 2013 and 2015, the BI team came to believe that training should naturally become a part of the work portfolio. At the same time there was a period of churn within the university as a result of voluntary severance and early retirement schemes for staff and a change in structures and senior management. This meant that some organisational change took longer than expected and staff were less able or willing to take part in large BI activities, as time out of the office became more precious. Hence lean training was introduced to act as a way of engaging staff in smaller scale changes that were less onerous or daunting.

LEAN TRAINING PORTFOLIO

The lean training portfolio commenced in autumn 2015 after a period of in-house development by one of the BI specialists, Helena Ziegler. Three types of training offered are 1) Lean @ Lunch, 2) Lean for HE (Higher Education) and 3) Lean for your Team. Courses are advertised via the university staff development course booking system, via the staff e-zine and by word of mouth (whilst BI staff are working with colleagues on other activities). Training is held in the Business Improvement room so that all BI materials are available and it also introduces colleagues to a location that will host future improvement work. Sessions are informal and refreshments are offered to reinforce a friendly environment. Feedback is gathered from attendees at the end of training via a short paper survey form (following the PDCA – Plan, Do, Check, Act – cycle). This is an effective way of gathering comments because once people leave the room there is less likelihood of them providing feedback.

As well as specific University of Aberdeen sessions, Lean for Leaders training has also been undertaken in collaboration with the Universities of Strathclyde and Stirling. Table 13.1 summarises the different lean training methods.

Lean @ Lunch

This is a one hour introduction to lean theory, concentrating on the two fundamentals (continuous improvement and respect for people), the five principles (value, value stream, flow, pull and perfection) and the

TABLE 13.1

Summary of Lean Training Methods

Training	Duration	No of attendees*	Frequency	Expected output
Lean @ Lunch	1 hour introduction	104	4 x per year	Generate discussion for future learning
Lean for HE (ILM accreditation)	2 days in-depth	32	2 x per year	Project proposal
Lean for your Team	Variable	65	Ad hoc	Lean champion Project proposal Comms board
Lean for Leaders	2 days in-depth	9	1 x per year	Project proposal Leaders to be lean champions themselves and encourage others to think in a lean way

* Figures as at September 2018.

eight wastes (Aberdeen uses the DOWNTIME acronym ie defects, over-processing, waiting, non-value added, transport, inventory, madness and employee potential). We also use Muda (waste ie consumes resources but creates no value), Mura (unevenness) and Muri (overburden) to illustrate standard lean concepts. Learning is shared via a presentation with opportunity for discussion and interaction, giving examples of previous BI activities within the university and externally, to show that it is not just a theoretical methodology. Attendees are encouraged to bring lunch along, with refreshments provided, and informality is key to gain interest. Learners are given a one page laminated "Quick Guide to Lean" to take away from the session, highlighting the key lean theory items ie the two fundamentals, the five principles and the eight wastes.

Lean for HE

Colleagues who want a more hands-on approach to lean generally attend this training. There is some repeat business from Lean @ Lunch attendees and the BI team also ask project leads (who have already been identified to fill that role from discussions with a project sponsor for example) to attend to ensure that they have an in-depth understanding of lean theory, tools and techniques prior to an improvement event. Colleagues who work on strategic university projects are also encouraged to take part eg the

Student Lifecycle build team attended training. The two days are a mix of theory, practical activities and teach back. The teach back is one of the most effective parts of the training as attendees have to directly apply lean theory to a work or personal situation and their feedback suggests this is very valuable to them, rather than making it part of a manufactured activity. Attendees are given a Lean for Higher Education handbook to take away with them to help reinforce the greater depth of understanding that they should have after two days. The training is accredited by the ILM (Institute of Leadership and Management) and attendees can receive a formal certificate subject to a fee being paid to the ILM.

The expected output from attendance is that a full project proposal will be developed, and a BI activity will follow (eg a rapid improvement event) with the support of the BI Team. An example of a BI activity resulting from Lean for HE was a project that placed year four and year five medical students into their general practice placement (primary care setting where they learn and can practice communication and clinical skills). The administrator for the placement task attended Lean for HE training in April 2016 and a Lean for your Team session was held for core staff in June 2016. This resulted in a review of the work area over winter 2016 that led to processes and IT systems being aligned to ensure that students received a consistent service and staff could work in a more standardised and efficient way. It was estimated that there could be a 30% saving in staff activity time once full process and system design was implemented.

Lean for Your Team

This model came into being as some staff, who had attended other lean training or had been involved in other BI events, asked about more specific training for their work area. The one hour Lean @ Lunch presentation is used as the basis for an introduction to lean but it is tailored to the individual work area. Once the presentation is complete the team are then asked to share their thoughts via coloured post its on a feedback grid to highlight what works well, what doesn't work well, what are the pain/pinch points and what are the suggested areas or processes for improvement. The team then decides which of the identified areas would be most suitable for a project and further scoping and analysis is undertaken to ensure that this is the correct priority. The expected outputs from Lean for your Team training is as per Figure 13.1 ie to ensure that the staff become a continuously improving team that becomes self-sustaining.

FIGURE 13.1
Diagram illustrating the link between "Lean for your team" training with other activities.

There are several examples of Lean for your Team success stories within the university eg the School of Biological Sciences admin team who undertook a session in January 2016 which culminated in an exam paper blitz in June 2016 that was attended by both admin and teaching staff.

Lean for Leaders

Lean for Leaders was delivered in collaboration with colleagues at the Universities of Strathclyde and Stirling and the training was held at Stirling University over a two day period, allowing for staff networking between universities during the formal sessions and informally. It is similar to the Lean for HE model in that there is a mix of theory, practice and teach back. Aberdeen attendees were nominated by their managers or were approached directly and attendees have represented Estates, Marketing, Student Recruitment and Admissions Services, the Institute of Medical Education, the Directorate of Digital and Information Services and CPD (Continuing Professional Development).

PROJECTS RESULTING FROM LEAN TRAINING

The BI team has undertaken an additional eleven projects as a result of lean training since autumn 2015. This has resulted in over 5,000 actual or potential hours of staff time saved with resulting improvements in staff collaboration, quality improvement and reduction of non-value-added work ie over-processing via duplication or reworking. Examples of projects are as follows.

Example 1: School of Biological Sciences Examination Administration

The School of Biological Sciences administration team has been an adopter of lean training and methods since the BI team introduced the lean training portfolio. The School Admin Officer attended Lean for HE training in October 2015 and this was followed by a Lean for your Team session with admin staff in January 2016. They identified various areas for improvement and decided to take forward an exam paper blitz in June 2016. Between January and June they were able to collect exam assessment data for each course eg when the calls for exam papers were sent out, how long they took to format the exam paper etc. This data was invaluable during the blitz, particularly when describing and evidencing the problem to other staff. The blitz outcome included the development and implementation of a SharePoint site to manage the exam process, reducing the amount of time that it takes to administer the documents as well as having much better version control and cutting down bottlenecks during the production phase. Whilst there were some technical difficulties with the implementation of the SharePoint system in the first semester of the 2016/17 academic year, the admin team have undertaken to ensure that the difficulties are solved and then re-double their efforts to ensure that the site is adopted as standard practice.

The admin staff are good examples of what we look for in a lean team ie they are eager to solve a problem if they encounter one and they are not afraid to experiment. Maree McCombie (School Admin Officer) commented in September 2017 that the Lean for your Team training "changed the mind-set of the team, it got everyone involved, it made us more professional".

Example 2: Estates Project Delivery Improvement

The "Delivery of a project in Estates" initial workshop took place in June 2017 after the Project Lead attended the Lean for Leaders course in Stirling in March 2017. A "project in Estates" was defined as

- Any piece of work (e.g. a refurbishment) managed by the drawing office
- No formal project board exists

- A value of £50,000 to £1 million
- Normally requires external consultants, external contractors and internal staff
- Normally requires planning permissions and a building warrant
- Budget and basic project brief agreed
- Might have a business plan

Problems and wastes identified included that
- The outline proposal was not always clear
- The budget had a loose estimate so that there could be finance issues
- There was duplication due to reworking and scope creep
- There was time difficulties as every project had to follow external procurement standards (eg Invitation to Tender regulations)
- It was difficult to have standardised ways of working
- There were communication problems

The team consisted of various Estates staff, an external consultant and an internal customer to allow for the full value stream mapping journey and relevant feedback from all stakeholders. A SIPOC exercise was undertaken to highlight the seven high level process steps which was expanded to a full AS IS process mapping that illustrated that there could be 59 steps from a project conception to delivery. There was a huge range in activity time and waiting time depending on the project scope and the number of external consultants and contractors involved in delivering the projects. A significant amount of time was undertaken by university staff during the procurement part of the process as they would have to put together information for Pre-Qualifying Questionnaires (PQQ) and Invitation to Tender (ITT) for consultants and contractors to bid for as there are statutory waiting times for bid management under UK government mandated procurement requirements. Consultants and contractors then had to spend time bidding for the work with no guarantee that they would be successful and this sometimes made the work less attractive for them.

The key change from the project was to move to "term contracts" for projects of value between £50,000 and £1 million (term contracts were already in use for Estates maintenance contracts under £50,000). Under this type of scheme contracts are set in place for a fixed period of time; consultants and contractors submit information about the building/ refurbishment work that they can undertake; quality standards are set at the start of the contract; and it avoids Estates having to manage the

PQQ and ITT exercise every time they need a piece of work carried out. Expected benefits included

- A reduction in staff activity time making workloads more manageable (cutting 22 steps from the original process mapping exercise)
- Reducing scope creep
- Reducing variable between projects
- Improving quality of the work with less ongoing snagging

As of autumn 2018, the University of Aberdeen has signed up to a national (UK) construction framework for projects that incudes design, tendering and construction. This has been a large time saving as the Estates section was expecting to have to set up term contracts by themselves. The Project Lead has estimated that it cuts out an eight week period of tendering etc from the schedule and the main contractor acts as a project manager rather than this role being carried out by the university drawing office staff, thus helping to further cut out wastes as identified earlier. Bob Watson, Project Lead commented:

> I found the experience of undertaking the lean workshop and subsequent project to be a very engaging process. The project looked at how I run my construction projects, looking at each process step, which highlighted how much work goes into a project. This also illustrated to others, that even the small projects can take as many process steps as larger projects. Having carried out the initial review we have now implemented a couple of major changes in the procurement process for the contractors, which has saved my team significant time and effort. We are also looking at how we can improve the procurement of our external design teams, and would hope to have this implemented in the next 6 months. Some things still take time to change. If you haven't been leaned get leaned on, it's well worth the effort.

Example 3: Student Recruitment and Admissions Improvements

The Student Recruitment and Admissions Service (SRAS) section have participated in a number of BI activities since 2013 ie they have been a key stakeholder in strategic projects for student recruitment, admissions etc. The home/UK recruitment team took part in a Lean for your Team session in November 2016 where they identified various areas for improvement and two activities were undertaken. The first of those was a review of student ambassador processes ie registered students who are employed by the university to help SRAS with recruitment activities. A separate review was held to improve the booking of private visits to the university – the university offers prospective students an opportunity to come and visit Aberdeen by themselves or with parents (rather than having to attend a large-scale open day).

In addition to the Lean for your Team session, the SRAS Enquiry and Conversion Manager also attended the Lean for Leaders course at Stirling University in March 2017. A two-day rapid improvement event "E-communication to pre-registered students" took place in May 2017 and involved staff from SRAS, Marketing and academics schools. There were various problems identified ie e-communication delivered via different teams, using different software and using a variety of templates. This meant that pre-registered students could be receiving communications from different teams on the same day in inconsistent branding, leading to a confusing message being received. The BI Team used standard lean methodology, tools and techniques to help the group identify the issues and reach a solution.

Day one was spent on the AS IS process mapping to understand the different sub-processes that different areas of the university used to communicate with potential students. From that analysis, the group identified a number of wastes (eg overlap and duplication of information) and opportunities for change (eg sharing and repurposing content across SRAS, Marketing and schools). On day two the group designed the TO BE process with the principles and products needed to implement a new system.

The principles included:

- Enquiries and offer holder communications would be made via a single CRM (instead of multiple systems and email accounts)*
- Ad hoc messaging should reduce as there should be better planned messaging
- Calls to action to be clear in messaging
- Ensure e-communications (e-zines) fit with other social media messaging

---

* The University of Aberdeen moved to a MS Dynamics CRM (Customer Relationship Management) system from summer 2018 onwards and the project mentioned helped to embed standardised ways of working prior to the new IT platform being developed and implemented.

An action plan was put into place to

- Review all current schools and SRAS e-communications
- Agree brand/tone/template for e-communications
- Create an e-communications plan for 12 months in advance (to aid the recruitment cycle)
- Set up a better tracking, i.e. evidencing what works and what doesn't
- Inform relevant colleagues about changes
- Refresh post graduate coordinator meetings to share best practice

Megan McFarlane (Enquiry and Conversion Manager, SRAS) was Project Lead and her thoughts are:

> It would be hard to overstate the improvements to the service we are now providing to our customers following this project. Moving to a centralised model, where School staff still get to provide content, but central communications staff use this to design attractive messages sent from one place, has led to huge benefits to the customer and the staff experience. Open and click through rates are tracked and used to improve future content, and there is a culture of continuous improvement in this area. Getting everyone in the room for two days and following lean methodology has led us to this point, and from surveying the sector, it is clear we are now one of the leaders in this area.

LEAN TOOLS AND TECHNIQUES

The BI team use a variety of standard lean tools and techniques during lean training and projects. During an initial Lean for your Team session, there is normally a brainstorming session of pain/pinch points on coloured post its and they are then affinity sorted to work out the scale of a problem. Process mapping is then undertaken (colour coded to immediately highlight where the issues are) with measurement of the number of steps, activity time, waiting time, number of wastes and number of opportunities for change. Outputs are presented via an A3 report that staff can place on a noticeboard to make activities highly visible to colleagues (Figure 13.2).

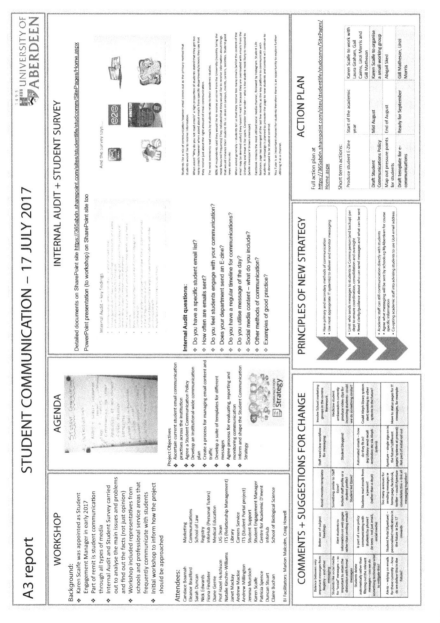

FIGURE 13.2
A3 report for Student Communication workshop – 17 July 2017.

Colleagues in SRAS, Marketing and Communications have embraced visual management via whiteboards in the corridors next to their offices in the main university admin building. They are used in a variety of ways

- The international recruitment office indicate their current locations by placing their photograph or avatar on the country they are currently visiting
- The Go Abroad team use to highlight the number of applications they have received
- The undergraduate and postgraduate teams use to flag key dates eg open days or deadlines for application
- The communications team pin up newspaper cuttings from press releases that they have circulated

Whilst the white boards are used in a more informal way, rather than formally recording performance, teams are tasked with tailoring them to the use most suited to their work area. As well as making the information available to the team's immediate work colleagues, they are also viewed by other colleagues within the main admin building eg staff from other professional service areas or senior managers.

A WORD OF CAUTION

Whilst lean training can be a good way of engaging with staff there are certain aspects that a BI facilitator should be aware of. Be careful that a Lean for your Team session can turn into a "group grump" (group listing of problems only) if it is not handled appropriately. Asking what works well before asking what doesn't work well should allow participants to reflect on the good things in the work place, rather than just concentrating on negative aspects. Team dynamics can make or break a session and that is why Lean @ Lunch or Lean for HE sessions may be better in that individuals can raise issues that they wouldn't raise in a session with their immediate work colleagues. There can sometimes be a considerable period of time between the training and the workshop/project so the key is to keep the momentum going and not allowing incremental workarounds to cloud the original problems. However, this time period can be beneficial for gathering data and analysing it with enough time to do so rather than rushing into a project without enough preparation. A successful outcome relies on attendees being engaged and proactive at the initial session and being self-sustaining throughout and after a project (real continuous improvement). There can be frustration for BI team members in that they can see areas that would be good for projects but they don't progress after the training is over. Staff can promise to "get back to you" (develop and then proactively contact you) with a project proposal but they don't do so and then the employee engagement waste comes to the fore. Focus BI resources on a project that is interesting, has a good project lead and proactive staff. There is no point in "flogging a dead horse" (putting lots of effort into a project when there is very little business benefit) if the BI facilitator has to be the person reminding the project lead to action items, particularly at the proposal stage. A facilitator can end up project managing the project lead which results in lack of ownership and problems with implementation.

BENEFITS OF THE LEAN TRAINING APPROACH

Introducing lean training at the University of Aberdeen has realised several benefits.

First, staff have a structure and methodology to help them with their change journey. Asking people to change what they are doing without giving them a framework to refer to is risky and compromises the success of any endeavour.

Second, the BI team can coach staff through a project proposal and preparation for a rapid improvement event (and during and after the event too). This can be particularly important if someone is undertaking a project lead role for the first time. The BI team can assist in scoping the project area, can help to formulate the project goals, can give advice about which staff to engage with and can really challenge the project lead and project sponsor to think about what success will look like. They can also buy a cup of coffee when all seems lost!

Third, staff may feel more able and motivated to change if it is at a local level and the change is less risky.

Fourth, project leads and teams have real ownership of a project as they may have suggested the idea in the first place. Once they have delivered a project successfully then they may be open to more change thus displaying real continuous improvement behaviour.

Finally, from a BI team and university perspective, projects have taken place that would never have happened otherwise.

IN CONCLUSION

The University of Aberdeen "lean training to lean projects" approach developed as a result of organisational change within the university and also the BI team believing that it should be an activity that is part of the overall lean programme it provides to the institution. The team had to change the way it engaged with staff to sustain interest in using lean to make improvements ie by using our lean training portfolio. A more tailored training approach ie Lean for your Team can result in significant benefits for individual areas eg staff time savings, more collaborative working etc. The BI team can showcase improvements in individual areas to cross-university audiences to encourage change in other areas ie by acting as knowledge brokers. The team intends to continue to use this approach alongside engagement with large-scale programmes and other projects.

Section IV

Technology

14

Machine Leaning – Adopting Lean into a University IT Culture

Brian Stewart, LeeAnne Klein, and Melanie Clements

CONTENTS

OVERVIEW

University of Alberta's central IT department, Information Services and Technology (IST) began its Lean journey in 2016, in collaboration with the Facilities and Operations department. The two departments in true Lean fashion partnered to train and orient staff to Lean principles and techniques. Its trajectory since then has proven to be uneven as initial enthusiasm has given way to a more informed reality. Initial ideas flowed quite freely, but as time passed this flow grew increasingly stilted, with workable ideas only coming every few months. Such is not unusual with any new initiative as the Gartner Hype Cycle articulates, where initial inflated expectations give way to the realization of the difficulty of actualizing a change. Nonetheless the concept has taken root and while overall progress has not been as extensive as hoped there is a solid base to build on. This chapter charts IST's Lean journey to date and reflects on what it has achieved outlining the considerable effort expended to encourage Lean thinking and ideation.

INTRODUCTION AND COMMUNICATION OF LEAN

Lean in IST started in March 2016 with seven participants attending Lean Leadership, a two-day course introducing the concepts of Lean, Lean thinking and setting up a lean practice, aimed at Supervisors and above. This was followed by a series of yellow belt training sessions that provided 66 yellow belt employees. This provided a basis of knowledge within the department to begin leaning out our services and processes.

To gain additional awareness with staff in IST and to broaden the understanding of waste we ran a series of Lunch N Lean's, lunchtime sessions led by our contract black belt. A total of 95 people attended these sessions. In total approximately half of IST's staff have had exposure to Lean training at some level.

Further awareness was provided through a campaign launched by our Communications Team that published newsletter articles focused on Lean initiatives every couple of months. These included project stories, participating staff comments and videos. Presentations at Supervisors' meetings were also part of this campaign.

A Lean Council was formed by the Deputy CIO to assist with building the Lean culture. The council consists of volunteer members from a range of IST units that have a passion to advance its adoption. This followed other similar councils in organizational change management and benefits realization that have proved effective in introducing new thinking into IST. The concept is to provide a collaborative forum for interested staff of all levels to share their experiences, ideas and insights, into how a new idea can be brought into practice into existing work practices.

Ideas were initially generated through a process improvement steering committee, consisting of the leadership of IST. The recommendations were broader than Lean, but several ideas that could be achieved through Lean were obtained. Further ideas came out of brainstorming sessions at the end of each Lunch N Lean session. To facilitate ongoing idea generation a Lean Hopper has been added to the unit's web portal to allow submissions via a Google submission form and drop ins are encouraged. Despite these early wins, the initiative began to stall and was under threat of complete stoppage. More recently, several initiatives related to Lean such as Root Cause sessions and Service Reviews have generated new ideas that can be added to the Lean Hopper and provide renewed interest in the methodology. A list of IST Lean projects is in the chapter appendix.

U OF ALBERTA'S FIRST LEAN PROJECT

To begin the introduction of Lean we followed best practice and selected a project that would be small enough to accomplish in a relatively short time yet big enough to be noticed. This is a little more complicated than first reading would reveal as IT departments are made up of a myriad of integrated and interdependent systems, processes and policies, making selection of a separated component very difficult. All overlaid with the byzantine complexity of a large research-intensive University. Nonetheless we did manage to select a suitable candidate, *the creation of a virtual machine.*

After selecting the process, we struck a Lean team that would be working on it. The operational team lead was very supportive and willing to participate and cooperate with the Lean team to make the necessary improvements. A Virtual Machine (VM) is a non-physical computer that exists within computing hardware. They have generally replaced single dedicated physical machines as servers allowing greater efficiency and resource utilization – a Lean story in itself.

The Virtual Machine (VM) Creation process includes the time and activities from the original request submission to the time the VM is handed off to the client. The current process, owned by the Director of Server & Application Hosting, was estimated to take 6 days from request to provision to the user. The actual work involved to provision a VM was estimated to be approximately 2 hours. The gap represented an obvious choice for a Lean review.

The Lean team was led by a contracted black belt, consistent with the Lean approach, who guided the analysis, selected the appropriate metrics and most effective tools. The team analyzed the process to find out where the over-processing and excessive waiting were happening and what was causing them.

The team found several reasons for the delays:

- Ineffective information processing that required staff to go back and forth through the chain to get responses to questions.
- Three days to obtain firewall approval.
- No tracking of request and client expected delivery date.

These were responded to by creating a requirements form in our IT Service Management system (ITSM) ServiceNow, to capture all information at the beginning eliminating the need for the back and forth. Additional staff were trained to undertake firewall rule approval and tracking of client requests and delivery was introduced.

The outcome of the project led to the service provision becoming more predictable with turnaround times reduced. We have also added monitoring to see how often we meet the customer's required date. As of May 2018 we have met the customer required date 88% of the time.

First Project Learnings

The project initially took longer than expected as the team needed to understand how to relate their activities to the Lean context. In the main this is due to IT departments seeing themselves in more technological systems environments than process and procedural ones. Indeed, this is one of the biggest challenges of leaning IT. The systems mindset fits well with Lean, however the application of it requires nuance that is not without challenge to adopt. It is likely at the heart of why we are finding it difficult to obtain recommendations. The interconnectedness of IT components requires a deep understanding of the interdependencies and how each element fits within the system of systems. Abstracting a slice for closer examination is therefore somewhat counterintuitive to this mindset and requires an adapted Lean approach.

Since the initial project we have undertaken several more, the table in the Appendix at the end of the chapter provides a summary of these projects. These have proven successful within themselves and have improved different aspects of IST's performance. What remains more elusive is the creation of a Lean consciousness within the department. Those units that are more process oriented pick up Lean quicker and are more desirous of developing and implementing projects, as is reflected in the project list. Another constraint is the ability to influence process or system end-to-end elements outside of the control of IST. For example, the digital issuing of tunnel permits requires amendments to the e-signature procedure which is governed at the institutional level. Thus requiring greater effort and time than the process optimizing would take.

LEAN REINVIGORATION

As mentioned previously ideas for Lean projects grew fewer over time, threatening the whole initiative. To address this, we have linked other quasi Lean activities to provide ideas for project development, Service Reviews and Root Cause Reviews. These are essentially Lean exercises as they have been designed and undertaken from a Lean consciousness, moreover the consulting lead has Lean expertise and experience and employs it throughout.

Root Cause Reviews

Root Cause analysis is a familiar Lean technique that is used to assess systemic failures in processes. IST has embraced this concept to analyze and repair identified issues in service delivery with the reviews being a collaborative team effort focused on reducing incidents/waste, (service failure) within a particular service. In keeping with the Lean approach we use the DMAIC (Define, Measure, Analyze, Improve and Control) methodology as the foundation for the review framework. Although we do not use a strictly Lean approach with accepted terminology as the reviews are not Lean projects.

Approach

The reviews are initiated by looking at available data to identify service areas with the highest volume of incidents/waste. The data in the main comes from ServiceNow software, which is exported to Tableau enabling more robust analytical tools to provide insights into service performance from several perspectives, in particular allowing several criteria to be used to establish the urgency and importance of a given service failure review.

The selection is undertaken with the delivery team's leadership and the lead consultant. Once selected, the leaders; prioritize review activities, gain alignment on the focus area for the reviews, and then identify team members to participate in the review (e.g. service owner(s), team leads and analysts who provide the service).

- The Root Cause Review team identifies the best method to collect additional data for their area. Typically, this involves diagnosing the cause of the incident as it is being resolved (going to the Gemba) which requires participation of all the individual contributors/analysts who are responsible for delivering the service.
- Once enough data has been collected, the Root Cause Review team comes together in a workshop, where a 5-Why strategy and fishbone technique (Ishikawa diagram) are used to brainstorm the root of the problems and generate solutions, with the Control Impact Matrix used to finalize improvement ideas. Larger activities that would not be achievable with the operational load of the teams will be relayed to the Lean Council for the creation of more formal Lean projects.
- Upon completion of the review and implemented improvements, sustainment is achieved through ongoing monitoring through the capture and tracking of data to validate the changes have resulted in an improvement.
- The Root Cause cycle is then restarted on another target, where we look at the data to identify services areas with the next highest volume of incidents/waste.

To date we have undertaken two Root Cause Reviews: Classroom Projectors, and Printers and Scanners. They yielded several action items that have been assigned to the teams to address, monitor and review to ensure improvements have been made and changes adopted. Several of the action items are now feeding into Lean projects, providing fresh impetus to the Lean initiative.

In addition, a significant benefit has been the identification of poor data quality relating to service delivery. Data was being gathered in a transactional manner to enable remediation of a service failure. It was not being gathered to enable elimination of the cause of the failure. Without the impetus of ongoing Root Cause analyses there was no reason to gather such information, significantly lowering the value of our data repository. In response we leveraged the Root Cause Reviews as an opportunity to improve data literacy and assist teams with greater understanding of the need for more complete data sets to both initiate service repairs, but also to prevent ongoing service failures. This represents a cultural shift that will require ongoing reinforcement for the department to fully adopt. Nonetheless it is a critical foundational component of IST's drive to evidence based decision making.

Service Reviews

It is generally the case that internal service units design and deliver services for logical and appropriate reasons to meet a need in the organization. It is also the case that these services continue to be provided without ongoing review as to their continued appropriateness, need or relative value. In response to this pattern IST is undertaking Service Reviews to assess the need, value, effectiveness and efficiency of its service catalog. Essentially this is being driven by the need to provide sustainable services within increasingly tighter budgets and to enhance the value IST provides to the university through highly valued services. In essence it can be seen as the other blade of the scissors to Root Cause Reviews, one determining the why and what and the other the how, where and when.

Methodologically Service Reviews involve a broader analysis of the entire service model and overall customer experiences, analyzing all aspects of the service from a system perspective to determine interdependencies and key drivers. IST has been developing this methodology in-house using a range of approaches and adopting and adapting components that can blend into a comprehensive analytical framework.

Service Review Framework

The Service Review Framework incorporates several different methodologies and tools.

1. The first stage of the Service Review involves multiple workshops where service owner(s), team leads and subject matter experts (individual contributors/analysts) analyze their service model.
   - For the Labs & Classrooms Service Review we used the Strategyzer Business Model Canvas (Osterwalder & Pigneur, 2010).

- For the Client Support Service Review we used an adapted version of The Grid (Watkinson, 2017) assessment tool developed by Matt Watkinson.

2. The second part of the review is focused on understanding our customers and analyzing the value proposition of the service.
   - We conduct interviews with our customers to find out more about their needs, wants, values, pain points and barriers to using the service.
   - And we analyze the value customers can receive from our services with the Strategyzer Value Proposition Canvas (Osterwalder & Pigneur, 2014).

3. The third stage involves setting the direction, defining measures and identifying improvement initiatives.
   - We use the Lean continual service improvement method Using Lean CSI to enable fast-safe-reliable Change Management (Smith, 2018).

4. The Service Review is a highly collaborative team effort, with Lean thinking and mindset integrated throughout.
   - Involve and equip people in the process – staff engagements, customer interviews, team participation.
   - Focus on the customer.
   - Highlight potential waste/non-value-added activities and opportunities to reduce variation.

Similarly to the Root Cause Reviews, we use the Control Impact Matrix to prioritize improvement ideas and pass larger initiatives identified by the Service Review team through to the Lean Council.

CONCLUSION

The impact of introducing the Lean mindset into a culture cannot just be considered on the basis of the Lean project portfolio alone. The fundamental value of Lean is to change how activities are approached, to initiate different thinking and to question commonly held assumptions and understandings with a new lens. In this broader sense Lean has been more impactful in IST than the portfolio might at first admit. The new ideas coming from the quasi Lean activities will provide fresh impetus, resulting in new projects and increased willingness for the use of Lean.

The key learning from IST for the broader Lean community is that of leaning a computer or machine based culture, one focused on the intricacy of systems within systems that have very distended value chains and non-linear end to end process lines. In such a milieu it can often be unclear where to start and how to know if the impact makes any significant difference or if the initiative is worth the effort. All in an environment subject to relatively sudden significant technological disruptions that can make many of the existing processes redundant. IT therefore represents a unique challenge to Lean adoption. Almost paradoxically however Lean concepts and tools are essential for the application of digital technology to business problems as they provide the analytical framework to identify opportunities for digitization, automation and robotification. Thereby fulfilling the potential for enhanced value creation through the elimination of non-value-adding activities. Therefore, machine leaning has the potential to move the IT function in organizations away from running increasingly marginalized infrastructure and declining relevance to a source of strategic value through the adept use of digital technology to solve wicked organizational problems.

APPENDIX 1: COMPLETED PROJECTS

Lean Initiative Name	Problem	Solution	Savings	Type of Waste Eliminated
Expense Reports	Finance was spending too much time reconciling expense reports and chasing down report details	Process was analyzed from start to finish with representatives from all involved groups. The overprocessing was 100% eliminated. The process and accountability had been changed but that change had not been communicated down resulting in unnecessary work being done	4 days of effort per year	Overprocessing, waiting, non-utilization of talent
IST Offboarding	Completely paper based, incorrect information on the paper form, no process owner, too many teams involved, missing equipment and unusable cell phones	Determined who actually does what, who should be doing work and redistributed the work where it makes sense. We now have someone overseeing the whole process. There is now visibility and consistency in the process. The paper process has been automated into our Service Management tool. The completion rate can now be tracked	Overprocessing and back and forth are reduced. Before: paper based. 50% of assets confirmed returned, 30 min per person to initiate, 10% unusable phones. After: automated. 100% of assets confirmed returned, 1 minute per person to initiate, no unusable phones	Overprocessing, waiting, non-utilization of talent, motion and inventory

(Continued)

Lean Initiative Name	Problem	Solution	Savings	Type of Waste Eliminated
Creation of a Virtual Machine (VM)	The VM Creation process includes the time and activities from the original request submission to the time the VM is handed off to the client. The current process was estimated to take 6 days long. The actual work involved was estimated to be about 2 hours. Requirements needed weren't clear and requests come in different formats	Before: Time delay – lack of information creating back and forth during intake. After: requirements form built into Service Management tool. Before: up to a 3-day delay for firewall rules. After: More people trained to do firewall rules. Before: did not track when customer needed VM. After: Can track and report how often we meet customer required date	System is more predictable and turnaround times have been reduced. Data checks how often we meet the customer's required date. As of May 2018, we have met the customer required date 88% of the time	Overprocessing, waiting
File Folder Access	Process to give a user access to a network file folder contains unnecessary delays and incomplete information. Not capturing the right information at the start. Not sure how to find the right information at the ServiceDesk level	Walkthrough the process with all involved analysts. Document what information was needed at which stage and move as much as that to the first level support analysts as possible. Created a form in our Service Management tool to capture requirements, a knowledge base article to help ServiceDesk find the information needed	Before: 12% of all tickets were unnecessarily escalated to Tier 2 support. After: 6% escalation rate	Overprocessing, waiting, non-utilization of talent

(Continued)

Lean Initiative Name	Problem	Solution	Savings	Type of Waste Eliminated
Tunnel Permits	Getting a permit to perform network work inside the tunnels beneath the University contains some delays and overprocessing	Meeting with IST and Facilities & Operations (the owner of the process) to walk through the end to end process. Some delays were able to be fixed by introducing notifications. Recommendation: include a 'Requested by' date on form, formalize process around network line inspections. Future: electronic signature or approval options. As this is not an isolated need, an informal University level committee has begun to meet		Overprocessing
IST Onboarding (in progress)	Completely paper based, incorrect task list on the paper form, all involved teams not included, no process owner, no sense of urgency to do this right	Determined who is involved, in what way, when and what information is needed. Decided what common onboarding tasks should be completed by Supervisors in a consistent way. Presented the group's vision of an ideal onboarding to a focus group of Supervisors. Agreed on a process owner. Automated the workflow with timed tasks and notifications inside our Service Management tool	To be determined once a baseline number of onboardings has been completed. Expecting savings in time, equipment being ready on time, consistent onboarding experience	Overprocessing, waiting, non-utilization of talent, motion and inventory

REFERENCES

Osterwalder, A., & Pigneur, Y. (2010). *Business Model Generation: A Handbook for Visionaries, Game Changers, and Challengers*. John Wiley and Sons: New York.

Osterwalder, A., & Pigneur, Y., et al. (2014). *Value Proposition Design: How to Create Products and Services Customers Want*. John Wiley and Sons: New York.

Smith, D. (2018). Understanding Modern ITSM Strategies. https://www.brighttalk.co m/webinar/using-lean-csi-to-enable-fast-safe-reliable-change-mgmt/?utm _campaign=communication_reminder_starting_now:registrants&utm_med ium=email&utm_source=brighttalk-transact&utm_content=button. Accessed September 2018.

Watkinson, M. (2017). *The Grid: The Decision-Making Tool for Every Business (Including Yours)*. Random House.

15

Can Information Services Lead a Network of Change Agents in a HEI?

Linda Spinks

CONTENTS

HOW DID WE GET HERE?

As a Business Change Manager within University Information Services (UIS) at the University of Cambridge I have been promoting the concepts of continuous improvement for the last 14 years. To me, it made absolute sense that implementing IT solutions on top of poor process was a recipe for disaster! More and more engagements involving the review of business processes resulted in recommendations for process change prior to the development of system solutions. Often, however, the recommendations to change business process were ignored in favour of creating IT projects to address the issues. This approach frequently resulted in high investment and aesthetic improvements without actually addressing the root causes of the issues. Inevitably when the same business areas are reviewed four or five years later, the same issues exist but are simply supported by more up to date IT solutions.

The light bulb moment came for me when I attended an Efficiency and Effectiveness in HE session (presented by Sarah Lethbridge and Christine Stewart) in London in February 2014, where I realised that I had actually been practising a number of Lean principles without realising it! With the support of my line manager, I was able to embark on training, (achieving Lean Six Sigma Black Belt qualification in May 2015) and attend events organised by Lean HE, although this was more about personal development than any mandate from senior management to implement a Lean culture. University Information Services (UIS) itself has been undergoing a period of change in recent years, however in my role within the relatively recently established Delivery Management Office there was a clear mandate for continuous improvement and the vision that UIS would be recognised as the place to go for support in all things relating to Business Improvement.

BUILDING A NETWORK OF CHANGE AGENTS, HOW IT HAPPENED

As the single resource for Business Improvement, it became clear that if we were going to really promote a Lean culture at Cambridge I would need to spread the knowledge. However, after gaining my Black Belt certification I realised that in order to gain buy-in for the adoption of Lean principles in a HE environment any training would need to be tailored for the sector. A conversation with Mick Gash from the University of Nottingham during the 2016 Lean HE Conference in Stirling resulted in an invitation to observe their "Introduction to Lean in HE" course the following March. After my visit to Nottingham, I was provided with the course content and proceeded to adapt it for use in Cambridge.

After running a small pilot session with colleagues from my own area, I was able to integrate the training into a major piece of process improvement work that was underway with the Research Operations team and ran three sessions before creating a publicly bookable course available to staff and students across Cambridge via the University Training Booking System

(UTBS). The results were astounding, with sessions being booked almost as soon as they were published. This high level of interest continues (autumn 2018) and sessions are being run almost on a monthly basis.

Feedback has been collected from each session of the training and I have responded wherever possible. Key areas of feedback in the earlier sessions were around the questions of "What next?" The initial response to this question was to set up a "Business Improvement at Cambridge" community page within our Moodle VLE environment. This enables members of the community to not only access resources (such as templates, slides and links to external sites like Efficiency Exchange) but also to hold discussions with other members of the community. When members were polled as to whether they wished to remain as part of this virtual community, all responded in the positive.

A series of Business Improvement at Cambridge seminar sessions are also underway. These take place approximately once per term and are in the form of a one-hour session held at midday, so minimising time away from the day job. The seminars aim to encourage sharing within the community, so the session kicks off with a twenty-minute presentation by someone who has had some success in applying the principles that they learned on the training course. This is followed by the introduction of a new technique or approach that was not covered in the training. Time is also available for general discussion and networking over tea and biscuits. These have been well-received by the attendees and will continue at least during the 2018/19 academic year.

I have also been asked to deliver cut-down versions of the course in order to promote the Lean way of thinking within teams. These have ranged from thirty-minute sessions delivered as part of a team "away-day," to three-hour abridged versions designed to ensure full coverage across a HR delivery team. In many cases, these tasters have resulted in some individuals signing up for the full day course.

A number of delegates at the training have also shown interest in gaining further knowledge and professional qualifications. As a result of this I have been working with Claire Lorrain at the University of Winchester to facilitate the delivery of accredited Green Belt training. The pilot for this was delivered in July 2018 and plans are underway to make this a regular offering.

One of the other outcomes of the training sessions has been the enthusiasm to embark on Lean initiatives across the institution. I am often contacted post training and asked to give advice on how they can approach these initiatives. This supports the vision that I had when identifying the training need, as I am able to act in a consultative fashion, advising others and providing a sounding board for ideas and suggestions. As a lone resource this ensures that my time is utilised as efficiently and effectively as possible and allows me to concentrate on more strategic activities.

Where larger groups have been involved a variety of mechanisms have been used to track the projects being undertaken. The Service Operations Team within UIS have set up a SharePoint site to monitor and track activity. An A3 template has been set up within our Confluence platform, so that project managers and business analysts within the UIS Delivery Management Office can utilise it within their projects. There are also plans to add further templates to the Confluence site.

Why Is the Course So Successful?

One of the key things reported following attendance at the training is that it provides a structured and logical approach to improvement – the "Improvement Kata." One delegate commented that the "Improvement Kata as a way to take manageable bite-size steps to a larger goal" (Figure 15.1).

This strikes a chord with people regardless of whether they are applying these principles to a process improvement initiative or a "pure" IT development project, so is starting to form part of a universal language across the organisation.

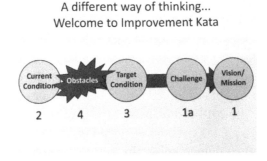

FIGURE 15.1
An illustration of improvement Kata.

Who Are the Change Agents?

In the twelve months to August 31st 2018, 304 delegates have attended "An Introduction to Lean in HE" training. These have come from across the University, with some targeted sessions for particular institutions. A breakdown is shown in the following table (Table 15.1).

Looking specifically at the UIS portion of the community, there is an interesting breakdown across the divisions. In total 33% of the UIS headcount have attended training (103 people), with 58% of these being from the Infrastructure team, incorporating the frontline support group as well as all other infrastructure service areas. This is due to a conscious decision by the Infrastructure leadership team to look at the way that IT services are supported in order to fulfil their vision of being "the sole provider of Core IT for the Collegiate University."

An example of this is the team responsible for the Cambridge Data Centre. Building on the service operations group vision, they have identified a number of "Challenge Statements" such as "To provide secure, reliable, and resilient Data Centre and equipment rooms for hosting the University's Core IT Systems." These are further underpinned by "Next Target Condition" statements such as "To streamline the process of conditioning IT infrastructure equipment, from purchase to production-ready deployment". By utilising a Kaizen approach they are making great progress towards achieving their targets. This clearly demonstrates that an IT organisation can not only drive the adoption of Lean across the institution, but in fact it can apply the principles to its own processes.

TABLE 15.1

Course Attendance (Introduction to Lean in HE) by Institution/Dept

Institution/Dept	Participants
University Information Services	113
Research Office	52
Cambridge University Library	27
Human Resources Division	27
SAH	21
Academic Division	14
Finance Division	7
*Other	43
Total	**304**

* Other incorporates 26 distinct institutions where less than 7 have attended.

With regards to activity across the broader university, initiatives are underway within a number of areas including Research Operations, Cambridge University Library and the School of Humanities and Social Sciences.

The Research Operations Contracts Team have been working to reduce contract turnaround times by decreasing the amount of paper in the process, as well as improving communication and clarifying the risk management process across the university. This work resulted in the successful submission of a poster presentation at the INORMS (International Network of Research Management Societies) conference in June 2018 with a poster entitled "Applying Lean Principles to Research Operations".

The Finance team at Cambridge University Library were so inspired when they all attended the "Introduction to Lean in HE" training that they wanted to get started straight away. They particularly engaged with the concepts surrounding Voice of the Customer and as a result they quickly performed a stakeholder analysis, so that they could really start to understand their customers. A session to consider their vision and challenges followed which has set them up to start to really make a difference. The gratifying aspect of this work is that the whole team is engaged and committed to the initiative even though they are aware that they are constrained in some ways by other longer term work surrounding the University Finance System. They see that any work that they do locally can then be used to feed into the larger ERP programme.

The Graduate Recruitment Manager at the School of Humanities and Social Sciences (SHSS) has been using Lean principles to improve graduate admissions processes within her school. Following a survey of 2017 graduate applicants there were strong indicators to suggest that the length of time taken to make decisions on applications varied between the departments of the school with a range between two and eighteen weeks. Following a workshop with graduate administrators from across the school, key process information was collected using a technique based around SIPOC. This provided valuable information about the process and identified a number of issues including unnecessary printing of application materials, duplication of record keeping and too many levels of academic review. Once these issues were identified it was possible to make a number of recommendations to assist departments in decreasing processing time, so improving the applicant experience.

FEEDBACK FROM THE CHANGE AGENTS THEMSELVES

A survey carried out across the "Business Improvement at Cambridge" community asked a number of questions and generated some interesting and sometimes unexpected responses.

There were 44 respondents, 57% of whom were based in non-UIS departments (central administration (40%) and other institutions (17%)).

Question 1 – How Did You Hear about Lean at Cambridge?

34% had heard via word of mouth, with 59% hearing via targeted internal communication activities. It is reasonable to assume that those that heard via internal communications are individuals belonging to institutions where targeted improvement activity was/is being carried out. Interestingly, amongst the comments made, a number of managers who have attended training have subsequently recommended that their staff also attend.

Question 2 – When Are Lean Principles Applied?

41% stated that they use Lean principles wherever possible while 39% said that they also applied them to specific projects. 30% said that they applied Lean principles as part of their day-to-day activities. Individual comments included:

- "It helps me to sketch out project layouts and optimise my workflow."
- "For looking at university policies and strategies, they are just not good."
- "Apply general principles day to day; plan to make Lean process improvement part of BAU for the whole team."

Question 3 – Do You Understand How Technology and Lean Can Interact?

79% of respondents replied that they do, with 13% being unsure. Additionally the majority of respondents from within UIS stated that they understood how Lean can be applied within an IT organisation. Comments included:

- "Lean principles can be applied to the way we work internally (e.g. the way we manage projects, or the way we manage service desk calls in a Lean way) as well as to the specific technology projects that we work on, i.e. helping other teams to work in a Lean way and developing software systems that support Lean working."

- "Lean is very important to be able to create new IT system and maintain existing ones. Lean principals are part of DevOps approaches and conducive to Continuous Delivery, Continuous Integration and Continuous Testing."

When asked about how Lean principles have helped them to enable change a number of responses were received, a summary of which are shown:

- "They have given me a structure and help me to depersonalise and make it a process the whole team works on together."
- "Everyone wants to do less mundane, repetitive work, so we have reduced this aspect of our daily duties to concentrate on more analytical work. Lean has helped us with this."
- "Having a toolkit that is logical and simple to introduce has helped."
- "It has helped to identify areas that need reviewing. By looking at Lean principles and comparing an ideal situation to the current situation, it can help to determine what changes should be made."
- "They provide a proven methodology to analyse processes and suggest changes which gives the proposals more weight (or should do)."
- "A small shift of mind-set and some tools to visualise change for myself and others."
- "The body of work produced, having applied Lean principles, provides a compelling argument to adopt revised procedures, by highlighting inherent weaknesses."
- "Helps to make everyone feel engaged in the changes that need to be made rather than feeling they are being told to do things they may not feel committed to."
- "I have felt more confident that what I was proposing was making sense and that there was a case for suggesting efficiency savings."

SUCCESSES

From my own perspective as a Lean advocate there have been many successes. Firstly the sheer volume of people interested in attending Lean events has been a colossal, and for the most part unexpected, success. Not least because there has historically been a fundamental disconnect between the IT community and the broader "business" community. Secondly, the last twelve months haven't been simply about people attending training and ticking a box on their personal development plan, for the most part there has been a desire to be part of the broader Business Improvement community and a keenness to not only learn more but to put that learning into practice, even if just on a small scale. Thirdly the concept of making small, incremental improvements and being empowered to make local decisions where appropriate has resulted in an openness to change.

At the more local level, members of the community were asked about their successes with Lean. A selection of responses follows.

- "I only went on the course a few weeks ago, but I think the way I approach my work making small improvements that add up to something much bigger is more or less a Lean approach and has worked very well for me."
- "In setting up a new workflow for an eSales product, Lean principles were considered to ensure the product was set up in the most streamlined way from the start."
- "My team is becoming aware of what they do, why they do it and suggesting refinements."
- "I have used it to create project proposals when before our aims were unspecific. We have also used this so that we could feedback on proposals for the fieldwork policy. They are trying to create a system and a policy at the same time, and I am able to specify the concerns of the students in a way that management understand."
- "Working out a new way of processing former Postdoc records and reducing the amount of time it takes so the majority is now automatic."
- "We now have more procedures (forms pre-filled for data collection purposes) and an expected time-line to pass on to prospective customers. This stops us re-inventing the wheel every time we go to on-board new customers."
- "During the last year we have managed to create Test Automation Services which are providing additional levels of QA and allowing the CamSIS (Cambridge Student Information System) team to deploy security patches, database upgrades and maintenance packs more frequently and with higher levels of confidence. Automation suites which were run individually on local computers are now centralised

and run as part of a Continuous Integration Model using common methods and common technologies."

- "Incremental improvements in Kanban board used for Live Operations; it is still not a good board as it is too busy, but at least it is something to build on."
- "I have convinced my colleagues that moving numbers round in spreadsheets is wasteful activity, and that we can have tools to do this. The value they add is in interpreting and acting on the data."

CHALLENGES

Spreading the word about Lean has followed a predominantly bottom up approach, and although some senior management have attended training, there remains a disconnect between what is happening at the grass roots level and decisions and initiatives being discussed at much higher levels. It is hoped that this will change in time as local successes are celebrated and shared with the broader community.

Introducing the concept of the Voice of the Customer has resulted in many discussions about the fundamental concept of "customers", particularly within the IT community. This was addressed by clarifying the term in its broadest sense as the "recipient of the output of a process".

Local challenges reported by members of the Business Improvement Community have a number of themes:

- Time constraints – not having or being allowed the time to take a Lean approach
- Buy-in and understanding from management and colleagues
- Resistance to change
- Resistance to anything that appears "commercial" or sounds like "consultancy-speak"
- Avoiding tackling too much at once
- Knowing when to apply IT or non-IT solutions to identified problems

To address these challenges it is important to ensure that Lean practices become part of our way of working rather than something that has to be planned in as extra work.

THE INTERACTION BETWEEN TECHNOLOGY AND LEAN

As can be seen by some of the feedback documented previously, IT professionals within UIS are embracing Lean and applying the principles to pure technology projects. The Data Centre team are actively looking at how equipment is commissioned from purchase to production-ready deployment as well as defining the minimum standards for IT equipment to be housed at the Data Centre. Project managers and business analysts are also including Lean in their toolkits, so that they are able apply it to the way that projects are managed as well as to the project solutions themselves.

One such project looking at Post-Graduate Funding has focused on both business process change as well as technological solutions. Once complete this project will revolutionise the way that post-graduate students are funded at Cambridge. Although in its early stages, the project has already adopted a Lean-Agile approach. Lean-Agile applies the mind-set of Lean to the software world while incorporating the lessons of Agile that are useful. "Lean Business Analysis Values" have been defined within the project team by considering the customer value added activities, the business value added activities and the non-value added activities.

The first of these values refers to producing what is needed when it is needed rather than the more traditional approach of completing all analysis upfront. Similarly, effort has been made to work with the right people at the right time regardless of any historical silo behaviour. This is underpinned by an approach of building in quality at the outset rather than leaving quality checks to the end of the process and avoiding unnecessary steps wherever possible.

KEY LEARNING POINTS

I always make it clear that although I am based in an IT organisation, technology solutions should be enablers to enhance good business process, not fix poor process. Process improvement should therefore precede IT solution development where possible.

Sometimes it is difficult to get people to think beyond the idea that there is an IT solution for everything, and once fixed on this any change ends up being solution driven. Other changes are typically harder to manage, so often are set aside in favour of perceived easier to implement technology fixes.

It is important to maintain the sense of community, so that even if the Lean advocates are spread far and wide across the organisation, there is a mechanism to allow them to get together and share experiences. We at Cambridge are operating on minimal budget to support this, but providing tea, coffee and biscuits and allowing people to share experiences is highly effective in keeping up the momentum. It is important that these sessions are relatively short (so that there is not too much of a time commitment) and accessible. We change the venue each time due to the broad geographical spread of offices around Cambridge so that everyone who wishes gets a chance to attend at some point.

Working with other Higher Education Institutions has been key in allowing us to get to where we are. Being part of a global network allows us to share techniques and experiences with our "competitors" – a situation which certainly would not happen in the commercial sector. We do not have to constantly reinvent the wheel and often there is a good chance that someone else will have addressed the same issues at some point in the past. For me this is one of the great benefits of working within the Higher Education sector and I truly hope that such collaboration will continue long into the future.

Always avoid using "technical" or even "business" terminology; remember who your audience is and adapt your language accordingly.

Time is often the issue that people complain about when they are trying to make changes on a local level. This is partly because, in our case, Lean is not yet quite embedded in day-to-day working. Change agents are sometimes not given the mandate or opportunity to step away.

SUMMARY

So returning to the question "Can Information Services Lead a Network of Change Agents in a HEI?", the answer has to be yes it can, but it is reliant on the drive and creativity of individuals who are willing to lead the charge, as well as the ability to communicate in a non-technical way with colleagues from across the institution.

Fundamentally it doesn't really make a difference whether the drive towards a Lean way of working is based in IT or any other area of a university, it is more about the people within the organisation with the passion and drive to get the message across. I am fortunate, that working within a university, I have been afforded the support and autonomy to go out there, find out about Lean and implement it as I have seen fit. It remains to be seen whether the current interest will continue; I will continue to hold introductory courses and grow the community for as long as the need is out there.

At Cambridge we have examples of Lean initiatives being carried out within IT areas, within business areas, and also collaboratively across both IT and business: so we know that it can be applied across the board.

16

Lean, Kanban and Agile, A Story of Continuous Improvement in a University Software Team

Richard Arkless

CONTENTS

BACKGROUND

I am (at the time of writing) part of a small team working on the final phase of a project to build a central system to hold all student assessment marks, calculate course (module) results, progression decisions, degree classifications and publish all the information to students. The project has been run over several phases during which we have steadily expanded and improved the functionality as well as on-boarding more and more users. We are now in the final phase of the project, rolling out to the remaining Schools as well as fixing bugs and delivering some final usability and stability improvements. From initiation right through to these final stages, we have used Agile methodologies to deliver the project and also to allow the team to keep a focus on continuous improvement.

What Is Agile?

Agile in software development is a blanket term that covers many different tools, techniques and ways of working. Like Lean, it has at its core a focus on customer value, the promotion of continuous improvement and the reduction of waste from the software development process. It also aims to create value by involving the customer throughout the development process to help deliver the right product.

Agile therefore differs from the traditional waterfall approach. With waterfall, customers are expected to specify their full requirements upfront and these are then in turn documented by business analysts and delivered by software developers, with a typical delivery schedule of six months to a year. This limited and fixed-point interaction with the end user and the fact that business needs can change significantly in the length of time between requirements capture and build delivery, means the final product is often not what the customer needs.

Agile on the other hand is set up to deliver software as quickly as possible with projects being broken down into smaller pieces of work, with sets of features being released to users as soon as they are ready and therefore delivering value much earlier. These smaller bits of software will then build into the complete system over the time of the project. This iterative and incremental approach also provides development teams with earlier insight into a system's usage and what is and is not working which means they can refine the system in response to that learning.

What Does Agile Mean for Us?

There are a wealth of Agile tools and techniques that can be employed to help deliver customer value and improve how software team's work. I have just tried to describe the context in which my team used Agile to support continuous improvement and deliver our project. We have tried various bits of Agile over the years – some things we struggled with and somethings worked well and so we've evolved our approach over time but broadly speaking we will do the following on our projects:

1. Break the project into manageable pieces

   Big detailed requirement documents or specifications written upfront are gone. Instead we write a couple of lines on a card that describes what the user wants to do, or what the problem is that we're trying to solve. We refer to theses as 'user stories' and they provide the starting point for discussions on what software we need to build.

2. Get users involved throughout the development process

In an ideal world, an end user would be a full-time member of the project team but in most cases, this is not possible. In a university for example, users tend to be students with their own learning commitments, or front-facing staff where budgets or business requirements do not allow them to be seconded. As such, we seek out different ways of ensuring customer engagement. In particular, if users could not come to see us, we would go out and see them. We also encouraged users to give us feedback, get involved in testing and we would regularly go to our customers to demonstrate software in development to gather their user input.

3. Keep the team flexible

Roles in the team are kept flexible to keep development flowing. A developer may work with users to write stories, a business analyst may pick up testing if there is a backlog.

4. Small batch release of software

Releases are every two weeks in order to get working software deployed to live and therefore adding value as frequently as we can. Small releases also reduce the risk of breaking things (generally, the bigger and more complicated the change, the more change of introducing bugs) and where bugs do exist in small releases they are much easier to track down and fix.

5. Daily stand-ups

To facilitate team communication and to build a shared understanding of what is happening on the project we use daily stand-ups. These are face to face but occasionally take place online if there are team members working from home. The format of the meeting is; what you did yesterday, what you plan to work on today and anything blocking progress. Anything blocking development is followed up after the meeting to keep processes flowing. The frequency of the meetings means we can keep them short and face to face, interactive meetings allow for better quality and clear communication than via email.

6. Retrospectives

After every release the team meets to review progress, plan what is coming next and to review any problems. We will discuss how we can adapt our working practice to address any problems and re-review at a future meeting. The retrospectives are vital to ensuring we continually improve as a team.

7. Manage work in progress

We use an online tool for managing development work in progress which allows us to record user stories and bugs. These can then be assigned to different users and moved through various workflow steps until completed. This system also allows us to manage our work in 'sprints' which are a time boxed period where we focus on development, and then at the end we release the code to live.

Our workflow for a sprint is as follows:

- Ready for development
- In development
- Ready for testing
- In test
- Done

'Done' is defined as the point the release is ready to be deployed to live. All development work has been undertaken with technical documentation as well as system and user testing completed and passed.

A PROBLEM

However, whilst these Agile ways of working contributed to a very proficient development and delivery cycle, we were falling over once software was released to live. Roles and responsibilities were not defined or agreed which meant post go-live support was not consistent and handover documentation was often not completed on-time.

This lack of an effective handover led to failure demand characterised by a significant amount of support calls from end users to the operations team. So, whilst the software was a success in terms of it working correctly, customer satisfaction did not mirror this. Users were asking 'how do we use this new feature?', 'why doesn't this button work like it used to' or 'where has this screen gone?'. This meant that the project team, who were involved in the next delivery phases, became embroiled in day-to-day support having to pick up questions from the operations team, and the operations team were being overloaded.

As bad as we were at failing to get implementation documentation done in time, we were equally bad at estimating how much effort was needed to do it and we would usually underestimate. Documentation was not prioritised and there was often a backlog of processes and features that needed to be written up. As the system and number of users grew, the demand on support grew and that made the lack of useful reference materials even more apparent. We delivered regular training sessions on the system (so users were not completely in the dark) but it was clear that they also needed good reference material for use outside of the training.

A Change to the Team

It was clear that the activities necessary for a successful handover could not be absorbed into the world of the project team if they were to focus on the next software delivery. As such it was decided that a new role was needed – that of implementation specialist. This implementation role would cover anything the end user needed to help them use the software effectively. This means documentation (e.g. user guides and standard operating procedures), training materials, a formal hand-over to the operational support team and communications to users to let them know what was being released and when. All of this can be challenging as constantly evolving software means the implementation specialist has to respond to these regular changes. Therefore, as this was both a new role and an area we had not been getting right, we were conscious other changes might be required to support the role.

A Change to Our Workflow

First of all, we decided to change our definition of 'done' (when a feature is ready for live).

Now rather than 'done' being when development, testing and sign off have taken place, a few additional steps were added to each delivery cycle: We came up with the following:

- Details of the change are recorded in a communication ready to send to users when the software is released.
- For new features guidance documentation must be prepared for users and the operational support team.

- For updates to existing processes and features the guidance must be updated accordingly.
- For bug fixes where users have been aware of the problem, details of the resolution must be communicated to them and associated support calls closed.

IN A NUTSHELL…

What Was the Problem?

- High demand on the operations and project teams for user support post-implementation.

Impact

- The project team was being slowed down and it was impacting how much could be developed.
- The high demand was reducing the quality of support that could be delivered by operations.
- End user processes were delayed while they waited for support and information.

Root Cause

- Reference documentation for users on new features was often missing or incomplete and existing documentation was not being updated.

Proposed Solution

- When we build a feature or a bug fix, we will create the documentation for users and operational support at the same time.
- We will always tell users about a new feature or fix when we release it.
- *Most importantly*, we will change our meaning of 'done' so that nothing will be released until the relevant documentation and communications are completed and therefore our workflow will contain these additional steps.

What Do We Think Will Happen?

- We think we can write the user documentation like we build the software (using the same small batch approach), and still maintain a good velocity (the number of features and fixes done over a period of time).
- Our velocity may be slower compared to earlier project phases, but we will reduce failure demand once a feature or fix is live (so hopefully we can balance that out).

How Will We Know If Our Solution Works?

We did not have much to measure against as we were still near the beginning of this phase of the project with most of the team being new. We did not know what our velocity would be, and we were without statistics to illustrate what the demand on the operation and project teams was from users. However, we were confident we could improve documentation and that this would not prove too onerous; as fixes that did not change the way users worked would not need documented, and better documentation would reduce support calls. What we did know was that from previous projects our average velocity was 5.5 features a week so if we could get close to this we would be delivering at a reasonable rate.

WHAT WE DID

Once we had defined the post-implementation processes, we wanted to see if we could re-configure the university's online tool to incorporate these steps. Unfortunately, we could not implement a change without it impacting all users and we were not ready to do this. So at this point, we decided to move away from the online tool and use a physical tool instead – namely a whiteboard. This would let us experiment with our new processes before making the move to changing the standard workflow. Also, we were aware of the use of Kanban boards and that some software teams favoured these over electronic tools and have seen some great examples of visual management in practice at the 2016 Lean HE conference. So, this was the perfect opportunity to try this approach for ourselves.

We came up with a simple design for a Kanban board that would represent each step in our new workflow process. We kept it simple with the view that we could change it easily (Figure 16.1).

Our new workflow had additional steps at the start for the analysis, and at the end for the implementation.

Our implementation steps are:

- Ready for implementation
- In implementation
- Ready for release

The implementation specialist would have control over when something was released to live.

Next, we needed to physically create the board. We had no usable wall space, so we used a couple of wheeled whiteboards on which we drew the columns and headings and added all our work in process with sticky notes. For continuity and consistency, we kept some of the priority and issue numbers used in our online system. We continued to use the online system to hold the details of each user story or bug, such as notes from developers and conditions of satisfaction for testers. It made sense to keep this electronically as it would have been too much information to fit on each card.

How It Works

Each card on the board represents a piece of work. The Agile process of breaking down our work meant these were each about the same size. Starting from the left, the card moves across the board as each step is completed until reaching the final column, at which point it's done and ready to go live.

After a process step is complete, the card moves into the next 'buffer' column ready for someone to pick it up and perform the next process in the workflow. A few days before each scheduled release (for us every second Wednesday) we'd review what was in the 'ready' column and prepare it for go-live. After the release, we would clear the column.

Output

We also wanted to monitor output by measuring our velocity (the rate at which we could get features to 'done'). For this we simply counted all the

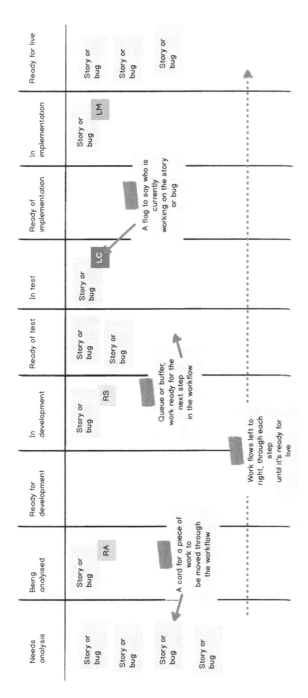

FIGURE 16.1
Mock up of team board.

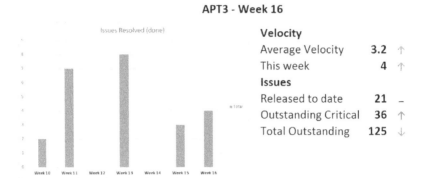

FIGURE 16.2
First set of measures for team board.

features that had been added to the 'ready for release column' each week and logged it in a spreadsheet. We also kept a count of the outstanding issues in our backlog.

From this we were able to generate statistics and graphs that we could print out and add to the board. We wanted to have this high-level visual representation, so we could all see where there were problems, and also what we were achieving (Figure 16.2).

WHAT WE OBSERVED AND LEARNED

At the time of writing we are six months into our experiment of incorporating implementation activity into development workflow and it has been quite successful. We learned a lot more about how we work and the visualisation of processes and increased planning meant other additional improvements began to suggest themselves.

Physical Kanban Boards

We had been using the same standard workflow steps for a few years and this was meeting our needs. However as soon as we decided to move onto a physical board, we began thinking of additional steps that we could include. We started out just wanting to include the implementation steps:

but when we designed the board we added the analysis steps too as we now had the flexibility to do so. Since then we have also added an estimation step, and we are actively considering other step indicators to help highlight problems (Figure 16.3).

Daily Stand-Ups

The Kanban board has significantly improved our daily stand-up providing team members a visual cue for discussions and making it clearer across the team exactly what they have been working on. Also, prior to use of the board, the online system's ticket numbers were frequently referenced at our stand-up meetings. The statement 'I'm working on 36' often led to 'What's 36 again?' and a protracted discussion about the ticket. In contrast, now the description is on a card in front of us, clarity has improved and discussions are more efficient.

More Involvement of the Operations Team

We have included our operations team in the stand-up as the board helped give them a view of what's in progress and therefore what's coming up. It has also given them the opportunity to point out anything on the board

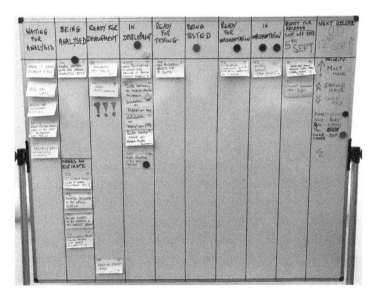

FIGURE 16.3
Current team board.

that is generating a lot of support calls and to ask if we (the project team) can prioritise it.

Signalling When Something Needs to Be Done

We located the board in a spot where most of the team could see it and we found this was helpful. A person moving a card from one column to the next was a signal for the work to be picked up and moved to the next stage and the team preferred the visual prompt to the emails used previously. It also improved planning in the team as people could see what work was coming their way. Further it engendered a sense of accomplishment and achievement being able to progress the cards. It also assisted with better workload planning as individuals would clearly see what was coming up and what might be involved within them.

Highlighting Bottlenecks in the Process

Having the board in a prominent position meant that it was very clear when bottlenecks started to occur, and both the team and the project manager could see that there was a problem when a column was filling up with cards. We would address this at the daily stand-up and agree how to re-direct resource to get the work flowing again. We would also discuss these bottlenecks at the next retrospective to identify the cause and find solutions to prevent this happening in future.

Limiting Work in Progress

Progress limits were not considered at first, but the board instantly created these for us. If a column filled up on the board then another card could not physically be moved across. We came to treat this as a positive as there is no benefit to adding extra work to a queue that is full. It forced us to focus on clearing the bottleneck in the full queue. Further, with the bottlenecks and backlogs being so visible, we made more effort to look at the cause of these to try and prevent them happening in the future. We have also decided to explore the use of work in progress limits in future to see how we could create a more even flow of work through our processes.

Monitoring Our Output

Whilst we had the functionality to produce monitoring reports via our online system we had not made much use of this in the past. Now that we were trying something new with implementation added to the process, we needed to monitor this in order to know what pace we were working at. We stuck with our simple monitoring approach (counting up the features ready for release) and a few weeks into the project we were averaging a velocity of 3.8 compared with 5.5 per week before the addition of the implementation steps. We had expected we would run at a slower rate so we were not too concerned by this and we also noticed that across the weeks, our velocity was steadily increasing so it is likely that we can improve upon 3.8. Plus, during this period we operated with some team instability as members were deployed to other projects. This both accounted for the lower velocity and provided us with some useful information for senior management to illustrate the impact of losing team members on the team (Figure 16.4).

Visualising Problems

The visualisation let us see quickly that there were some issues with the quality of the work that we were releasing to live, e.g. that there were a small number of instances where bugs introduced impacted critical processes. However, identifying this early (as opposed to a traditional waterfall project where this might not have been noticed until the lessons learned review) meant that we could take steps to mitigate this problem. Firstly, we took steps to improve the testing of products and secondly, we measured the number of bugs we were creating in each release and added this to the Kanban board. Measuring the bugs would help give an indication of whether the improvements made to testing were working.

Estimation

Tracking how much work was undertaken has helped us to estimate how much work we would be able to do in future. This is great for project managers and has helped us with our prioritisation as we have a better

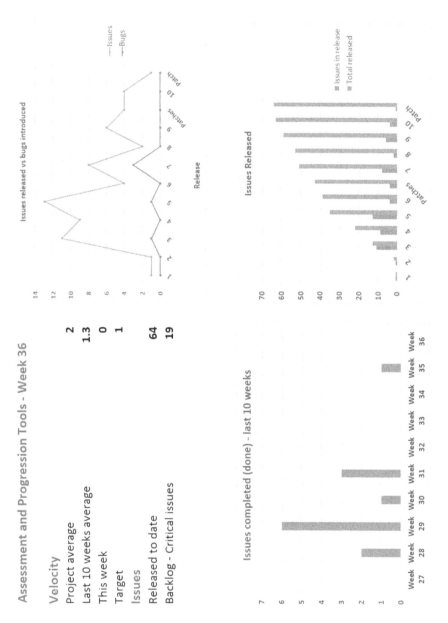

FIGURE 16.4

Current team measures for the board.

idea of the number of features we can deliver during the remainder of the project.

It's Nice to Show What You've Achieved!

As the cards moved through the process to 'done' we kept them on another board. Over time (as we were releasing every couple of weeks) the completed work built up and filled the board. This gave a nice visual representation of what the team had achieved. The team remarked how much they liked seeing the build of completed work and they complained when I needed to clear the board!

Negatives

Not everyone in the team was convinced of the benefits of a physical board and some said that they preferred the electronic version. In particular it was not ideal for the team's occasional home-workers; and when they were not in the office, their cards had to be moved for them. For a more distributed team the board might not work at all. It also took a little bit of effort to maintain the board (this was not measured but should be in future) and it was something that could slip. However, if it was slipping, it often provided another indication that the team was becoming overburdened. If the project manager was missing their weekly statistics, it was a signal that a deeper problem could potentially exist.

WHAT'S NEXT?

One of things we found is that once you to start to experiment like this to make improvements, you want to do more. At this point we still have a few months' work left on the project, so we will continue to refine our board and the visual management outputs.

Our handover to users has improved but we would like to try and find some measures for this as at the moment the feedback is anecdotal. Also, we still need to make some improvements to our handover process to operational support. We want to have them more involved at the start of the process so that they can see new features from the early stages of development.

We are thinking about how we can expand our use of visual management. We have visualised one of our workflows, and measured output, but can we also visualise outcomes? We present regular project updates for management teams on progress and increasingly there is a desire to see what benefits delivered. We would like to try and present some of this information on our boards too. If the boards are updated on a regular basis and we can present the information clearly enough, perhaps they can replace traditional management reports altogether. Anyone wanting a quick update on progress would be able to visit and take a quick look at the board.

We also want to improve flow. We found that the rate at which we deliver is sometimes a little uneven. This can be down to changes in team resourcing levels but when the team is stable we would like to investigate whether it is possible to create a steady flow of features to live. This may mean increasing the frequency of our releases to live even more as we already know there are benefits to frequent, small releases.

We would also like to measure more. This experiment has demonstrated that even simple measures can be useful. For us, just counting what was done in a week was a great start but we want to get better at measuring impact, for example tracking how many supports calls a release generates.

This has been a good experience for the team. Committing time to thinking about how we work has been an interesting experience and has really benefitted us. It is easy to put off analysing your current practice as the day-to-day work will always seems more important and that it should take priority. It almost felt like experimentation like this was not an effective use of time when we were very busy. However, the changes we made here did not actually take a huge amount of time to implement and once we started, it was easier and less time consuming than we thought. As we already had some continuous improvement built into our process (as part of retrospectives) we were really building on existing practice.

Our recommendation is that if you have had it in mind to do something like this, go ahead and do it. It does not have to be complicated to be successful. We took elements of existing Agile and Lean thinking to build an approach that worked for us.

I was particularly inspired to try and use the physical Kanban board after reading 'Lean from the Trenches' by Henrik Kniberg. We can always seek to apply Lean to our own work: if there is something that you think can work for you or would like to do; plan it, try it, measure it, improve it.

17

Every Organisation Needs A Mole!

Stuart Morris

CONTENTS

Some of the most common challenges in implementing Continuous Improvement (CI) or Lean across any organisation is obtaining buy-in from all your staff and developing the culture of identifying and addressing waste. This chapter highlights one aspect of the work at the University of Lincoln CI Team towards solving this problem, with the team's star Twitter correspondent Muda Mole.

INTRODUCTION

No CI team can address every issue as it arises, and neither should they. Responsibility for making changes and implementing them should be owned by the areas with the issue, who can be facilitated to address it and develop a solution by a CI team. CI is about empowering those that do the work to improve the way they carry it out and our role as CI practitioners is to support them in that work.

To help at the University of Lincoln we have run very popular CI Awareness Training, however CI shouldn't be down to "one off" activities and we are aware that we need to keep the message fresh and topical; not just something learnt on a course some years or months ago. Our aim is to develop a culture across the University whereby staff identify any wastes within their processes and help them meet the targets of the strategic plan. The first step is to educate staff in what the 8 Wastes are and how they are encountered in all aspects of life not just at work. This way when colleagues become used to recognizing wastes in general life they may be able to relate them to work processes.

In the past organisations have tried numerous ways of publicising their message, such as newsletters and pamphlets; but there is always a cost implication to these methods and an environmental impact from the large amounts of paper being used to spread the message. So how about a way of reaching possibly millions of people, and not just within your organisation but worldwide, to publish your message at a low cost and relatively low impact on the environment? Twitter is that tool and has the capacity to reach an audience that you would never expect (as we have found) to receive your message and to hopefully develop a group of likeminded individuals that can cultivate a culture for change.

IT'S ONLY COMMON SENSE

When something is "new" people often have difficulty understanding how the concept will relate to their daily routine or experience "fear" of its consequences on their daily activities. CI was once explained to me as "just common sense but sense isn't common" and whenever we train staff we highlight how they carry out CI at home and then ask: why don't they always think about that approach in their work environment? Most people don't realise they follow CI concepts "it's just common sense", but when it is put into perspective they see the opportunities available to them to develop further at work and make their working life easier.

SO WHY A MOLE?

Within any organisation there are numerous processes to carry out its functions. One of the aims of CI is to eliminate waste from these processes and at the University of Lincoln we use the acronym PETEWORM to identify the 8 Wastes:

- People's potential (not using)
- Excess inventory
- Transport
- Excessive processing
- Waiting time
- Over production
- Rework
- Motion

Having a "worm" as the issue, what would be better than a "mole" to devour them; remove the wastes?

WHY CALL HIM MUDA?

At the University of Lincoln we try to keep the majority of Japanese terminology out of our approach to CI as people may not be that familiar with the language, however, with Muda being the Japanese for 'wastefulness', it links in with mole to name the character. A benefit of the Japanese terminology in this area is that in a process we also need to remove the burden on staff and the variation in the way a process is performed. These two concepts are known as Muri and Mura and therefore with Muda we now have a family of three moles to help pass out our message.

SO HOW DOES A MOLE TWEET?

Every Monday morning Muda Mole has a "moan". Using some aspect of the local, national or international news we try to link in the concepts of the 8 Wastes and how they can be interpreted in that story. This is then converted into an A4 poster with a phrase relating to the Waste and an image (including Muda Mole somewhere in the picture). This poster is then tweeted and additional comments relating to the story and CI are included.

SO WHY TWEET?

There are numerous books on CI and Lean relating to its implementation in manufacturing, service industries and other sectors but to the uninitiated these may seem daunting. Some may feel that CI is a dry topic and by using current news events with a little humour, the aim of the tweet is to show that CI can be found in all aspects of life and is not something to do after your work is completed or when you just have free time. If people laugh at the picture or message then maybe this will show that CI is not something to fear!

Muda knows how much people "love" a good 100 slide PowerPoint presentation but maybe they don't always have the time to sit and discuss the virtues of CI. The concept of Twitter is to connect people with similar interests and to keep them up-to-date; it is a simple way to connect with a large audience, Muda Mole has 237 followers (@UoL_CI) at the time of writing. A tweet size has now been extended to 280 characters and this small size means you must ensure your information is concise and relevant so you attract the readers' attention.

The first waste within PETEWORM is People's Potential and the lack of utilising it. Connecting via Twitter to experts around the world lets us utilise the potential of all Muda's contacts, and by using this public forum Muda's followers also share their words of wisdom. Muda now follows over 100 likeminded people and they communicate, share best practice and pose questions to develop each other.

Whether Muda's followers are experts in the field of CI or those with little exposure to the methodology, the way the information in his tweets is portrayed hopefully allows his audience to understand the reasoning behind identifying wastes and eliminating them.

HOW TO GAIN FOLLOWERS

First you need to have something people want to read about. Would someone want to read a tweet about CI or Lean? All Muda's tweets relate to wastes within either local news, or further afield if needs be, this allows readers to relate to the topic.

Twitter allows topics to be grouped for people to find using hashtags #. Every Muda Mole tweet includes the hashtags #ContinuousImprovement and #HateWaste so if people search for Continuous Improvement they will find all his tweets. By linking his tweets to any trends using the appropriate hashtag the audience can reach millions.

FOLLOWING AND FOLLOWERS

Muda regularly searches for CI or Lean on Twitter to make sure he is up-to-date and to see people that are tweeting about these topics. If someone's tweet is interesting Muda will follow them to learn more. Once you follow a person on Twitter you will see every tweet they send and you can also send them direct messages (not visible to other Twitter users).

When someone finds your tweets interesting they will hopefully follow you and if they do Twitter sends you a notification. When you receive this notification look at their profile and see if they are someone you feel has something you want to read and if so follow back. If for some reason you feel the follower is inappropriate, and you don't want them following you, Twitter gives you the option of "blocking" preventing them from seeing your tweets.

TWITTER ETIQUETTE

Twitter sometimes receives a bad name usually when inappropriate content has been tweeted by someone. University of Lincoln's Communications, Development and Marketing team run a short course for staff to learn the basics and the best advice they gave was "if you can't put it on a billboard outside your grandmother's house don't put it on Twitter". Remember

Twitter is a way of broadcasting your message, make sure it is something that people will want to hear, not something that will offend and anything you tweet will represent your organisation. Simply put "Think first Tweet second".

As Twitter broadcasts to the world it is an excellent medium to act as a "shop window" on your CI activities. Ensure your biography is completed to let your followers know who you are and why you are tweeting, you can even add your website address to direct them to your activities on the web or other social media platforms (Facebook, Instagram, Snapchat, etc).

To begin with create an appropriate Twitter name; ours is @UoL_CI as we are the University of Lincoln CI Team so hopefully the name is easy to find (remember to keep it short as if people want to use your name in a tweet, it is included in the character count of 280 maximum).

If you read a tweet you like, share it; this is retweeting and if someone retweets your message Twitter lets you know. All your tweets are visible to your followers but if you want to highlight a tweet to an individual use the @ symbol and their Twitter name but remember your followers see it too (use the direct message option for private conversations). If you want to show someone's followers your reply to them include a . in front of the @ and this makes the tweet visible to all their followers too.

Often you want to direct a reader's attention to something you may have found or created that is online and Twitter allows you to share the link (though you may wish to shorten it using Bitly.com) within your 280 characters. This way if you want to pull people into your website Twitter is an excellent way of expanding your audience.

The main thing is to interact. If someone emailed you with a question or comment, would you reply? The same rules follow on Twitter and who knows what you might learn.

WHAT SHOULD YOU TWEET?

Simply anything! Muda sends his Monday Moan most weeks but if something catches his eye he tweets about it. During workshops, training events or conferences updates on the content and progress are shared with his followers along with photographs of the event taking place.

Any event that CI has some relevance to is tweeted to show the followers that CI is all around them and is nothing to fear.

HOW DOES MUDA KNOW IT WORKS?

Twitter allows you to view various analytics of every tweet to see how you have engaged your audience, you receive notifications if someone likes, replies to or retweets your message and speaking to staff around the University they mention Muda and have even asked if he will attend workshops. Muda has followers as far away as Australia reading his comments so he truly is a global mole. Whilst his main aim was originally to help staff at the University of Lincoln understand the 8 Wastes he is now making people further afield think about CI in their daily activities and possibly removing some of the concerns they may have about the topic.

If you want to see what Muda is "moaning" about each week, just search Twitter for #MudaMole's Monday Moan and follow @UoL_CI.

Lastly – Who doesn't love a small mole in a builder's helmet? (Figure 17.1).

FIGURE 17.1
Muda Mole.

Section V

Sustaining

18

Head, Heart, Hands: The Three Essentials to Sustaining Lean in HE

Valerie Runyan and Jennifer Bremner

CONTENTS

INTRODUCTION

Macquarie University (www.mq.edu.au) is an internationally known public university located 15 kilometres from central Sydney, Australia. Since its inception in 1964, Macquarie has grown into a large, modern campus with 40,000 students and 2,000 staff. It is ranked number 9 in Australia (US News, Best Global Universities Rankings, 2018) and is in the top 200 Universities in the world (Academic Ranking of World Universities, 2017.)

Macquarie University is located in the Macquarie Innovation Park District, with more than 300 leading companies located on or around the Macquarie campus, providing students and faculty with career, research, collaboration and innovation opportunities. The university campus is set in 126 hectares of stunning parkland, and in recent years the university has invested $1 billion in infrastructure and facilities.

This chapter will discuss how the Business Process Improvement Initiative (BPII) became a part of Macquarie University's story. It will consider the importance of core dependencies for a successful implementation of Lean, including (1) executive support, (2) the unit leader and (3) a high functioning central team. These three components are essential for the sustained success of an institutional implementation of Lean.

We will explain why these three components are necessary, and why it is imperative to sustain the support of each level (head, heart and hands) to maintain the momentum of the methodology and ensure it is adopted as 'business as usual'. Motivating and mobilising staff across the organisation is only sustainable when these three essential components are in place.

In addition, as Lean HE develops and becomes business as usual, challenges arise which can shift the momentum and establishment of the methodology. Addressing these challenges and embedding a culture of continuous improvement is no small feat.

THE HEAD: EXECUTIVE SUPPORT

In 2013, the newly appointed Vice-Chancellor and President led a consultative process to establish a long-term strategic framework for Macquarie University. Focus groups, town halls and surveys were conducted to ensure a representative input from staff. Seven key priorities were identified as the key drivers to ensure success of the strategic framework. The seventh priority identified that Macquarie University needed to improve its support services, to ensure that staff could realise the aspiration and vision of the other six priorities.

The Vice Chancellor appointed the COO and the Deputy Vice-Chancellor Students and Registrar (S&R) to lead and deliver on this seventh priority. The university community was clear in their feedback that the model would need to be one that was transparent to staff, and developed trust, ownership and accountability. The university needed to re-focus the organisation's core activities of teaching and research around a concept of 'a university of service and engagement'. The university's leaders also knew from the outset that they wanted to improve the support processes, because it was understood that people were the organisation's most valuable asset. They also knew that it was not possible to instigate the level of change that was envisaged without using the staff's knowledge and expertise. The leadership resolved that if the staff understood the problem, they should be allowed to design and implement the solutions.

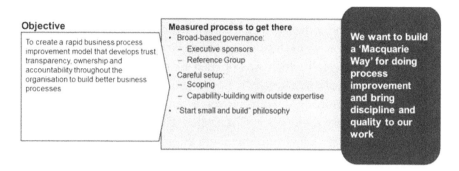

FIGURE 18.1
Macquarie Way.

To deliver on this initiative, the COO and the Deputy Vice-Chancellor S&R appointed a Director to lead and manage the BPII. The next order of business was to establish a Reference Group and select a business improvement methodology that would align with the culture envisioned model at Macquarie.

The COO, DVC S&R and the BPII Director purposely placed the initiative as a stand-alone unit, with the Director reporting to these two senior leaders. It was important that the initiative did not report to a functional unit such as IT, HR or Finance, to ensure the staff understood that this was a business process improvement initiative with no hidden agendas (Figure 18.1).

Five key stakeholders were asked to join the COO, the DVC S&R and the Director to establish the Reference Group. This group would be the key driver in establishing the business process improvement initiative. The Reference Group members were selected on what they could bring to the table, not on what positions they held. No nominees were allowed to replace a member at a meeting, and if a member missed two meetings, they were asked to resign from the Reference Group. This group needed to ensure it was a high functioning team that could make decisions and enact them in a timely manner. The group met four times prior to the launch of the university wide methodology, achieving the following in this short period of time:

- The recommendation to use Lean methodology
- Criteria and prioritisation for the selection of university wide business process improvements
- The project plan
- The communication plan
- The staffing complement

The COO, DVC S&R, the Director and the Reference Group all had key roles in the roll out of the communications of the Lean HE methodology. It was important that all areas of the university received these communications, including a Town Hall which was opened by the Vice-Chancellor with over 150 people in attendance.

To ensure the senior leadership's involvement remained visible to staff across the university, the Vice-Chancellor, COO, DVC Students and Registrar and Reference Group members all participated in welcoming and thanking staff for participating in Rapid Improvement Events (RIE's). Some staff had never met these senior leaders prior to their being involved in an RIE. On a number of occasions the Vice-Chancellor told staff that, not only was it important that they changed university processes, but that if anyone stood in their way to let him know and he would remove them. This was a very strong statement, and it removed any doubt that staff were empowered to change a process, and that, in fact, there was no excuse not to.

Following the launch of the methodology the Reference Group met monthly; then as the methodology became established across the university it met quarterly. The Reference Group moved to an advisory role to the Director. Its role was to deal with any obstacles, and report back to the Director on feedback from the university community and development steps the initiative should consider for continuous improvement.

Once the meetings became quarterly the group did discuss whether there was still a need for a Reference Group. But, following discussions with the Director, the group continued as it was perceived that there was value in having this well-respected group as part of the team; in fact the group's involvement was an important factor in the acceptance of the university wide methodology. Staff across the university were well aware that the BPII was owned by two Senior Executives who had been appointed by the Vice-Chancellor, a well-respected and high-functioning Reference Group, and the Director. Project staff saw this group as integral to their success; they knew these senior executives had their back. In addition, because the BPII had such a small staff complement (three) the unit needed the reputation and support of the Reference Group to maintain a high profile across the university.

THE HEART: THE INITIATIVE LEADER

When deciding on the leader of the BPII it was important that the Director understood the business of higher education and the culture they would be working in. The Director did not have a business process improvement background; but had extensive senior management experience in higher education. She had also worked at Macquarie University and had developed a reputation of trust and transparency with staff and the senior leaders.

The Director needed to understand the necessity of communicating, listening and delivering a project outcome. They had to be aware of their own feelings as well as the feeling of others, and have the ability to express their point of view judiciously and with empathy. A high priority of the Director was to be the 'face' of the initiative, to develop trust with senior executives, middle management and staff across the university. Without trust and transparency the initiative would not have succeeded.

With three staff members, the BPII team did not have room for egos. Although every staff member had a role to ensure the success of the initiative, they all were required to have the capacity to roll up their sleeves and complete mundane tasks, leading by example.

It was the Director's role to drive business into the unit, and to deliver the results of the project. Planning, delegating, evaluation and reviewing were key components of the role. When Macquarie's BPII commenced, the three staff members felt the remit of the unit was to deliver a new process through an RIE. It was then the responsibility of the project group and the business process owner to implement the new process.

The BPII team quickly realised that a key measure of its success was if and how well a new process was implemented. The Director needed to ensure the methodology was followed and projects were delivered well and on time.

In the initial stages of the implementation of the Lean methodology and RIE's, staff continually asked for mini RIE's, as five days for a standard RIE had lost its initial shine. The Director was required to stand firm to the standardised methodology, to ensure the experience was the same for staff across the organisation and that the rigor of the methodology was not compromised.

An escalation process was developed by the Director, based on the Vice-Chancellor's comment about removing anyone that got in the way. Facilitators and project participants all knew that any issues could be escalated to the Director who would in turn escalate the issue to the Reference Group or the Executive Sponsors. It should be noted that although there was an escalation process, this process was never used. The knowledge that there was an escalation process was enough to empower the staff to solve problems themselves.

THE HANDS: THE BUSINESS PROCESS IMPROVEMENT INITIATIVE TEAM

The essential aspects of the BPII team's work are communication, facilitation, negotiation and project management. These skills are particularly important to demonstrate effectiveness to senior leaders and to attract and mobilise staff from across the university. Effective facilitation enables staff to adopt, interact with and deliver the chosen process improvement methodology. The methodology can be taught, but it is the essential skills of communication, facilitation, negotiation and project management that make the difference in being able to deliver improvement.

During the establishment phase the business process improvement team had two members who reported to the Director. The team was collegial and collaborative in nature and together developed a structured sustainable approach to the delivery of process improvement. Additional support came from other areas of the university with the backing of their respective areas (the Sustainability office and the Library). These additional staff also contributed to and used the structured approach to process improvement.

A key requirement of the BPII team during this phase was supporting the Director by communicating effectively about the nature of the initiative and the methodology being implemented. Part of this communication was an explanation of why the Lean methodology was chosen, and how it fit with the university culture and strategy.

The structured approach to facilitation and project management ensured consistent delivery of process improvement based on Lean HE methodology. The team worked together to create a process map of the improvement process, and developed tools to support each of the process steps. For example, problem definition and scoping were conducted in the same format for each process to be improved; rapid improvement events followed an established template, with some variation depending on the group in the room. The structured approach also assisted with another important element of getting the initiative off the ground, which was to clearly demonstrate that the methodology worked with quick win improvement events both from within one area and across the university.

During the implementation phase for the initiative, this structured approach enabled the small central process improvement team to deliver multiple projects at once and to show that there was a replicable way to achieve positive results. Because of the way the initiative was set up and structured, from the beginning the team were able to be independent and neutral in their approach to the improvement of processes and the implementation of change. The key traits that made this team function well within the university were excellent communication with all levels of the organisation, an understanding of the nature and culture of the university, as well as a demonstrated commitment to continuous improvement by asking for and incorporating feedback into their way of doing things.

Facilitation, communication, project management and negotiation skills are paramount in enabling team members to engender trust and confidence, and to form cohesive project teams comprised of disparate individuals (from different areas with different agendas) to effectively deliver on projects that improve processes.

These skills enable the central team members to:

- Empower staff to look for opportunities to change that can benefit themselves and the students.
- Impartially facilitate groups to improve their own processes.
- Explain and train in the fundamentals and principles of the Lean methodology.
- Identify key issues preventing areas from achieving their strategic goals.

Extensive facilitation of large and small groups is essential to the delivery of Lean process improvements. A facilitator that creates an inclusive, safe, neutral and non-judgemental space for all participants enables an honest and frank discussion about problems with a process. This facilitation approach also empowers cross-functional teams to seek and find solutions to common problems they encounter. Process improvement stems from the understanding of the process by those who work in it. A skilled facilitator elicits this understanding and creates a shared approach by providing skilled questioning, active listening, clear reflection and a structure space.

The empowerment of university staff who participated in RIE's also contributed to their ongoing development within the university. They often reported that having their perspective listened to and seeing their ideas implemented improved their confidence and enabled them to be more proactive and engaged in their work. The initiative worked with over 1,000 university staff through RIE's, training and process reengineering for specific projects. These people became an important part of communicating about the BPII initiative as they spoke about their experiences and became change agents.

Knowledge of the higher education sector, and the culture of the specific organisation, is also extremely important to enable adaptability and understanding of challenges. For example, it was necessary in the Macquarie context to first explain to staff what a process was, so we had a common definition. We also had to be explicit about what a process was not. For example, we trained all staff to see a process as a way of doing something independent of a system. So that they could see that processes do not fix IT systems, they interact with them; and that processes do not change policy, they enact it. Knowledge of the higher education sector and the organisation increased the credibility of the central team engendering trust with RIE participants.

The delivery of Lean process improvement was done using a variety of consistent and structured tools. These tools were refined and adapted, as appropriate, based on feedback from each session. This improvement of the structure and tools was done collaboratively by the team, which required complementary skill sets such as an ability to analyse evidence and metrics, as well and the ability to write meaningful and targeted content.

The roles within the team reporting to the Director need to be interchangeable in their delivery of improvement events and projects, to ensure they could support one another. They also need to collaborate effectively to combine their strengths, so that projects were always moving in the right direction. The BPII team at Macquarie University worked effectively by working on all activities together. The team was action oriented and focused on results.

Each member of the team, from the Director to facilitator, is required to manage ongoing and often complex relationships. Building and managing relationships with internal and external stakeholders at all levels of the organisation enables the team to create a reputation for impartial and effective change management.

The successful delivery of projects builds momentum for the improvement initiative. Project management and high-level problem-solving skills are required to enable the BPII team to deliver on multiple projects at once. Across 2016–17 the Macquarie University BPII team successfully delivered 52 improvement projects.

As Lean HE developed and became 'business as usual' for Macquarie, several challenges shifted the momentum of the initiative. Process improvement and the use of Lean HE continues at Macquarie University and is now embedded in specific areas of the university. Lean HE is used to improve processes in areas such as Finance, HR and the Library, while the central process improvement team is tasked with focussing on key projects and support services.

While delivering on projects, the BPII team also developed and delivered training packages, which offer benefits from the shared understanding of Lean HE and how process improvement works at Macquarie. The training sessions included introductory, process improvement and facilitation training, to create a network of champions and key staff who embrace and promote Lean HE across faculties and support services.

CREATING CHAMPIONS AND FACILITATORS

The core BPII team trained facilitators to conduct RIE's and Lean workshops in the Library, the Faculties of Human Sciences and the Faculty of Arts. The staff who participated in BPII activities with the central team often became advocates for the BPII initiative and Lean in HE approach. When the BPII team began training facilitators and collaborating with faculties, these advocates supported and encouraged the nominated facilitators.

The BPII piloted a one-on-one training approach, to train nominated staff to use Lean tools and the Lean methodology. These staff could run RIE's and improve processes within their areas. This training program, although intensive, was designed to ensure staff would have the same experience regardless of where they were participating in an RIE in the university.

Macquarie employees undertaking this partnering and training were nominated by the Faculty General Manager or Director of their area, and then received support enabling them to run RIE's. The support and partnership that the BPII team offered was one-on-one training prior to each of the eight RIE stages. BPII staff were present at each stage, and the RIE workshop stage was co-facilitated by the nominee and a BPII team member. This approach involves potential facilitators learning about the Lean methodology, viewing an RIE and then doing an RIE as a co-facilitator. This happens in rapid succession to enable the new facilitator to put the theory into practice as quickly as possible.

The benefits of this approach were to have embedded champions of Lean thinking as the 'way things are done' at Macquarie, while providing staff development and improved processes. The challenge in this approach is keeping the facilitators and champions within the organisation and in enabling them to keep using and honing their skills. It is important to ensure that continuous improvement is kept on the agenda and that a methodology is explicit. Process improvement is not something that will just happen 'naturally'.

BENEFITS, CHALLENGES AND KEY CRITERIA FOR SUCCESS

Sustaining Lean in an organisation requires the continued support of the Executive and a group of senior staff who advocate for and provide practical support to the Business Process Improvement leader and team.

At Macquarie, it was important that the initiative was seen as a neutral stand-alone unit, that reported to the COO, DVC S&R and the Reference Group. Had the team reported to a specific area within the organisation instead of directly to the Executive, this could have threatened the neutral status of the team and lead to process improvement being concentrated in specific areas instead of being about cross-campus, end to end processes.

The goal of the Director and business process improvement team is to have the staff who work in the process own the process, and truly engage with the improvements they have designed and are implementing. This not only improves processes but it also begins a cultural shift towards process improvement by staff. The staff who redesign the process get credit for the improvements, and the business process improvement initiative is promoted and seen as an enabler for change. The projects are delivered by the rapid improvement team, and communicated by them with the assistance of the business improvement team. Communicating this in a way that ensures the initiative is sustainable is fundamental in maintaining the visibility and effectiveness of the initiative.

CONCLUSION

The Lean methodology is a vibrant and powerful change management tool. Staff are empowered to make decisions, change processes and improve the staff and student experience. The organisation needs to be ready for this change, and if so will embrace the methodology.

Key findings by the initiative leader and business process improvement team have been:

- The Lean methodology is an enabler for an institution's cultural change process, and it empowers staff to take the responsibility and ownership for purposeful and continuous change.
- The methodology needs to be clearly explained, inclusive and transparent for project participants and the wider university community.
- In order to achieve institutional acceptance of the methodology, visible and continuous support is required from the Executive Team.
- Communication of roles and responsibilities of all staff across the university need to be clear when introducing and using the Lean methodology. It is a new way of thinking and reporting lines are not the deciding factor for the change implementation.
- The BPII team is a support team, working behind the scenes to assist the project team to achieve their goals and ensure the business has ownership of the change process.
- The BPII team does not need to be a large central team, but one that is collegiate, high in emotional intelligence and understands the common goals.
- To sustain the methodology across the institution, the methodology needs to be shared and embedded in the functional units for ongoing success.

The work of the BPII team and project groups needs to be underpinned by a sustainable, replicable and measurable approach. The value of Lean is that it leverages existing knowledge and resources and improves cross-functional processes. It can also change the culture within an organisation; it has the potential to be transformative. Realising this potential was a big part of the BPII team's agenda. Improving staff and student experiences, reducing waste, stopping repetition and saving or generating money all contributed to the success of the BPII unit; and the ripple effect at all levels of the organisation made positive changes for individuals and cultures within the organisation.

19

Lessons from Implementing Lean at the Veterinary Teaching Hospital

Chris Shannon

CONTENTS

INTRODUCTION

This case study describes the implementation of lean at the Veterinary Teaching Hospital at the University of Queensland. Implementation included embedding lean in the hospital strategic plan, running a rapid improvement event (RIE) on 'scheduling elective procedures/ surgery for small animals' (a key process in the daily life of the hospital), implementing changes and addressing cultural and behavioural change within the hospital. The author facilitated the RIE, and subsequently worked with hospital leadership, providing additional support and advice to resolve issues that arose during and post implementation. The author wishes to acknowledge the excellent work done by Ellen Balke in co-facilitating the RIE.

The case study contrasts the teaching hospital implementation with the broader unsuccessful attempt to implement lean at the university (which the author was also involved in). Issues of scale, ownership of end-to-end processes, leader commitment and the role of the lean consultant are considered to offer practical advice based on this experience.

BACKGROUND

The Veterinary Teaching Hospital (VTH) is part of the University of Queensland (UQ) and trains undergraduate and postgraduate students in veterinary science and veterinary technology programs. The VTH is based at Gatton, 87 kilometres west of Brisbane, where the main university campuses are located. Gatton is the largest town in the Lockyer Valley, a fertile agricultural area between the coast and the mountains which provides much of the local produce consumed in South-East Queensland.

The VTH runs as a commercial operation within the School of Veterinary Sciences. The hospital employs 123 staff, including 57 veterinary clinicians, trains over 350 students a year and treats 17,000 cases a year, including 8,000 small animal cases. Many of the small animals are domestic pets although the hospital also treats native animals, exotic birds, reptiles and small mammals. The annual expenditure budget of the VTH is approximately $12M. The VTH consists of four distinct units: the small animal hospital; equine hospital; production animal service (mobile service for farms); and the Dayboro practice (a separate practice located approximately 130 kilometres north-east of the hospital). Supporting the units at Gatton are shared services including the hospital reception and administration teams, anaesthesia, diagnostic imaging and kennels.

Senior management were aware of operational inefficiency and cultural problems in the hospital. Surgeries were frequently rescheduled and animals were kept under sedation for long periods. Staff routinely worked long hours and the cost of overtime was ballooning. Nursing staff complained about disrespectful behaviour by clinicians. The current state was not optimal for patients or staff, and did not provide the student learning environment to which the hospital aspired. In 2016, the hospital Business Manager attended a lean awareness session for managers in the Faculty of Science (co-facilitated by the author) and saw that lean could help to address the hospital's problems. She embedded lean in the operational plan for 2017 and sought the author's assistance in facilitating lean implementation.

IMPLEMENTING LEAN AT THE VTH

Using the University of St Andrews '8 Step Model' as a guide (Table 19.1) (Robinson & Yorkstone, 2014), the author worked with leadership and stakeholders to define and scope the work to be undertaken. A working party established to lead lean implementation within the hospital identified *scheduling elective procedures/surgery for small animals through the Hospital* as a priority process to fix. 'Elective' surgery in this sense means necessary but non-emergency procedures. Animals are brought to the hospital by owners, or referred by veterinary practices, a clinician assesses the animal and, if necessary, a procedure is scheduled. This process is the main driver of daily activity in the small animal hospital, accounting for over 50% of all cases seen in the VTH, and impacting on all the supporting units.

Between November 2016 and February 2017, two all staff information sessions were held. The senior academic and professional staff leaders in the hospital attended both sessions. They outlined the problems the hospital faced and why they had chosen lean. The author gave presentations on lean and explained what would happen before, during and after the three day RIE. These sessions included very candid discussions and Q&A. While the staff all agreed they could not continue to work in the same

TABLE 19.1

The St Andrews 8 Step Model

Request	An area of work is defined or a request for assistance is made
Scoping	Goals, project team and resources are agreed with stakeholders. The key question is 'what is the problem we are trying to solve?'
Training	The project team are introduced to lean thinking and techniques
Planning	The project goal, approach, timetable and data requirements are reviewed and agreed by the team
Redesign (event)	New process and action plan are created
Implementation	New process put in place and action items are completed by team members
Review	Progress is monitored
Feedback	The project is signed off and feedback is taken

Adapted from *Becoming Lean: A Pocket Guide* (2017).

way, there was some scepticism that lean would help to solve what seemed to be intractable problems.

In scoping and running the RIE, the author led the development of a high-level process map (Figure 19.1), a BOSCARD (Appendix 1 – for more information on BOSCARD, refer to Chapter 11 by Mark Robinson), a value statement for the process, current state process map, future state process map (Figure 19.2) and an action plan. In addition, the team drafted a set of principles for the hospital to use in implementing change.

During the RIE, the author covered the two fundamentals of lean and spoke a lot about making the process flow and the theory of constraints. The surgery scheduling process included two common service providers (diagnostic imaging and anaesthesiology) who service multiple teams without effective communication or information sharing between the teams. The two services were constraints (theory of constraints says there is only one bottleneck or worst constraint at a time) where work would back up, but also had regular periods of inactivity due to poor scheduling of patients. That is, the process bottleneck(s) had downtime between periods of being overloaded.

The St Andrews model (Table 19.1) is similar to other kaizen/RIE models and frameworks. A 2014 review of kaizen literature across multiple industries identified model convergence around waste elimination, cross-functional teams who have authority to change processes, inclusion of 'fresh eyes' in the team, the need for management support, emphasis on action orientation, and reward and recognition (Glover, Farris, & Van Aken, 2014). Two differences between this convergent view and the St Andrews Model presented in the Guide are emphasis on the need for customers to be part of the RIE team, although this is variable across industries (Glover et al., 2015) and the absence of reward and recognition built into the St Andrews Model.* In the author's experience, including customers in the team is essential. Given the size and complexity of universities, this often means other staff as internal customers of the process, and of course students.

The main activities that take place in an RIE are:

- Confirming the process scope and purpose (it is surprising how often the team will spend an hour or more on day 1 of the RIE revisiting where the process starts and ends, and what the purpose of the process is).

---

* In conversation, Mark Robinson from the University of St Andrews has advised that they do seek to include clients in the RIE teams whenever possible, and that lean now forms part of the St Andrews reward and recognition system.

High Level Map

Process Name: Scheduling – High level process map
Process Owner:

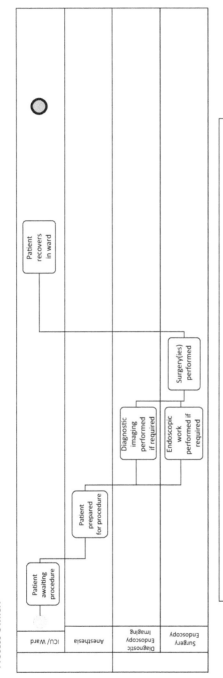

The high level process map is intended to capture the main steps in the process and assist in identifying the right people to include in the kaizen team. It is not meant to be a comprehensive view of the process or to capture all the possible paths a patient could take.

FIGURE 19.1

High-level scheduling process.

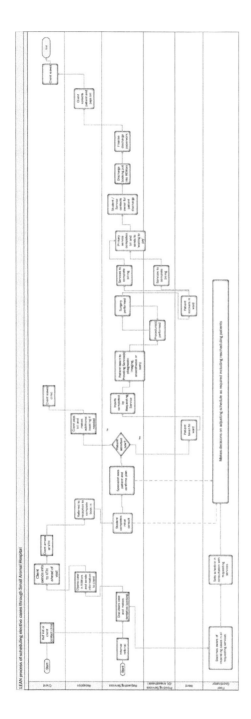

FIGURE 19.2
More detailed scheduling process.

- Mapping the current state process. The reason for spending time mapping the current state is to create a shared understanding of the process and to generate discussion and ideas for improving it.
- Sharing and discussing ideas for the future state process.
- Designing the ideal future, and (if needed) interim state(s).
- Compiling the action plan to move from current to future state.

People who are unfamiliar with RIE often question the need to schedule them over several days. It seems inconceivable that you would need that long to review a process, and seems wrong to even call such an event 'rapid'. The rapidity relates to concentrating effort on solving a problem in a focused burst rather than forming a working group that meets once a month and seemingly takes forever to make progress. The author prefers to use the term 'process improvement event' or PIE rather than rapid improvement event. This sidesteps the confusion about 'rapidity' in the event, and also allows for a little fun, assuring everyone that it is as easy as pie, everyone loves pie etc. However, for consistency with the common language used in this book, they are referred to as RIE in this chapter.

Concern about the time required for RIE can result in them being scheduled too tightly and the team not having sufficient time to complete their work. The author has facilitated RIE ranging from a single day to 5 days and has concluded there is no ideal duration; it depends on the complexity of the process and the level of lean maturity of the organisation. However, if your organisation is new to lean, it is advisable to allow more time rather than less. Mark Robinson uses the cricket game analogy – a long RIE will take around 5 days. Runs will be scored, wickets will fall but you cannot say in advance quite when these things will happen. If you finish the RIE early, get the team started on implementation.

Two points worth remembering about the investment of time in an RIE:

- The team members are stepping out of their normal jobs to help solve a problem for the organisation. Therefore the organisation should take the new process seriously and genuinely try to make it work.
- Other people inevitably cover the work of the team members during the RIE. They are contributing to the problem solving effort as well. Everyone has skin in the game.

Not covering all of the lean principles and tools in an RIE, and introducing other concepts such as theory of constraints is fine. The team is there to solve a problem and the facilitator has to guide them to the solution. It is not feasible to cover all aspects in every RIE. For example, Taiichi Ohno, creator of the Toyota Production System, has said identifying which type of waste something is does not matter. 'Don't bother thinking about what type of waste is this? Just get on with it and do kaizen' (Miller, 2013: 175). Besides, you will cover lean principles and wastes generally in the pre-RIE training. RIE can be hard work, though very rewarding, to participate in. Spending several days focused on analysing and improving a process takes a lot of energy and commitment. Sometimes there are arguments, sometimes tears, usually laughter and always determination to get it right. It is true that, 'there is nothing more powerful than participating in a five-day kaizen and personally creating significant improvement' (Fiume, 2007: 48).

Implementing the changes after the RIE required very strong commitment from the team and hospital leadership. While the team were enthusiastic after the event, they returned to busy jobs and struggled to find the time to make the changes they had discussed, or even to meet regularly to review progress. This is a common problem when implementing lean in busy organisations. They also found that while staff had agreed the old way of working was not sustainable, some staff were reverting to old behaviour during busy times. There were many learnings along the path to implementing process changes in the VTH. Two that are particularly worth sharing are discussed next.

1) *Review your end-to-end process but prioritise your top few changes* – the team designed a comprehensive end-to-end future state process with over 30 action items required to fully implement the new process. It was too much to take on at once. We ultimately agreed two rules which would be enforced, and which actions items had to support:
   - No animal will move to the next step in the process until all inputs (see Table 19.2) are complete (the hospital equivalent of 'don't pass defects down the line').
   - No scheduled procedure will start after 3pm (this would inevitably result in overtime and tired staff).
   In order to achieve those two things, the process had to flow smoothly and correctly. Whenever the hospital failed to achieve those two things, they needed to understand why, and fix the problem. The action items that directly supported achieving these two rules were the highest priority; the rest could be done later.

2) *Focus on your culture as much as your process* – in the months following implementation, the hospital could see the potential benefits from the new process but in times of stress people reverted to their previous behaviour. Process specific metrics were not enough so the team devised a second set of culture specific metrics (refer to Table 19.2).

Within a month of introducing these new measures the hospital reported improvements in the culture which translated to adherence to the new process. Management support for reinforcing the agreed behaviour was essential. There is a power imbalance in the clinician–nurse relationship (similar to the professor–administrator relationship), and nursing staff had to feel empowered to speak up for the new process. Hospital leadership had to back them up; and they did.

Other post-RIE initiatives that have been introduced include holding daily stand-up meetings, conducting daily lightning walks (a quick tour of the kennels to discuss on site the condition of each patient) and the use of a large LCD screen as a primary visual display of patient status directly from the hospital case management system.

The hospital has reported very positive results from the RIE and other actions on their path towards becoming lean. Specific to the scheduling process, the hospital reported substantial reductions in rescheduled

TABLE 19.2

Outcomes and Measures of Success

Outcomes	Measures of Success
The hospital will know the process is improving through:	Increase in number of days when staff finish work at scheduled time
	Decrease in number of procedures rescheduled because of delays in completing procedure inputs (request form, bloodwork, Vetpay consent, clinical discussion)
	Reduction in patient waiting time in shared services (Anaesthesia and Diagnostic Imaging)
	Reduction in downtime in shared services
The hospital will know the culture is improving through:	Observable increase in respectful interactions between staff, and reduction in complaints about disrespectful behaviour
	Observable increase in staff using data to inform problem solving and decision making
	Increase in number of ideas coming from staff and percentage of those ideas which are implemented

surgeries, overtime being paid and client complaints. The overtime savings have been redirected into purchasing new equipment. The cultural change at the hospital has also been significant. Staff complaints have reduced, morale has improved and student satisfaction has increased. In one instance, a locum clinician who had previously been at the hospital a year earlier returned and expressed great pleasure and surprise at the changes he observed, 'The case flow is much more efficient and things are just better in general'.

DIFFERENCES BETWEEN HOSPITAL AND UQ IMPLEMENTATIONS

The implementation of lean at the VTH commenced in the context of a broader unsuccessful attempt to implement lean at UQ. The author worked on both implementations and offers the following reflections on why the implementation at the VTH is succeeding while the larger attempt at UQ did not. Noting that the hospital has achieved success with lean where the university did not is not a criticism of UQ; it is simply a description of the current state. Consistent with lean requiring a no-blame culture, the important thing is to understand why one thing works and the other does not, and what can be done differently in the future. Comments follow on how common this experience is, the scale of change effort, ownership of end-to-end processes, explicit leader commitment and the ongoing role of the lean consultant in the change process.

UQ'S EXPERIENCE IS VERY COMMON

The UQ attempt to implement lean was part of a program of process improvement work overseen by a steering committee of senior staff. It was driven by a central project team consisting of a mix of external appointments and internal secondments. The project team were provided with lean training, with two members of the team tasked with identifying, scoping and delivering process improvements via RIE, with a focus on improving the student experience. They took on big problematic processes which ran across all or most schools and faculties and multiple support units. They also ran lean awareness training for hundreds of staff across the university. Despite an initial wave of enthusiasm, within a year UQ had stopped using lean and taken a different approach.

False starts and failed first attempts are common when trying to implement lean in large, complex and mature organisations. Academic and management journals are littered with case studies of failed lean implementation. Some articles focus on the struggle to implement changes from particular improvement events (Farris, Van Aken, Doolen, & Worley, 2008; Van Aken, Farris, Glover, & Letens, 2010) while others describe system wide failures to embrace lean (Emiliani, 2013). Frequently cited reasons lean implementation fails include lack of alignment to organisational strategic direction (Chiarini, 2013; Fiume, 2007), organisations focusing on lean tools rather than lean leadership (Dombrowski & Mielke, 2014), and barriers to implementation of improvement event outcomes not being removed (Fiume, 2007). Starting lean by running RIE is also very common. RIEs play an important part in reinforcing lean culture (Fiume, 2007; Van Aken et al., 2010); however, an event is by nature episodic and should not be the primary means of implementing lean. Unless supported by an appropriate organisational culture, the benefits gained from process improvement events typically dissipate within 9–18 months (Glover, Farris, & Van Aken, 2015).

SCALE AND OWNERSHIP OF END-TO-END PROCESSES

As noted at the start of this chapter, the VTH employs 123 staff and teaches 350 students a year with an annual budget of $12M. It runs as a discrete business unit within the university. Although the staff working in the hospital are part of the School of Veterinary Science, the hospital can be viewed as a distinct entity. UQ has 6,700 full-time equivalent staff, 51,000 students and an annual budget of $1.75 billion. The university has 6 faculties, 8 institutes and at least 4 large divisions of non-academic staff providing support services ranging from finance, HR, building maintenance and ICT support through to library and legal services. The scale of the two entities is vastly different, and scale creates challenges.

Within the VTH, the decision was made to start with the process for scheduling small animal surgery. This served to address one of the biggest pain points in the hospital. While the hospital relies on other parts of

UQ for some services, scheduling surgery is unique to, and owned end-to-end by, the hospital. This undoubtedly helped in implementation and provides an important clue to success. The hospital leadership did not have to convince anyone else to implement the change. All staff attended information sessions on lean and it was understood lean would be implemented across the entire hospital over time. The size of the VTH made implementing lean in an integrated way manageable. The project team were drawn from all the units impacted by the scheduling process, and this represented most of the units in the hospital. Information was shared with those units not initially in scope.

While the UQ team attempted to liaise with key stakeholders across the organisation, the size and complexity of the university made achieving full coverage difficult. Implementing change across UQ required liaising with multiple stakeholders and at times felt like seeking permission even though running RIE was endorsed by senior management. The size of the university is such that not all organisational units could be represented in the RIE team, and UQ simply did not yet have a culture of accepting changes determined by a small team of staff drawn from across the organisation. While the RIE teams embraced this new way of thinking, it was not successfully communicated to the broader university. RIE teams set out with action plans to implement future state processes only to run into current state thinking and behaviour.

One reason for taking on big processes was that the cost of running an individual RIE can be high, at least in terms of people's time commitment to it, so it was felt that they had to tackle big processes to generate sufficient return on investment. Examples of the RIE that were run are academic progression (what to do when a student is failing their courses), and sending students on overseas exchanges. It may have worked better at UQ to accept at least part of the cost of early RIE as investment in the cultural change and professional development, rather than individual improvement efforts that each needed to yield a positive return.

LEADER COMMITMENT

The hospital leadership team was aware that starting on the lean journey then failing and abandoning it would be worse than not starting at all. The two most senior academic and professional staff in the hospital are the Academic Superintendent and the Business Manager. Both were fully committed to implementing lean. They attended every scoping, planning and information session in the lead up to the RIE, attended the event itself and were instrumental in making the changes work afterwards. They provided essential support to staff in challenging behaviours that were inconsistent with the agreed principles and the lean approach. They stuck to the message that the purpose of implementing lean was to improve both patient outcomes and staff working life. They were adamant that lean was not a cost cutting exercise, and backed this up with action. The goals were clear and easy for staff to buy in to. The RIE team's authority and autonomy were never questioned by leadership. In fact, when there was pushback by other staff, leadership spoke strongly in support of the changes and reiterated an early message about implementing lean – hospital staff had agreed the current state was not sustainable and the hospital had to change. The case for change had come from the staff, not management.

The university level change project was funded centrally and overseen by a senior steering committee which was initially enthusiastic about lean but which also spoke of seeking 'quick wins', and which was removed from the actual workplaces where changes would occur. As time passed and the RIE teams struggled to effect change, university leadership felt that lean was not having the desired effect and the return on investment was too slow. Within a year, the university had stopped talking about lean and changed its approach.

As stated earlier, this is a familiar story across many different industries. Implementing lean in large, mature organisations is difficult to do. The role of the lean leader is to inspire the organisation to build a culture of continuous improvement, and to develop the organisation's ability to identify and eliminate problems. Staff must feel empowered to contribute. In order to do this effectively, leaders must first understand lean themselves, and accept that it requires a long-term commitment to cultural change with an unspecified financial return. Fiume has written a very good book chapter on this topic (2007).

ONGOING INVOLVEMENT OF LEAN CONSULTANT

A key difference in approaches taken with the VTH and with UQ is that the author remained involved in the lean implementation with the hospital after the RIE. By viewing the hospital as a long-term client, the author was able to stay connected to the implementation throughout the year, meeting regularly with the hospital Business Manager to discuss issues that had arisen. The distance between the main UQ campus where the author works and the Gatton campus (87 km) is a challenge. A visit to the hospital required half a day when travel time was included. While this resulted in less frequent visits than would be ideal, it also put pressure on the hospital to make the drive worthwhile, and it sent an important message to hospital staff; the work was sufficiently important that the author would regularly make the trip to see them.

The volume of work attempted by two facilitators in the UQ-wide attempt precluded this sort of ongoing partnership from developing. They scoped processes and facilitated RIE but largely left implementation to the team members, process and business owners.

From a personal development perspective, the VTH approach has benefited the author. It has allowed opportunity to see implementation issues first hand, to understand the challenges the team faces and to introduce new tools as required. It has also resulted in better knowledge transfer to the VTH, building the capacity for future process improvement without as great a need for a facilitator or internal consultant.

ADDITIONAL ADVICE TO CONSIDER IN IMPLEMENTING LEAN

UQ's story is typical of the path large and mature organisations follow. Big 'transformation' projects are often not understood to be slow-burn, incremental cultural change; they are thought of as high profile, high return activities. In the rhetoric of change, 'transform' often connotes speed. Pressure is applied to deliver quick wins, but quick wins do not translate to sustained improvement. The challenge for any organisation is to learn from experience and do better in the future. It is useful to remember that while people today view the Toyota Production System as a highly sophisticated system, Toyota struggled too. Reflecting on the early years of development, Taiichi Ohno described it as highly experimental and largely trial and error. 'Nobody knew if the Ohno system would work. Nobody else was trying it'. Toyota tried many different ways of doing things, measuring and assessing the results of different options, changing them and trying again when the results were bad (Miller, 2013: 80).

Successful lean implementation requires demonstrable leader commitment and patience. Leaders not allowing sufficient time for changes to take effect will be disappointed by the results. Do not underestimate the challenge it presents to senior leaders to support something that can require a long time-frame to be fully implemented, which requires ongoing, visible support, and which will have an unspecified ROI. It is a different way of doing business.

In the early days of lean implementation, do not seek a positive ROI on every RIE or improvement activity. Consider part of the cost of the activity to be professional development for the staff involved, and the cost of a culture change process. Also, be prepared to run RIE on small processes.

Lean is built on the foundation of respect for people and determination to continuously improve. These two fundamentals are incredibly important. Most leaders say that 'people are our most valuable asset' but not all leaders back those words with actions. Lean is predicated on that belief, as evidenced by Toyota's famous maxim 'Before we built cars, we built people' (Dombrowski & Mielke, 2014). You have to demonstrate respect for people if you want them to buy in to your culture. The ability to continuously improve requires problem solving skills at all levels of the organisation, possessed by people who believe they have the support of management to suggest and implement changes. Liker and Ballé wrote that 'The key to becoming lean is not to apply the lean tools to every process but to develop the kaizen spirit in every employee so they can solve each unique problem with the appropriate approach' (Liker & Ballé, 2013: 19).

The purpose of lean is to make problems visible. Doing this requires a no-blame approach. Problems occur and mistakes are made despite the best intentions of all concerned. A blame culture simply compels people to conceal problems or attempt to shift blame when problems become known. An organisation which seeks to attribute blame to individuals will not become lean. People who come to work with the intent of doing their best for the organisation and who act with integrity should not be blamed when things go wrong. They should be acknowledged for trusting the organisation enough to make the problems known. Lean demonstrates that when things do go wrong, it is the fault of the process, not the people.

APPENDIX 18.1 – VTH BOSCARD

Process Name	VTH Scheduling	Process Owner	Academic Superintendent
		Business Owner	Business Manager
Date Raised	7 December 2016	Date scheduled	Feb 2017

Background	The VTH has identified the need to streamline its process for scheduling patients for procedures. The current process frequently results in schedules being missed, staff being required to work additional hours, patients being anesthetised for longer periods of time, and staff being frustrated and dissatisfied.
Objectives	1. Create a streamlined process for scheduling patients into procedures; 2. Identify and fill information gaps; 3. Develop and implement appropriate performance measures for this process.
Stakeholders (and benefits)	Key VTH staff identified –

Scope	Within Scope	Patients admitted through UQ VETS Small Animal Hospital, Gatton.
	Outside Scope	Patients admitted through the Equine Specialist Hospital Clinic, the Dayboro Hospital and the Production Animal Service.

Process A map of the process at a high level (6 or 7 KEY steps)	The process starts with a client making a booking for a patient to be admitted to the hospital, and finishes with the patient being scheduled for discharge. High level map attached.
Information (and data)	• Number of patients admitted to wards per day for past 90 days; • Number of procedures per day for past 90 days, including by type of animal and type of procedure; • Number of patients requiring multiple procedures; • Number of procedures rescheduled or affected by noticeable incidents of delays, and reason for rescheduling or delay; • Number of procedures with unsuccessful outcomes, by animal and procedure type; • Teaching outcomes and requirements.

Constraints	EBA, lack of information, veterinary legislation, existing budget and staff plan.

Assumptions	Assuming executive level support to change processes and associated staff behaviour.

Risks	The risk of doing nothing is the VTH does not improve, and staff dissatisfaction increases. Changes to the process might adversely impact student learning experience. Changes might have an adverse impact on other services not fully involved in the improvement event (equine, avian and exotics, GP, CSC, production animal).

Reporting	Stakeholders within the VTH, School of Veterinary Science, Faculty of Science and relevant parts of UQ.

Deliverables	Streamlined 'future state' process with clear plan for progressing from current state to future state. Streamlined 'interim state' process (if required) to ensure incremental improvement while the VTH moves to the future state. Knowledge transfer to key VTH staff and kaizen team.
Project Resources	Chris Shannon (SMP) 20% FTE VTH staff as required – kaizen team membership to be determined. Ellen Balke (Insight 2 Results) – as required up to 20%

BIBLIOGRAPHY

Chiarini, A. 2013. *Lean Organisations: From the Tools of Toyota Production System to Lean Office*. Milan: Springer-Verlag Italia.

Dombrowski, U., & Mielke, T. 2014. Lean Leadership – 15 Rules for a Sustainable Lean Implementation. Paper presented at the 47th CIRP Conference on Manufacturing Systems.

Emiliani, B. 2013. Lean Management Failure at HMRC. *Management Services*, 55(4): 13–15.

Farris, J. A., Van Aken, E. M., Doolen, T. L., & Worley, J. 2008. Learning From Less Successful Kaizen Events: A Case Study. *Engineering Management Journal*, 20(3): 10–20.

Fiume, O. 2007. Lean Strategy and Accounting: The Roles of the CEO and CFO. In: J. Stenzel (Ed.), *Lean Accounting: Best Practices for Sustainable Integration*. Hoboken, NJ: John Wiley and Sons Inc.

Glover, W. J., Farris, J. A., & Van Aken, E. M. 2014. Kaizen Events: Assessing the Existing Literature and Convergence of Practices. *Engineering Management Journal*, 26(1): 39–61.

Glover, W. J., Farris, J. A., & Van Aken, E. M. 2015. The Relationship between Continuous Improvement and Rapid Improvement Sustainability. *International Journal of Production Research*, 53(13): 4068–4086.

Lean Team (Ed.). 2017. *Becoming Lean: A Pocket Guide*. St Andrews, Scotland: University of St Andrews.

Liker, J., & Ballé, M. 2013. Lean Managers Must Be Teachers. *Journal of Enterprise Transformation*, 3(1): 16–32.

Miller, J. 2013. *Taiichi Ohno's Workplace Management, Special 100th Birthday Edition*. McGraw-Hill Companies Inc.

Robinson, M., & Yorkstone, S. 2014. Becoming a Lean University. *Leadership and Governance in Higher Education*, 1: 41–72.

Van Aken, E. M., Farris, J. A., Glover, W. J., & Letens, G. 2010. A Framework for Designing, Managing and Improving Kaizen Event Programs. *International Journal of Productivity and Performance Management*, 59(7): 641–667.

20

Cardiff University. A Lean University or a Better University?

Sarah Lethbridge

CONTENTS

CREATING THE LEAN UNIVERSITY PROGRAMME

The first word in the book *Lean Thinking* (Womack and Jones, 1996) is muda – which is Japanese for waste. The authors of this book then go onto to talking about the acquisition of 'muda glasses' i.e. the ability to spot wasteful practice wherever you go. One of the most troubling parts of being a specialist in improvement thinking are those 'muda glasses' which, over time, resemble less like glasses and more like permanent muda laser eye surgery. Given this effect, in 2006, as somewhat of a pioneer of muda laser eye surgical techniques, whilst working within Cardiff University, Professor Peter Hines was very keen to engage in discussions with the then Vice Chancellor of Cardiff University, David Grant, to propose and commence the £1/2 million pound Lean University programme. Professor Peter Hines was the then Director of the Lean Enterprise Research Centre (LERC), a fairly autonomous unit within Cardiff Business School, created in 1994 by Peter, as well as Daniel Jones, one of the authors of *The Machine that Changed the World* and *Lean Thinking*.

The LERC, in the 10 years since its inception, had worked with many large organisations, such as Tesco, to bring about positive improvement and change and had become experienced in 'action research' i.e. learning about Lean whilst also getting involved, helping to apply it. The LERC did much to galvanise different perspectives and approaches to the adoption of Lean within the UK and beyond and so it was perhaps only right that it should then use its expertise to help the organisation that it was part of.

The initial drivers for the Lean University project for Cardiff University have been officially listed as thus (Hines and Lethbridge, 2008): as a mechanism to improve bureaucratic structures and processes that weren't responsive and sensitive to customers' needs; that unprecedented growth due to a relatively recent merger with a large medical school meant that there were clunky and confusing adoption of different practices across the organisation; and finally, as a response to increasing commercial, competitive pressures within the UK and Global Higher Education sector. If the University were 'more Lean', it would achieve a competitive advantage.

From the LERC's perspective, the drivers for the project were twofold: to improve the environment within which it worked, increasing efficiency and effectiveness, and to also, as the 'world's leading Lean academic research centre', pursue a particularly unique 'academic challenge'. In 2006, Professor Peter Hines and I delivered a presentation at the Lean Educators Forum in Worcester, Massachusetts entitled 'Cardiff. A Lean University? I Wish!'; a title, not of my choosing (and one that still causes me pain) where the prevailing message was that academia was the last bastion of organisations yet to be 'touched by Lean' and that if we could bring Lean to the exceptionally 'challenging' University sector, by God, Lean really *could* be deployed anywhere!

And so it began, although it began in a rather unique way and one that I've never encountered since when working with numerous organisations to help them to deploy Continuous Improvement and Lean. As the LERC was keen to pursue the academic challenge, half of the project would be 'ours', to examine and research the challenge that was applying Lean to the University sector. The other half of the project would involve creating a central team, within the Strategic Development Division, who would be in charge of running the day-to-day operational approach to Lean change.

From the LERC's perspective, Year 1 was meant to be 'light touch' and 'low profile' in order to understand how best to adopt and adapt Lean thinking to the University sector. On reflection, it was surprising therefore that the central Lean Thinking team, with complete support from the

LERC it has to be said, should pursue an operational plan that sought to touch every single part of the University. The programme would comprise of three different elements as shown in Figure 20.1.

1. Strategy: Learning from the LERC's research into Lean sustainability, one of the key enablers of success was that organisations pursued strategy deployment, that Lean and Continuous Improvement was a senior decision to cascade and translate change throughout the whole organisation.
2. End to End: These were designed to be classic 'value stream' projects which examined and improved key processes that spanned a range of Schools and Divisions (now called Professional Services). They were: 'Procure to Pay' – how to buy and pay for external services; Programme Approval – setting up a new degree programme of study, and Supporting Research Funding – initiating a new research project, maintaining it and closing it down.
3. Continuous Improvement: These projects referred to Lean projects that were smaller in nature and were mainly initiated by a sponsor asking the Lean Team to come and help them to solve a particular issue or problem. These projects were more bound in terms of scope.

The central team consisted of four full-time members of staff working on the project, one of whom led the programme. The LERC team comprised of numerous different researchers such as Professor Peter Hines, all of whose time equated to four full-time equivalent members of staff. I was

Strategy	• Vision
	• Alignment
	• Prioritisation
	• Measures
	• Action Plans
End-to-End	• Current State
	• Future State
	• Implementation Plans
Continuous Improvement	• Specific Problem
	• Limited Area
	• Limited Tools

FIGURE 20.1

The three elements of the Lean University project.

the only researcher from LERC that was 100% funded by the project and Lean University was the first time that I led a Lean project by myself, that of 'Supporting Research Funding'.

TRIALS AND TRIBULATIONS

Up until the Lean University project, most of the Lean work that I had experienced involved a senior person within an external organisation inviting, and paying, for the LERC to examine their processes and help to bring about improvement. There was a sudden cachet to this arrangement. The host organisation and sponsor would already be hopeful of the progress and opportunity that the LERC could bring to their operation. Attention was immediate. Things were somewhat different when trying to enact change within the organisation in which you worked. 'Action research'/'quasi consultancy' projects with externals were largely short term in nature and nearly all had a defined end point. The mapping and investigative work would be done, improvements and conclusions reached, final presentation delivered. It was then the organisation's responsibility to implement the suggested changes and they could then hopefully relay the benefits of the improvement work to the LERC at a later point or we could research and investigate 'how well things had gone'. Lean University was the first time that I had experienced the trials and tribulations of being an *internal* change agent and as such, it was hugely illuminating to me and very important in terms of the development of my Lean knowledge. After a period of mapping and investigation, the team did not 'return home', we were home. In addition, it was very evident whether the project had 'worked' or not.

Early Lean University mapping workshops uncovered some very sensible, very useful improvement ideas. For example, within a project which looked at a backlog of legal tasks, one of the suggestions was to put model contracts on the internet and let researchers download and use them without permission from the legal team, a solution that Cambridge University already employed. Although it was appreciated that this would involve reassessing the organisation's approach to risk, a major shift, the Lean University project team thought that if 'watertight' but 'basic' best practice contracts were put up, something such as a standard Non Disclosure Agreement, this work could flow without joining a queue of activity troubling the very stressed and under pressure Legal Team. To use the Lean concept of 'runner, repeater and stranger' runner activity should seek to move to more of a 'self-serve' position to allow the Legal Team to use their expertise solely on the more complex tasks.

This improvement idea seemed relatively straightforward and relatively easy to implement, definitely worth a try anyway, so it was surprising therefore when this improvement was not instantly employed. After working on Lean University for a while, it began to become clear that indeed, it was not just this project that suffered from the strange phenomenon of perfectly sensible improvement suggestions not able to be implemented.

When asked why this would be the case, replies were largely either – lack of senior support for the change or that everyone was too busy to do the work needed to make the change. Both of which responses were likely very correct. Once you are a recipient of the muda laser eye surgical procedure, neither answers seem to make much sense however.

The longer the Lean University project went on, the importance of leadership as a key determinant of success became ever apparent. Actions happened when those in charge wanted them to happen. In addition, it became clear that there was a key difference between leaders expressing support for the initiative and those who were actually interested and would participate within the initiative. That is not to put all of the blame at these leaders' door, far from it, this situation merely illustrated a failure to effectively communicate the need for change and how and why Lean could help.

What's more, some tensions began to occur between the implementation team and research team in that their objectives were slightly different. Obviously, the implementation team's primary focus was making change. This was of course a goal of the research team but they were, for academic purposes of course, keen to spend time thinking about definitions and ensuring methodological rigour and as this project was just one of their many projects, availability was affected. This is not to say that definitions and methodological rigour are not an important part of successful improvement work, rather, that the urgency for change was different and the implementation team were keen to push on and not wait for the academics.

As progress was slow, soon it became obvious that the support of the LERC somewhat dwindled too. As many of the academics were working on multiple tasks, in the face of adversity, perhaps also affected by the reduced cachet that comes from internal change, they were easily distracted by other assignments and more pressing research questions.

Thus far, a somewhat bleak tale, however, it would be wrong to suggest that Lean University (2006–2009) didn't achieve positive outcomes.

KEY SUCCESSES

One of the most impactful elements of the Lean University was the Lean Skills for Managers programme, latterly, Lean Skills for Leaders programme. This programme involved working with several School Managers, some of the most senior Professional Service staff within the University, and other middle/senior administrators who were keen to learn about Lean.

The programme's aim was to share Lean knowledge with them which they could then incorporate within their approach to leading and managing. Each participant was assigned a 'Lean mentor', one of the members of the Lean University team, and they each set on working their own Lean improvement project within their own organisation. Suddenly, it became clear how different outcomes could be achieved when leaders owned the change and were responsible for its success within their own departments. How different than a change team attempting to drive both 'bottom up' change (encouraging those doing the value work) and 'top down' change (influencing senior members of staff to improve) when the change team itself possessed zero line managerial responsibility.

One of the notable successes occurred when the School Manager (who participated in the first Lean Skills for Managers programme) and Head of School within Nursing and Midwifery, both new in their roles, together adopted a Lean programme to first understand the School, and then improve it. They did this by firstly talking with staff and students to identify issues and problems at School level and then developing a strategic action plan about the order of how they were going to attempt to tackle them. One by one, different projects were initiated, projects which ranged from streamlining committee structures and improving the processing around their BSc in Clinical Practice. Whilst most affected staff and students agreed that this work made things better, measurement was undisciplined, so it is difficult to share the tangible before and after benefits.

Lean University also started to highlight another phenomenon of Lean improvement and change, that of the perception of 'project failure' when not all actions were completed. There should be an appreciation of *progress*, even when projects do not fully reach their potential. Within the 'Supporting Research Funding' project that I led, some of the improvement actions that the project teams identified were not completed, however several tactics *were* adopted. Tactics such as the addition of a standard operating procedure/visual management checklist being added to the paper files (likely now superseded by digital systems) to help to prompt when key actions within the research project were required.

Improvement is inherently a good thing to do, the right thing to do. It is somewhat strange to think that an attempt to improve an area could ever be a 'failure' when some good activities and achievements were made. Most projects didn't complete all of the actions that they identified, however, whilst somewhat guilty of researcher bias, it was often clear how the experience of a Lean approach to work and change moved the area on, regardless of whether those working within wanted to admit as such.

GROWING OUR KNOWLEDGE OF HOW TO APPLY LEAN WITHIN ACADEMIA

As previously discussed, Lean University was a very important project in terms of my Lean development. It enabled me to learn about how hard it is to make Lean work and gave me many lessons about how to improve my approach to improvement (Lethbridge, 2010). The experience definitely taught me the importance of measurement within change. How it wasn't enough to tell a story of how Lean improved things, concrete and tangible measurements were required – 'this process used to take 25 days to complete, now it takes 5' and as a consequence, this kind of 'before and after' story is now something I insist upon in my teaching of Lean (although whether people choose to follow that advice is questionable of course).

The biggest lesson was the importance of leadership within the process. It is not enough for the change agent to lead the project, although this is very important, senior leaders must *participate in and own the change.* Lean is not something that can be delegated. It must be led from the top, particularly within complex, highly autonomous organisations such as

Universities (Figure 20.2). As well as this top down drive, local leaders are also very important to create buy in and acceptance. The best way to 'convert' was through education, sharing key concepts and ideas and illustrating them as effective *leadership tools*. Indeed, some of the best Lean work was not declared as such, but merely declared as a proactive approach to leading teams.

In fact, leadership was such a strong determinant of success that 'pillars' of Lean improvement were seen to build around key individuals within the organisation. 'Platforms' of improvement that moved across University departments – those 'End-to-End' projects described earlier – were much more difficult to enact. (Pillar – a range of Lean tools deployed in a small defined area, often at the bequest of a leader who 'gets it' – narrow but deep. Platform – a thin application of Lean tools deployed in a large, cross departmental area – wide but shallow).

Indeed, on reflection, one of my key findings was how important it was to focus on 'point improvement' 'pillar' work in the early days of large system change. This is important because it focuses the lens of improvement within a locus of control that is manageable. Working closely with leaders to truly understand what is trying to be achieved, posits more chances of

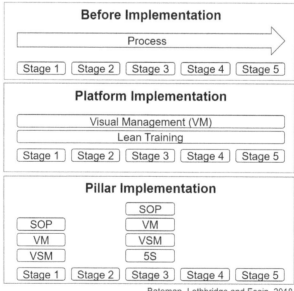

Bateman, Lethbridge and Esain, 2018

FIGURE 20.2

The pillar and platform analogy in process improvement work.

success within this type of organisational environment. Not only this, but in this case, it was actually important for the change team themselves to learn the best approach to trying to enact organisational change. Focusing on pillar/point activity in the first three years of the Lean University would, I believe, have been an excellent strategy designed to build support for the initiative and to organisationally learn the approach. The three large 'End to End' projects which 'touched' every part of the organisation were just too big to manage and convert.

In effect, it is my belief that that's what Lean University turned into as a change programme, something that focused on pillar/point work as a mechanism to enable improvement – however, what could have then happened was a later 'platform' approach which built on the support and understanding of those leaders who had all lead 'pillars'. To some extent, the enthusiasm for a system wide approach to improvement across a value stream had probably been 'used up' by the three 'End to End' projects. However, there should have been the courage and support to attempt this scale of initiative again once lessons had been fully learned. That in itself is the spirit of Continuous Improvement.

The Lean University programme formed one of the cases within a paper which looked at the use of the Pillar and Platform analogy within Public Sector process improvement (Bateman, Lethbridge and Esain, 2018) and it is hoped that the experience and learnings of Cardiff University, the first University in the UK to adopt a Lean methodology, has helped not only the University sector in general, but also large scale public sector change programmes.

In response to the twofold desires of the LERC to engage in the programme, to improve our University and better understand the 'academic challenge' of applying Lean in the University sector then both aims could be seen to have been successful. Lean University has definitely helped all those who worked within it to have a better understanding about how to enact organisational change and the University did progress over the course of those 3 years.

Thanks to the successes of the project, and the long-term commitment expressed by the University to develop and change, acknowledging that whole system change takes time, the Lean University team's work continued for many years after that first phase of the project ended and indeed, at times, the team grew considerably in size, but as I was pulled onto other projects, it would be wrong of me to comment on what was achieved in those latter years whilst I was not a close part of the programme. As an outside observer it was clear that following a 'boom period' the team then became smaller in size and was then subsumed within a newly formed team within Information Services, that of the Programme Management Office, whose role was to bring about technological improvement and change across the University.

INFLUENCE OF STRATEGY DEPLOYMENT AND LOOKING TO THE FUTURE

In 2012, Professor Colin Riordan joined the University as its new Vice Chancellor (VC). One of the first things that he instigated when he came was to instigate a new College Structure in order to streamline executive decisions and provide greater visibility. Previously, 27 Heads of School reported to the VC and Schools were fairly autonomous, particularly big and wealthy Schools such as Cardiff Business School! A College structure would enable greater clarity and speed of decision making and would help the organisation to collectively move together, onward and upward, as a more cohesive unit.

The second major initiative that he initiated was the creation of a new University wide strategy – The Way Forward (interestingly, but probably coincidentally, the same name as Ford Motor Company's 2006 strategy. To my Lean lasered eyes this strategy was everything that we were trying to achieve within the strategy element of the Lean University project. A consistent and stretching vision for the future which clearly expressed what the University had to achieve if it wanted to progress in the University rankings. Most importantly of all, this strategy had the Vice Chancellor completely behind it and now also the new College structure within which to communicate a new direction. For 5 years, The Way Forward was deployed and Cardiff University did indeed increase and improve its academic standing. Most pleasingly, The Way Forward was succeeded by The Way Forward (2018–2023) (https://www.cardiff.ac.uk/thewayfo rward) to continue the trajectory of progress. There is no doubt that this strategy has power and weight within the University. It motivates change and provides direction as to how to proceed.

So in 2018, the University is probably the most strategically aligned and focussed on improvement and change than it has ever been. The competition within the sector is the fiercest it has ever been; the political, social and economic environment that we operate within, has never been so tough and unforgiving. Of course, much has still to be achieved, but thanks to The Way Forward, we have the enabling strategic deployment 'platform' to help us achieve what we need to achieve. Interestingly, a 'Transforming Professional Services' programme has recently begun to again, challenge slow, bureaucratic processes that aren't sensitive to customers' needs. From my perspective, I sincerely hope that the lessons learned from Lean University, the good and the bad, are reflected and acted upon to help Cardiff University continue its pursuit of the (painful and challenging) activity that is positive organisational change.

REFERENCES

Bateman, N., Lethbridge, S. and Esain, A. 2018. "Pillar or Platform—A Taxonomy for Process Improvement Activities in Public Services". *Public Money & Management* 38(1): 5.

Hines, P. and Lethbridge, S. 2008. "Creating a Lean University". *Public Money & Management* 28(1): 53.

Lethbridge, S. 2010. The Ethnography of Organisational Change within a Lean University. Ethnography Symposium, The University of Liverpool. https://www.liverpool.ac.uk/media/livacuk/schoolofmanagement/docs/abstracts/ethnography2010/Lethbridge.pdf.

Womack, J. and Jones, D. 1996. *Lean Thinking*. Simon & Schuster.

Section VI

Culture

21

Developing a Culture – The Essentials for Continuous Improvement

Natasha Bennett and John Perkins

CONTENTS

INTRODUCTION

Middlesex University established the Business Enhancement Team (BET) in 2014 with the overall aim to support business improvements, enhanced ways of working and to facilitate a culture of continuous improvement across the University.

This empowerment recognised the importance of building an in-house change team with a strong commitment to lean and a sustainable model of working.

In this chapter we will explore our approach, toolkit and learning in building this culture of sustainable continuous improvement across the institution.

We demonstrate our overarching aim through:

- Process redesign, contributing to improved outcomes for students and stakeholders
- Identifying opportunities for capacity creation

- A focus on performance, data analysis and evidence-based decisions
- Cross functional problem solving
- The skills transfer of our improvement tools to contributing to improved working relationships and communication

The two lean principles of continuous improvement and respect for people are core to the belief that our approach offers both fundamental process improvements and the local engagement of staff. These expectations are an increasingly significant part of building the working culture at Middlesex. Continuous improvement and staff engagement feature explicitly as core work streams within our People and Culture Plan, as well as inclusion in our organisational values and the University Strategy 2017–2022.

We define continuous improvement as:

> An ongoing commitment to make both incremental and breakthrough changes to our processes and services, for the benefit of all members of our community.

OUR KEY DRIVERS

The challenge is to build a culture of continuous improvement that will be sustained for the long term; in response to increasing sector competition and expectations of efficiency and effectiveness:

Delivering efficiency and value for money is an absolute operational priority. All stakeholders rightly expect efficient use of resources and in the UK's current financially austere times, investment to maintain excellence in both education and research will often come through efficiencies. Thus, to meet the demands of competitiveness in the 21st century, universities must work in ever smarter and more innovative ways.*

Our People and Culture plan describes an environment where staff are engaged in a high-performance culture in which consideration for what we do and how we work can be continually improved. We see employee engagement as essential:

---

* Professor Sir Ian Diamond 2015 http://www.universitiesuk.ac.uk/policy-and-analysis/reports/Pages/efficiency-effectiveness-and-value-for-money.aspx

Only organisations that truly engage and inspire their employees produce world class levels of innovation, productivity and performance.*

In practice this means developing a culture where staff are actively involved in developing and designing changes in their own area of expertise. This is about actively encouraging local problem solving and decision making, creating a climate where challenge is expected, stakeholder needs are prioritised and improvements enhance the overall student experience.

Our approach supports the explicit university priority to provide effective systems and processes for our staff and students together with the value for money expectations facing the higher education sector. There is a recognition that we need robust processes to support both improved service design and delivery. These improvements must deliver positive outcomes for our students and free institutional resource for teaching and learning.

Four years into our evolution we are increasingly contributing to our wider organisational development expectations for a more agile and developed workforce particularly in support of organisational change, workforce planning and capability development.

OUR CORE APPROACH AND TOOLKIT

Our approach goes beyond process redesign or the facilitation of "rapid improvement events". Our work with teams seeks to embed a toolkit that includes (Figure 21.1):

- Process redesign
- Communication Cells
- Visual management and the use of operational performance indicators
- Standard work
- Creative problem solving
- Workplace review

---

* Engaging for success: David McLeod 2009.

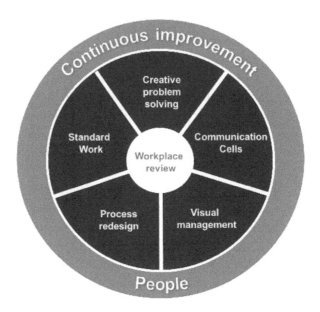

FIGURE 21.1
Continuous improvement toolkit.

Together these tools interlink to support a continuous improvement culture that is proactive, responsive and student focused. Whilst true to the core values and tools of lean working, we have taken a pragmatic approach, adopting the language and crafting the message for Middlesex University.

Key has been the introduction of *Communication Cells* – a daily forum (10 to 15-minute meetings) for teams to meet to discuss their workload, priorities and review performance. The use of visual management and performance indicators assist. Most significantly these forums are team led, with facilitation by all encouraged to share successes, lessons learnt and the opportunity to identify ongoing incremental improvements.

> The Comms cell has been an equalizer within the team. Regardless of grade or role, everyone has an opportunity to lead, raise concerns, ideas and ask 'what happened' to those raised previously.

To date we have 30 Communication Cells in place with over 300 staff trained, and an active community of practice membership of over 40.

The introduction of *visual management*, combined with operational performance indicators, is more traditionally seen in manufacturing and high-volume service industries. Core to our Middlesex toolkit, teams are utilising display boards to visualise the work of a team; whether this work is being done well or if the volume of work is being managed well. Intended to be highly informative they prompt the action of team members to focus and prioritise their efforts.

> Visual Management is an ideal tool for gaining a snapshot of performance at designated points during the day. The Duty Managers have found this very useful both to fill in the data on the board and using it for resource analysis; an excellent way to plan organise and prioritise all projects that now must be data-led.

The addition of visual operational *performance indicators* provide focus on the satisfaction of service users (e.g. time, data, quality). Ongoing work with both senior managers and planning is facilitating the opportunity to achieve a greater line of sight with Departmental and University KPIs.

The *workplace review* provides a regular opportunity for senior management engagement, challenge and support. At Middlesex the "workplace review" consists of a set of key questions and areas of focus that include performance, challenges and skills development. It brings a level of visibility and transparency which highlights how teams are using the tools and evidence continuous improvement activity.

Creative problem solving provides an objective structure which teams, or members from multiple different teams, are using to solve problems collaboratively. This structured approach is being utilised to establish clear problem and goal statements, understand the "current state" and encourage the analysis of "root causes" before agreeing a plan of action. This is proving invaluable.

The language of 5Why's and root causes is increasingly utilised and understood as is the discipline of monitoring the results of the actions taken: What works? What doesn't work? What can be done differently?

Together with process redesign, Communication Cells also provide the opportunity to identify larger scale improvements. We are increasingly using A3 problem solving in the identification of root causes, the exploration of options and solutions. Together with an increased focus on data analysis, this creative approach encourages evidence-based decision making.

The impact of this approach has successfully facilitated greater collaboration between process stakeholders and a shared awareness of the "problem" among multiple teams. In one example, 6 hours of problem solving led to clarity of action which resolved a longstanding issue for nursing students – they weren't able to receive their timetables online after enrolment. The approach was undertaken with representatives from Student Records, Timetabling, The Nursing Programme Team and IT, and achieved a reduction of duplication, over processing and delivery time and received positive feedback from the Director of Programme: "…we are thrilled to have got this far…after 4 years!".

Our toolkit has not been without ongoing learning and evaluation. Early feedback has led to an increasingly flexible approach and local ownership of the tools.

> Sometimes the methodology can seem a little clunky as it's quite stan-dardised but this is also one of its core strengths in terms of collaboration across teams using a common framework.

Our agreed priorities as a central team are to deliver:

1. Cross institutional reviews driven by the university strategy
2. An investment in skills transfer to ensure local ownership for improvements and capabilities

The project work we undertake follows five phases:

1. Start-up
2. Diagnostic
3. Design
4. Implementation
5. Embed and sustain

The delivery of large cross functional end to end processes includes the investment in skills transfer and the practical application of the toolkit described previously as a core deliverable of project work. Our measures of success relate to whether tangible benefits of an improved quality of service and increased efficiency are delivered, in addition to an improved staff experience. We see the embedding of these tools as having a critical and positive effect on this staff experience.

Examples of institutional wide end to end reviews to date include areas such as admissions; assessment; timetabling; overseas operations; research administration; and academic partnerships. Faculty or Professional Services reviews have included core processes and work with: student placements; departmental and programme administration; finance; human resources; employability; and student wellbeing.

The increasing emphasis on institutional end to end reviews not only delivers more effective processes but also breaks down silo working, increasing a collective understanding of our strategic aims.

> Working with BET connected the project we were delivering to the whole of the University; opened doors to other departments/people in the University and broke down barriers.
>
> The overall effect has been to move towards a more consistent and effective way of working as a team. It has helped instill a collaborative culture and gelled the team together. We will carry learnings from the project forward to continue improving processes and make our interaction with other teams more efficient.

Achieving these deliverables has forced us to adapt the structure of our centralised team in order to meet the demand for work. We find that our current flat structure enables us to support multiple, concurrent projects, both larger end to end institutional wide and smaller functional reviews alongside rapid improvement events, and problem solving.

Our increasing investment in skills transfer will enable over time a reduction in support for smaller scale improvement reviews (e.g. function specific) which should be led locally.

HOW DO WE MEASURE IMPACT – OUR BALANCED SCORECARD?

Our early experience was that the collection of baseline data, while essential, was not readily available. The reliance on anecdotal "evidence" was prevalent. This may still occur if unchallenged.

The lesson learned early on was that it's not acceptable to say "some of us think it feels better", "we will do that soon" or "I think it has gotten worse". "Some" is not a number, "worse" is not measurable and "soon" is not a timescale. Measuring benefits begins with understanding the current state of any situation, regardless of whether seeking to solve a problem, close a gap in performance targets or improve the efficiency of a process.

Our learning was that this must be done through collecting facts about the problem, opportunity or process. These facts can be described through the use of numbers, measurements and observations and therefore can become data to be used as a reference or baseline measurement, or for further analysis. For example, the number and type of enquiries received, the length of time taken to resolve/respond these enquiries, the route those enquiries have travelled in order to be resolved, and the transparency of the enquiry process.

It allows for a comparison "before" and "after" a change or intervention has been implemented. The ideal is to be able to demonstrate that a change has had a positive effect in addressing a problem, process or help to reach a target. At Middlesex, we aim to ensure that the positive effect of changes are felt by our students, staff and are demonstrable in more effective/efficient processes.

> I think it's very important that organisationally we start talking the same language and engaging fully in data led decision making. The BET process has provided us with a framework that enables that.

Our approach is to demonstrate a balanced scorecard of measurable benefits across our three overarching performance indicators:

- Sustainable Capacity Creation
- Student and Stakeholder Benefits (Quality of Service)
- Staff Experience (Figure 21.2)

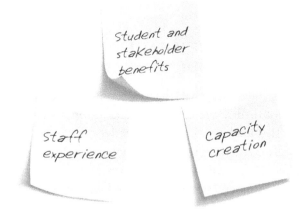

FIGURE 21.2
Our balanced scorecard.

We define *Capacity Creation* as released time (measured as a monetary value) which can be used for value added activities, resource flexing, productivity or savings. This has subsequently been adjusted to include the revised HEFCE (Higher Education Funding Council England) expectations of efficiencies including resource releasing, cash releasing and additional productivity gains.

There has been a concerted effort to focus on freeing up staff time to allow a greater focus on core or value add activity. The removal of process waste helps to identify the resource time recovered. In order to measure the value of this to the institution, the notional cost of time saved is converted to pounds and pence.

Student and Stakeholder Benefits measure improvements in service delivery through a wide range of quality indicators that include turnaround times, end to end process time, errors or rework, clarity of roles and responsibilities and measures of compliance.

We have found that it can be initially difficult to get traction by using terms like "service excellence" or "quality" as it can leave an amount of ambiguity about what it may actually mean; similarly, there can be some resistance to the terminology of "customer". Our focus is to seek tangible improvements to the experience of students and stakeholders whether we are focussed on a process, fixing a problem or looking how to hit a new target.

> I appreciate that at its inception the focus was efficiency and cost saving but I believe that a focus around students at the heart is what does and should drive the work of the team. If cost savings can be achieved this is a secondary beneficial outcome but doesn't fully capture the breadth/value of the work.

Measures for *Staff Experience* monitor the impact on job satisfaction using a range of staff engagement and people indicators.

We use our Staff Survey results to help establish baselines for staff experience across the University. Our current work has been to establish how to draw a stronger "cause & effect" relationship between the use of continuous improvement philosophy and the impact on specific survey responses which relate to communication, collaboration, change and empowerment of and for our staff.

Our evidence gathering includes the long-term changes in behaviours and practice that include how managers manage, the impact on collaborative working across the University and the sense in which staff at all levels and all roles feel empowered to make changes to the way they work and deliver services.

One of our long-term aims is to continue to explore correlations with our employee engagement survey scores.

> The capture and systematising of processes has delivered many benefits - firstly efficiency but also improved stakeholders relationships and empowerment of staff (Table 21.1).

OUR ROLE AS FACILITATORS AND ENABLERS OF CHANGE

BET works on the principle of "with you and not to you" working with colleagues, facilitating change. It is this impartiality that is vital in supporting genuine cross functional improvement and collaboration.

Or are we really project managers accountable for the delivery of improvements – including implementation and traction?

The investment in skills transfer is a priority with the emphasis on coaching colleagues to lead their own local improvements and in guiding managers and staff ahead of larger improvement projects. Our training provision concentrates on our core improvement tools, the use of operational data, problem solving and the realisation of benefits. Our practitioner development programme enhances this skills transfer.

The role of BET is to:

- Work with areas to identify the opportunities for capacity creation and improvements.
- Ensure that the recommendations and improvements identified are agreed and signed off by project sponsors and senior managers.
- Monitor progress of improvement plans.
- Escalate concerns where progress is not being made.

This demands close and collective ownership with sponsors, project leads and subject matter experts regarding project milestones, ensuring revised processes meet business needs and thorough stakeholder analysis and communication.

TABLE 21.1

Indicators of Benefits Realisation

	Potential Indicators of Benefit Realisation		
	Student & Stakeholder Benefits	Staff Experience Benefits	Efficiency Benefits including Capacity Creation[a]
Examples	NSS results improve	Staff feel the university learns from successes & mistakes	Capacity release (release of staff time)
	Welcome survey results improve	Staff feel empowered to make improvement suggestions	Hard costs (stationary, software, systems no longer required)
	Student progression rates improve	Staff feel able to make improvements happen	Cost avoided (prevented expenditure)
	Reduction in waiting time (Internal)	Staff feel local co-operation between teams is good	Additional revenue (protecting or generating new income)
	Fewer enquiries	Staff feel wider co-operation between teams is good	Enabling (e.g. improved compliance, supporting pre-existing business cases)
	Reduction of errors or rework	Staff are aware of how their service contributes to MDX objectives	
	Reduction in end-to-end process time	Staff feel their service/ School provides an excellent student experience	
		Increased skillset of staff	

[a] Further defined for HFECE efficiency reporting across cash releasing, resource releasing and productivity efficiency gains

The accountability for the realisation of identified capacity creation and the delivery of improvements lies with the appropriate senior managers and project sponsors.

Our programme is led by the priorities of the University strategic plan and strong Executive advocacy. Stakeholder involvement and senior sponsorship is fundamental in all stages of project scoping, delivery and design. Governance is monitored through our Steering Group, chaired by the COO with feedback and learning through our highly valuable Community of Practice.

Project prioritisation is dependent on a scoring matrix that includes defined criteria for strategic fit, sponsorship and scope together with a business readiness assessment that includes access to resources – both people and financial.

Ensuring active academic and student involvement allows a greater understanding of the student perspective as a key part of project delivery.

Opportunities for wider engagement include "report outs" and case studies to share outcomes and learning. This "story telling" from teams and advocates facilitates wider recognition of outcomes and benefits.

Increasingly close working with our Planning function enables vital collaboration around business intelligence and reporting. There is a recognised need for the shared prioritisation of programmes with IT to enable their ability to respond to systems requirements and feasibility options.

INSIGHT AND LEARNING – DEVELOPING MATURITY

This is not about the introduction of lean methodology in isolation. Much of our learning reflects the wider cultural impact of changes to our ways of working, highlighting the importance of a whole-system approach to organisational change. Our learning cuts across a range of issues that relate to people, process and systems:

- The need for clarity of expectations, roles and responsibilities; there can be a lack of oversight and accountability. This is complicated by the fact that ownership for any one complete process in a University often travels through numerous functions and teams.
- The importance of a line of sight to unit plans and strategic objectives.
- The shifting role of managers to coaches, in how they manage day-to-day.
- The importance of effective role modeling at all levels.
- The need for compliance and consistency – there can be a tension between the lean principle of a "best way" and a need to recognise exceptions.
- Over engineered processes slowing responses to students and staff.
- A lack of baseline data limiting short term opportunities for demonstrating improvements.

- Vulnerability where the use of data and performance indicators highlight inefficiencies.
- A lack of information or information sharing causing duplication and inefficiencies.

The importance of senior management endorsement and challenge is critical. Issues faced in some early projects included a difficulty in guaranteeing ownership beyond the formal project end and improvement plans were not always implemented. Our approach had worked well in engaging staff during the life of a project, but did not always extend to post-project life. A palpable dip in engagement and therefore the delivery of identified improvements could occur which allowed medium/long term plans for service improvement to gather dust in a dark corner the office, or a disused folder.

In response, we have developed a structured approach to post project sustainment through ongoing monitoring and coaching. This model of support follows four stages from beginning through to adopting, business as usual and leading.

This work included our ongoing participation in activities such as daily communication cells and workplace reviews, but also our continued support of activities that fostered collaboration through ongoing process redesign and creative problem solving. Often this facilitative support was contained assistance with planning for, and co-delivery, or lending experience which helped to move through the structure for creative problem solving session with the key stakeholders present.

We have developed key characteristics to objectively describe how teams were using the tools. Those characteristics were then plotted against a continuum from which four levels of "maturity" were defined for the adoption of continuous improvement behaviour and tools. The maturity scale has been developed to be evidence based and is used to assess the progress at the end of a project, and again every six months (Table 21.2).

The scale and characteristics are being utilised by managers to provide an overall direction to head in, which is seeing teams strive towards the "Leading" end of the continuum. The practical use in the Business Enhancement Team has been in our own visual management to help focus and prioritise the work of our "embed & sustain" function. Success here is for teams/departments to reach the next level of maturity.

To improve our "embed & sustain" function further, a deliberate move towards coaching has taken place. We are actively advocating ownership

TABLE 21.2

Maturity Assessment Model

	Beginning 1	Adopting 2	Business as Usual 3	Leading 4
CONTINUOUS IMPROVEMENT CAPABILITIES	Opportunities to release staff time identified at the end of a project	Staff time released at the end of a project	Staff time has been released within the team but outside a project lifespan	Active collaboration with other teams has led to the release of staff time outside of a project lifespan
	Service improvements identified at the end of a project	Service improvements implemented at the end of a project	Service improvements implemented within the team but outside a project lifespan	Service improvements implemented through proactive collaboration outside the team and outside a projectlifespan
	Opportunities to improve staff experience identified at the end of a project	Improvements to staff experience have been implemented at the end of a project	Improvements to staff experience implemented outside a project lifespan	Improvements to staff experience implemented through proactive collaboration with other teams, outside a project lifespan
	Team trained in the use of core tools	Use of some core tools evident	Use of all core tools evident	Use and advocacy of core tools evident
	Key processes documented and VoC collected at the end of a project	"To be" processes produced based on voice of the customer at the end of a project	"To be" processes created and implemented with VOC outside a project lifespan	Team proactively review processes with voice of the customer on an ongoing basis

(Continued)

TABLE 21.2 (CONTINUED)

Maturity Assessment Model

	Beginning 1	Adopting 2	Business as Usual 3	Leading 4
PERFORMANCE METRICS	Relevant baseline data collected during the lifespan of a project	Relevant baseline data used develop performance metrics during the lifespan of a project	Data collected on an ongoing basis to generate new performance targets outside of a project lifespan	New performance indicators developed consistently through data analysis
	Peaks and troughs in work demand established	Skills and resource needed to address the peaks and troughs in work demand are transparent	Demand-driven resource flexing informed by data	Resource flexed outside of the team to support university-wide peaks and troughs
LEADERSHIP, ENGAGEMENT AND CULTURE	Few of the Middlesex Values are role modelled by managers	Some of the Middlesex Values are role modelled by managers	Most Middlesex Values are role modelled by managers	All Middlesex Values role modelled by managers
	Few of the Middlesex Values are role modelled by team	Few of the Middlesex Values are role modelled by team	Few of the Middlesex Values are role modelled by team	Few of the Middlesex Values are role modelled by team
	Service Plan objectives visible and available	Activity implemented to Service Plan objectives	Progress & success against Service Plan objectives monitored and tracked using data	Collaboration evident with other areas to help shape future Service Plans
PEOPLE	Skills within team have been identified	Development for team planned and implemented	Coaching in place Success is recognised 1-to-1's are modelled around personal development	Best practices actively pursued outside of the team

of cultural and behavioural change, and the role of coach has been to provide insight and encouragement for change and improvement methods, by utilising the local subject matter expertise on more of a one-to-one basis. Through use of the GROW model and coaching for improvement (based on the coaching Kata) there has been a significant improvement in local ownership which has been shown by "distance travelled" using our maturity scale.

Other benefits have been the organic development of advocates for continuous improvement who are confident and capable when sharing their experience in successes and lessons learned with colleagues. This active *Community of Practice* has the specific aim to facilitate learning and collaboration among the many advocates of continuous improvement across Middlesex with the expectation that members will take active roles in improvement activity.

Our Continuous Improvement Practitioner Programme has a focus on a simple toolkit to build both skills and confidence in problem solving and continuous improvement. Specific objectives include to create an understanding of the core principles of lean and continuous improvement; to demonstrate how a continuous improvement toolkit can support service delivery together with the use of appropriate metrics and measures to evidence the benefits of change. Modules, together with the practical application of a local improvement project and a "report out," allows delegates to achieve accreditation through LCS. *Leadership workshops* support leadership groups to collectively explore the crucial leadership role in support of problem solving and improvements and service delivery.

In response to the pull for service-based improvement practitioners we are currently exploring the potential for *secondment opportunities* within BET. It is anticipated that this will further mature the role of the central team.

CONCLUSION

Our overall aim is to support business improvements, enhanced ways of working and to facilitate a culture of continuous improvement across the University. In this chapter we have explored our approach, toolkit and some of our learning for this to be sustainable across the institution.

We are committed to ongoing evaluation and review; success will only come from an ongoing institutional pull together with the demonstration of benefits. This proof of impact is bringing a greater understanding of the implications for our working culture; our values and the leadership of continuous improvement are key to long term success.

The inclusion of our institutional value: "We shape the future, continuously improving on what has gone before" is testament to the increasing acceptance of the language of continuous improvement.

From initiation, BET have built on the wider opportunity for a joined up approach to organisational development in recognition that continuous improvement is part of broader cultural change. Close working with Human Resources ensures the expectations, behaviours and practices of continuous improvement are increasingly part of recruitment, our leadership model and development provision.

Ultimately organisational change is demonstrated by individuals changing... and whilst we benefit from the strong advocacy and role modelling of our CFO – "You can't afford not to do it"; it is the testament of staff using the approach daily that brings the greatest satisfaction:

> I can't imagine going back to the way we worked. We are now able to utilise all the skills that we learnt in order to make our jobs easier and produce higher quality work. One of the greatest things to come out of it, for me, was how learning these new skills will help me develop my career in the future.

22

Growing a Lean Approach in a Changing University

Brent Hurley and Stephen Yorkstone

CONTENTS

INTRODUCTION

Edinburgh Napier University was a relatively early adopter of lean-type improvement in the UK Higher Education sector. The university has had some form of team implementing a lean approach since 2009. This case study looks at the various iterations this team has gone through, to explore lessons learned and explain how the current devolved approach has evolved. It examines the importance of influencing culture and supporting a decentralised approach through developing a suite of continuous improvement training opportunities, a mentoring programme and the establishment of a community of practice. It looks at the evolution of a Business Improvement Framework and the establishment of strong alignment to strategy through embedding Business Improvement in the University's strategic change portfolio. It is hoped that by describing the evolution that the approach has gone through this will provide the opportunity for colleagues to reflect on similarities or differences with their own approach, and that this will help to further shape their lean journey.

ABOUT EDINBURGH NAPIER UNIVERSITY

Edinburgh Napier University (www.napier.ac.uk) is an internationally recognised University located across three campuses in Scotland's historic capital city. Edinburgh Napier University is a modern public University, having originated from Napier Technical College which was founded in 1964, and gained University status in 1992. There are over 19,500 students of which 11,000 are based on campus and 8,500 are studying worldwide on transnational education and online programmes. Students are represented from over 140 countries worldwide. Edinburgh Napier University is the largest provider of Higher Education in Hong Kong with more than 3,000 students studying there.

Edinburgh Napier University is in the top five percent of Universities worldwide according to the Times Higher Education World University Rankings, and has twice received the Queen's Anniversary Prize for Higher and Further Education, most recently in 2015 for work in timber engineering, sustainable construction and wood science. The University employs 1,700 staff across a range of professional services departments and six Schools: Applied Sciences; Arts and Creative Industries; Business; Computing; Engineering and the Built Environment; and Health and Social Care.

Edinburgh Napier University's current direction is articulated in the ambitious Strategy 2020: Building Success. The vision is to be an enterprising and innovative community renowned internationally, with an unrivalled student learning experience. This vision is underpinned by four key strategic objectives and the University values.

Our strategic objectives are to: grow our academic reputation; deliver an excellent personalised student experience; foster innovation, enterprise and citizenship; and internationalise our work.

Our values are to be: professional, ambitious, innovative and inclusive.

EDINBURGH NAPIER UNIVERSITY'S LEAN JOURNEY 2009–2012

Edinburgh Napier University began its lean journey in 2009. The initiative was initially badged as "Continuous Improvement" and later as "Sustainable Futures." The avoidance of the term "lean" was intended to allow for flexibility in approach, and was also to distance the activity from unsuccessful lean branded initiatives in other local organisations.

The name "Sustainable Futures" was intended to reflect the goal of the activity in ensuring better use of resources to support the longevity of the organisation. The then University Principal took responsibility for the initiative, appointing a senior staff member as a direct report to champion the initiative full time. This senior staff member took initial line management for the team.

Two staff members were redeployed from an internal project management function, and significant external consultancy support was secured to enable a 5-day rapid improvement event type rollout. An external consultancy with proven success in deploying their model in the wider Scottish public sector was engaged to support this.

The team was initially tasked with identifying and implementing operational and process improvements to ensure optimal utilisation of resources. This approach led to some significant successes, however, the approach was also limited in its impact by the style of consultancy and its fit with the existing organisational culture. It was seen by some participants as too directive, and some of the rapid improvement events undertaken did not meet expectations.

The legacy of these early stages persists in a high level of lean understanding in pockets of the organisation, and has informed the development of an approach that works developmentally with the existing organisational culture.

EDINBURGH NAPIER UNIVERSITY'S LEAN JOURNEY 2012–2016

In 2012 line management for the improvement function moved from the Principal's Office to the Director of Finance, Planning and Commercial Services, and the university recruited two staff members with experience in lean in higher education and six sigma in the telecommunications sectors respectively.

The arrival of these two Senior Consultants led to a change in direction, with specialist expertise again able to support University wide staff in carrying out process improvement activities, and this time to develop a model in house to enable improvement. This model was explicitly developed with the aim of promoting the lean fundamentals of continuous improvement founded on respect for people. Support was primarily provided through workshop facilitation, training and coaching, consultancy, and rapid improvement events.

To maximise impact of the small team, training and coaching provision was key, and provided in partnership with the university's Human Resources (HR) department. This training took the form of a series of short half day courses introducing key concepts, such as "Continuous Improvement Tools and Thinking" and "Process Improvement." Alongside these courses a year-long programme based on action learning sets and coaching, known as "Continuous Improvement Partners (CIPs)" was developed.

In 2014 the "Sustainable Futures" function was restructured into the University's Information Services Department, to reflect the role that this part of the organisation has in leading change, and the synergy between change and technological innovation.

EDINBURGH NAPIER UNIVERSITY'S APPROACH TODAY (FROM 2017)

The Edinburgh Napier University approach further evolved in 2017 and is centred on a Business Improvement Programme as one of six programmes in a Change Portfolio approach adopted by the University. The staffing resource from Sustainable Futures was redeployed to form a dedicated Business Improvement Team.

The term "Business Improvement" is intended to describe all initiatives that relate to lean, process improvement and projects that have a significant process or systems improvement aspect. In this approach the focus is on alignment of change with strategy, with Business Improvement as a key enabler of all strategic change (rather than being a specific strategic objective in and of itself).

The key drivers for Business Improvement are a desire to enhance the student journey and to support academic staff. The aim is to release academic time for value adding activities such as research and teaching, rather than carrying out administrative activities.

The model can be characterised as a decentralised approach combining strategic top-down leadership and bottom-up empowerment of staff. This is built on the learning carried through from the Sustainable Futures team to today, specifically the importance of taking a developmental approach.

Strategic direction for the initiative comes from the University Principal and senior leadership team, initially being led by the University Secretary then the Director of Finance and Operations. The empowerment of staff is supported through a Business Improvement Framework, which amongst other things includes events which create and nurture an internal community of practice.

The rationale behind the model is a belief that by using a decentralised approach change is more sustainable, and longer term results will be achieved. The approach also reflects the reality of the organisation in two ways. Firstly, that an increased level of resource would be required if a centralised model were to be adopted. Secondly, that the decentralised nature of decision making in Universities means that a number of improvement services or support functions have emerged organically, and these can work better when co-ordinated, even informally.

In a rapidly changing Higher Education sector with internal and external changes, including leadership, it is hoped that an approach incorporating bottom-up empowerment of staff will be more resilient.

BUSINESS IMPROVEMENT FRAMEWORK

The Business Improvement Framework brings together both new and existing information on Business Improvement tools, training, "people who can help", external resources, FAQs and case studies, and is designed to support and empower staff to carry out improvements. The Continuous Improvement Partners programme is now part of this framework. For staff that have identified an area of their work where there is an opportunity to make an improvement, but are not sure how to begin, the framework is there to support them, their line Manager and their colleagues.

A series of tools are being developed to support the framework. One example tool, which supports HR's Organisational Change team is a Change Readiness Diagnostic. This anonymously allows teams to review how prepared they are for change, and links into appropriate levels of support from the Organisational Change and Business Improvement teams.

Another example of a newly developed tool is the Student Journey Map. Presented in the format of an "underground tube station map" it is being used by academic and administrative teams University wide to help them identify the greatest opportunities to enhance the student journey. It was initially used as a very effective tool at two separate workshops to engage with both front-line staff and with the University's senior leadership team. From both a strategic and front-line perspective there was a very consistent view of the priority projects and this approach helped facilitate decision making, with a Personal Development Tutor Project being subsequently initiated.

These tools are additionally part of the University's strategy to support our development into an increasingly innovative and enterprising culture, which includes our in-house approach to Design Thinking.

The framework is conceived on an affirmative approach. It is intended to support the empowerment of staff in their own areas by not putting in place a large centralised resource, but instead highlighting the existing good practice that already exists in many areas, and enable further growth from this position. It is hoped that this will lead to a sustainable model of change towards a lean culture that develops as a natural part of the way the university works.

The University's Strategy 2020 sets the tone for this, noting: "We value, recognise and reward staff contributions and achievement, and empower them to innovate and take decisions, so that the University is known as a great place to work."

For the decentralised approach to work effectively, it is important that staff have both the capability and capacity to carry out improvements. Although some central support is essential there is emphasis on individual staff members being supported initially, but then taking increasing ownership.

While the central Business Improvement Team only consists of one or two staff members, there are several staff across the University who take responsibilities for aspects of improvement, without full time responsibility for institutional Business Improvement. Most notably these include the Portfolio Manager in the Principal's Office, Project Managers in the Information Services division, Learning and Development and Organisational Change staff in HR, and Enhancement Leads in centralised academic administration – the School Support Service.

The capability aspect is supported in a variety of ways, primarily through the resources described in the Business Improvement Framework but also through other events and training. Business Improvement training has expanded to a suite of training options now including "Engaging with Change", and our HR Learning and Development team have responded to a consistent concern from staff members with time management and prioritisation training. Business Improvement training is targeted at both front-line and managerial staff.

With around 40 staff having progressed through the Continuous Improvement Partners programme, and many more having been involved in facilitated workshops, coaching or other improvement activities, there is a growing level of bottom-up capability in lean type improvement.

CONTINUOUS IMPROVEMENT PARTNERS INITIATIVE

Continuous Improvement Partners is a groundswell personal development initiative, where a small group of staff take part in an annual programme of 10 action learning sets and monthly mentoring, in order to develop skills in applying continuous improvement to their work.

Based on research undertaken by an Edinburgh Napier University research student, the programme was co-founded by HR's Learning and Development team and Sustainable Futures and started in 2014. By deliberately drawing together people from across different functions and hierarchies, the programme supports shared understanding across boundaries within the organisation.

Together the action learning sets and monthly mentoring relationships aim to enable a sustained difference to participants work and beyond. It hopes to show how a relatively small group of people consistently modelling positive improvement and the University values can have a significant impact on the entire organisation.

This training was recognised in early 2017 with a runner up award from the Institute of Continuous Improvement in Public Services (ICiPS). This is national recognition of the innovative work Edinburgh Napier is doing in embedding continuous improvement as part of how the institution works.

Participants have said:

"CIP has strengthened my belief in collaborative processes having more impact."

"The CIP programme has given me the tools/models I require to think of continuous improvement on a daily basis."

"Mentoring a CIP has enabled me to understand what it is like for academic colleagues in the university in a way I hadn't before."

IMPROVEMENT PROJECTS

Prioritisation of improvement activities has led to a programme of work focussed on delivering key projects and supporting colleagues to carry out a range of process improvements, initially focussed on supporting HR.

The model utilised when supporting staff in interventions is largely based on the University of St Andrews eight step approach to process improvement. For pragmatic reasons the approach is tailored to take account of the capacity of participants, and this is also reflective of the scale and complexity of the process improvement being undertaken.

BUSINESS IMPROVEMENT PROJECT EXAMPLE: END OF FIXED TERM CONTRACT PROCESS

A series of HR improvement events was initiated with the dual aims of enhancing processes within HR, and developing the skills within the HR team to facilitate improvements without external support.

The first process to be investigated was that of the end of fixed term contracts. In moving away from zero hours contracts the number of fixed term contracts was predicted to rise, and the steps required at the end of such a contract was unwieldy for managers and for HR staff.

The HR staff member managing the process noted:

> "A lot of time was spent on the fixed term contract process, and managers weren't always aware of what they needed to do. Sometimes our email asking if a fixed term contract was to be extended would be the first time a manager would find out about the process, which is something we wanted to work on and improve."

A half day scoping session clearly defined the problem, identified key areas for improvement, captured work that was required to be done in advance of the improvement workshop, and set the agenda for a three-day workshop several weeks later. The workshop was led by the Business Improvement Team, with HR staff members shadowing to enable knowledge transfer. At this workshop there were representatives from all the different HR specialities involved, alongside key customers. External advice was sought at key stages of the workshop.

On the first day of the workshop the group mapped out the existing process physically on the workshop space wall, discussed its pros and cons, shared research and ideas, and prioritised experiments. The second day focussed on carrying out these experiments, iteratively building the new process, and estimating its benefits. The final half-day focused on developing and finalising the new materials required to support implementation of the new process.

The improved process was designed to include better planning and clearer communication from the start, so it has fewer, more straightforward steps. It was estimated that the HR team could save around 27.2 days every year as a direct result of the improvements – for a one-off cost of 12.4 days in total for the workshop.

The emails now sent out to prompt this process are fewer in number, shorter in length and more focused in content. By setting out clearly what happens at each stage, the need for follow-up emails is reduced. Three letters have been reduced to one, and it is hoped that the new communications and guidance will make it easier for managers and other staff to understand what to do. Two authorising forms have been reduced to one.

Giving feedback at the time, a senior manager who is a regular user of this process said:

> "This makes it simple, puts appropriate responsibility where it should be and takes away some of the forms. It used to be so repetitive to fill in."

A fact sheet was developed for managers to be given on the very first day they take on fixed-term employees, further helping to build knowledge and manage expectations. Further planned developments include automating the emails from central systems, freeing up the HR team even more to focus on the other process improvements in the pipeline.

When giving feedback about the nature of the workshop, participants commented:

> "You do need to put the time into process improvement, but you'll be rewarded for it afterwards."

> "It was so helpful to get that time away from the office. I think if we'd been left to do it ourselves, and do it as and when, we may not have got it done as quickly. Going in day after day, it was great to know that that was all you were focusing on."

> "The facilitation was really good as well. I appreciated having [the Business Improvement Team] there to prompt us and guide us a little bit – well, a lot actually! It was a really worthwhile and valuable experience, and I'd recommend it."

BUILDING A COMMUNITY OF PRACTICE

A key aspect of the current approach is building a community of practice that transcends team boundaries, hierarchy and role within the University. This is supported through a number of initiatives, primarily branded as "BIG" in reference to the community of practice being collectively known as the Business Improvement Group:

- BIG brown bag lunch
- BIG little email
- Continuous Improvement Partners (Described in the section entitled Continuous Improvement Partners Initiative)
- BIG Events

BIG BROWN BAG LUNCH

The "BIG brown bag lunch" is an informal monthly opportunity for staff to meet up over lunch, network with colleagues, share experiences with each other, and learn something new. It was initially started by inviting all staff that had done some kind of process improvement training or improvement work within the University, and has expanded organically through colleagues forwarding it on to others that they think would be interested. The lunches are semi-structured with time for networking but also with some kind of activity or learning. This could be a topic for discussion such as "dealing with the unexpected", skills enhancement such as the "sketch noting" session or an opportunity to introduce visitors from other Universities and focus the discussion around their interests.

BIG LITTLE EMAIL

The "BIG little email" is a monthly email on a topic that is likely to be of interest to the community of practice. It could be a book review, a good idea, a cartoon, an overview of a conference or some reflections from a colleague that may help others or prompt thinking about improvement. A key development is that ownership has been pushed out to the community of practice and a different member is now writing the email each month.

BIG EVENTS

BIG events are an Edinburgh Napier University initiative designed to support the internal improvement community of practice. They are a type of mini-conference or seminar that brings together a cross section of University staff who have demonstrated an interest in improvement with two main aims: to upskill staff, with a particular focus on gaining knowledge from an external perspective; and to facilitate the opportunity to put the skills into practice through an action orientated approach.

As an example, two such events were run in 2017, with one participant's summary of the second event captured in Figure 22.1. A series of workshops at the first event culminated in all 40 attendees self-organising themselves into five teams, with each group identifying an achievable improvement activity to tackle over an 8 week period by the second event. These covered a wide range of improvement opportunities: enhancing social spaces, time management, collecting student feedback, communications techniques

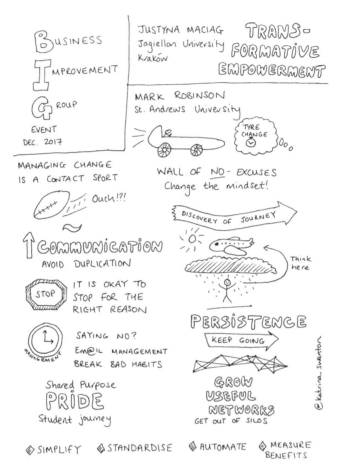

FIGURE 22.1

Sketch note of a Business Improvement Group event (Credit: Katrina Swanton, Edinburgh Napier University).

and even a quick reference guide to support staff "Who Ya Gonna Call." The aim of tackling small, achievable improvements was twofold: lots of small improvements are manageable, achievable and all add up; and small improvements allow staff to practice the tools, techniques and approaches that can be applied to more complex work.

All groups presented the outcome at the second event, with the focus being on describing what went well, but equally when things did not go well what the challenges were and how they could be overcome.

BIG EVENT SURVEY RESULTS

As well as stimulating improvement, the events were utilised as an opportunity to survey the attendees and take a snapshot of data around improvement in order to gain a sense of the University's progress on our lean journey.

Attendees reflected on what helped them to deliver improvements. Support from colleagues and personal research rated the highest, with both at 80% (Figure 22.2), with improvement tools and training also rating highly.

As a result of the first event 89% of those attending report gaining new skills or knowledge, and 81% report the ability to directly apply it in the workplace. The nature of the simplification was seen as resulting in savings of time (78%), effort (57%) and resources (39%). Most staff saw these savings as providing the most direct benefits for their immediate team (73%) followed by other professional services staff (69%), with better outcomes for students and academic staff identified by 46% and 35% of participants respectively. However, it is likely that participants identified the benefitting groups as those which they had most direct line of sight to, and it's expected that the secondary benefits were probably higher but less obvious.

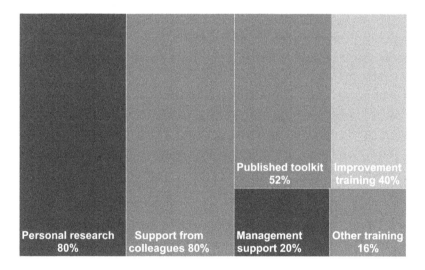

FIGURE 22.2
Elements supporting improvement initiatives.

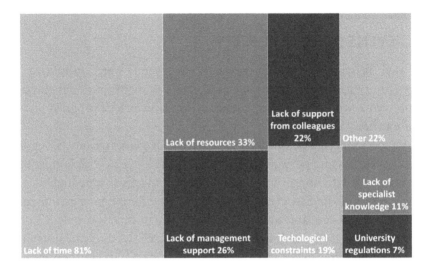

FIGURE 22.3
Challenges faced carrying out improvement.

Of the more specific challenges the biggest is perceived to be capacity. This is evidenced when staff were asked to select all the challenges faced in carrying out improvement initiatives from a range of eight options, and 81% of staff selected time, with the next biggest challenge (lack of resources) sitting considerably lower at 33% (Figure 22.3). When asked to pick the single biggest challenge from the same options 48% of staff still selected time.

It is of note that challenges such as University regulations and lack of specialist knowledge were not viewed as the largest barriers, but lack of support from colleagues and management were. Support from colleagues was both identified as the most critical enabler when present, but the largest barrier when not. This reinforces the challenges around culture, and the need for a long term approach that empowers staff rather than a quick fix, something that the decentralised approach aims to address.

As part of the BIG event, participants anonymously reported what motivates them to improve their work. While there are a small number of material motivations – "money", "Manager" and "financial incentives" – each of these were only mentioned one time in the data set. The overwhelming majority of motivations for improvement were non material such as "Recognition" or "Respect" and intrinsic in nature, such as "Satisfaction", and with just over 25% of respondents naming "Pride" as a motivator of improvement. The survey will serve as a baseline, to help establish the effectiveness of the programme.

CHALLENGES AND REFLECTIONS

There are a number of key challenges to Business Improvement or lean within Edinburgh Napier University. Some of these are specific to the decentralised model currently adopted and others are general challenges around implementing lean in HE.

The biggest challenge is the length of time that it takes to see the benefits through the current approach. Changing the organisational culture and upskilling staff to a sufficient extent that they can deliver measurable improvements takes long term commitment. Only around 2% to 3% of staff have successfully completed in depth improvement training, so it is clear that the shift to a culture of continuous improvement will take some time. The vast majority of staff engaged in continuous improvement are professional services rather than academic staff, hence this represents additional challenges in terms of differing cultures and engagement with change.

A devolved and organic approach without a large central team may make change harder to measure in the short term, although work is ongoing with the university's planning function to build improvement measures into our regular planning cycle.

It is hoped that a distributed approach allows for a "stickier" implementation than having a large centralised team. Rather than change being imposed upon the organisation, it is hoped that the Business Improvement Framework will enable staff to develop good practice further, creating a more sustainable improvement culture in the medium to long term, while avoiding some of the pitfalls brought by large centralised improvement teams.

A number of colleagues from other Universities, both within the UK and internationally, have visited for anything up to a week to observe our approach or carry out research. This independent perspective has offered us a number of valuable insights as we seek to enhance our approach.

The challenges faced in HE are to some extent no different to those faced adopting a lean culture in many diverse sectors. The biggest challenge is that, despite overwhelming evidence of the benefits of a lean approach, the organisational culture and established practices are challenging to shift.

To overcome these barriers, focussing on achieving each success one step at a time, and long term persistence are key.

It is fitting to conclude with comments from staff in Edinburgh Napier University actively involved in improving their work. Asked to give a positive message of encouragement, our community of practice responded with statements such as:

"Keep going, we can do it!"
"This really matters"
"We are making a difference"

23

Making Sense of Learning, Practice and Theory

Gretel Stonebridge, Claire King and Leanne Sowter

CONTENTS

INTRODUCTION

We've all read books about the theory of successful ingredients for developing an embedded continuous improvement culture. We might be tempted to lift ideas and methodologies or even copy what others are doing. We hope they will work.

Here at the University of Leicester we did just that a few years ago, and we are typical of all other institutions facing challenges in developing a culture where change and improvement are the norm against a fast moving and changing political landscape.

This chapter is about how we joined up practice and theory; how we used learning to involve both practice and theory to shape and implement our Leicester approach. The approach is about supporting teams in the work to improve the work and developing a culture of continuous improvement, but it is also about being positioned in the right place. Here we will explain what we learned and what we did.

UNDERSTANDING OUR CULTURE

As a large organisation the University of Leicester is very typical. It is facing many challenges which are set externally including government agendas, advances in technology, changing markets and so on. It is also typical in its reactions to pressures. As a good university it is seeking to improve, comply, change and become both leading and successful. This has meant, due to its size, that many different initiatives have been implemented in order to reach strategic aims.

The idea for continuous improvement originated about ten years ago was driven by our Chief Operating Officer and Registrar with a focus on professional services. At that time we explored the EFQM Excellence Model (this involved one of the authors of this chapter) and little attention was paid to model or methodology for improvement. There was an acute desire to join up services and improve the student experience.

Consequently the University of Leicester chose Systems Thinking. Using this method there were successes in learning and improving larger processes ranging from admissions, distance learning, recruitment and maintenance. Created within professional services in 2012 was a small Change Team which worked alongside staff supporting local improvements (this team included one of the authors of this chapter). With the appointment of a new Vice-Chancellor in 2014 the University developed a new strategic plan and from this the evolution of the student as the "customer" became even more of a focus.

In addition to the bigger improvement pieces which emanated from professional services, there were now a number of strategic projects.

The Change Team was able to observe the whole picture. It saw a number of organisational initiatives and it looked almost like an "archipelago" approach to change i.e. that there was lots happening and little joining up. It was as if the University of Leicester wanted to achieve:

1. Developmental change which was improving what we were doing day to day
2. Transitional change which was replacing what is with something new
3. Transformational change where the future state was unknown.

These levels involved different methodologies and terms. They all, however, relied on involving staff and were all happening at the same time. The Change Team was focussed on the day-to-day improvement and therefore saw work was either "feast" or "famine" because the same people were asked to support all the various projects. The team was curious to know more about engagement with improvement and views from staff.

To seek an answer the Change Team interviewed about 30–40 staff comprising leaders and team leaders who had been involved in local improvement work and asked:

1. Are you interested in change and improvement and why?
2. What are the levers for change?
3. What are the barriers for change?
4. How can the barriers be overcome?

There was a rich collection of views and points and they were mapped onto the Cultural Web (Johnson, G. 2009)

The Cultural Web (Figure 23.1) identifies six interrelated elements that help to make up the "paradigm" – the pattern or model – of the work environment. By analysing the factors in each, you can begin to see the bigger picture of your culture: what is working, what isn't working and what needs to be changed.

The paradigm at Leicester was:

> We want to change but we are too conservative and traditional focussing too much on the detail and therefore losing our way

The Culture Web was the first step in understanding how things work and it generated the following levers for change:

- Joining up with academic departments and the centre – Reduce silo working and thinking.
- Being better at communicating successes to get more interest – Create new and positive stories.
- Including people and time to create a culture for improvement.
- Understanding the importance of leaders to create environment for staff to be involved.
- Creating an approach which is accessible for all to grasp and fits our organisation and reducing emphasis on methodology and jargon.

FIGURE 23.1
University of Leicester Culture Web.

- Reducing the feeling that the continuous improvement team has to "sell" or "tell."
- Starting to grow an environment for learning, getting evidence to inform change and improvement and reducing the temptation to fix.
- Developing an understanding that improvement is not about information technology.

This exercise revealed a cross-section of our culture. We knew then that understanding your culture was the first step in starting to shape it. We realised that continuous improvement was more about culture than efficiencies and profit. We were now also curious to discover what others were learning about changing culture. At an event called "The

Great Culture Change Challenge" we worked with lean and improvement staff from the sector to create a Change Cake (Figure 23.2) with essential ingredients for culture change. The "cake" consisted of:

1. Foundation layer – Ingredients to start a piece of work
2. Middle layer and tier supports – Tactics and strategies to keep people and work on board
3. Top layer – How to get people to show what has been achieved and how to make the change normal (Figure 23.2).

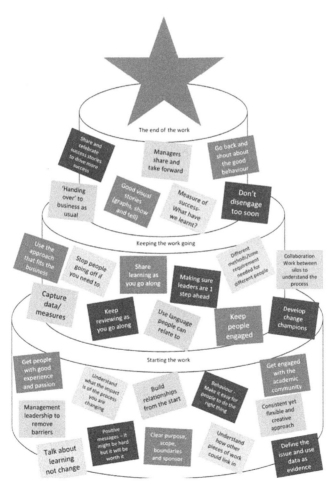

FIGURE 23.2
Change Cake.

DEVELOPING OUR APPROACH

From observing what was happening so far and plotting that on the Culture Web we had an idea of the levers and barriers for change.

The Change Cake added to the learning as we understood then what we were learning was not unique to us but common across the Higher Education sector.

To develop our approach we needed to make it fit our culture, it had to be accessible to everyone and not alienating. We also wanted the approach to be aligned to strategic direction and to be in the right place – not buried so far that no one could see it but also not seen as the "next big thing." It needed to have a place where it made sense for what the University needed to do – by being woven within and complementing other change initiatives. With this in mind we started to shape our approach to continuous improvement (Figure 23.3).

We developed the purpose of our approach which is:

> The Continuous Improvement Team are here to help you improve your work so you can provide the most effective and efficient service for your customers. We do this by supporting you in process improvement, delivering training and helping to develop a successful change culture.

Focused on learning and involvement rather than pushing, forcing or telling the approach comprises five guiding principles:

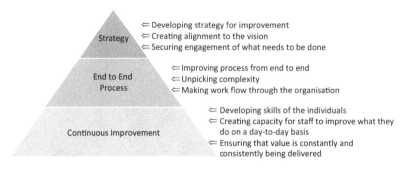

FIGURE 23.3
Where the approach fits in the organisation (Inspired by Christine Stewart from Macresco Ltd).

1. Putting the customer/student at the centre, understanding what matters to them and acting on that
2. Focusing on the flow of the process
3. Identifying and removing unnecessary work
4. Using measures to help understand and improvement performance
5. Involving leaders in the work, to see it, understand it and remove barriers

The Leicester approach to continuous improvement uses a range of tools that we learned work well, all underpinned with common sense. The approach is flexible and can complement or inform existing projects. Each piece of work is different and it is shaped according to what is required. In addition to tools the approach is as much about mentoring and coaching to support the people side of change.

Informed by the Levers from the Culture Web

From the levers we developed a continuous improvement narrative which sums up the ethos of the approach and provides details of the wider institutional setting (Figures 23.4 and 23.5).

FIGURE 23.4
Continuous Improvement Narrative part 1.

Strategic Plan	Our strategic plan describes our commitments and priorities for the future and explains how we intend to deliver these.
Key Discovery Strategies	Key Discovery Strategies have developed. These provide greater detail of how the overarching Strategic Plan will be attained. (Learning Strategy, Research Strategy, Enterprise Strategy, Finance Strategy, People Strategy, Digital Strategy, International Strategy and Physical Environment Strategy).
Continuous Improvement	Continuous Improvement at University of Leicester is about supporting teams to run the most effective services they can by facilitating pieces of process improvement work, delivering training in our approach and helping to develop a culture of continuous improvement.
Methodology	At Leicester, we have tried a number of different ways of doing change and improvement with some success and some failures. We have looked at what works for Leicester and brought together a way of doing continuous improvement that fits who we are. The Leicester approach is made up of a range of tools that we have learned work well here, all underpinned by a generous helping of common sense.
Culture	Whilst continuous improvement is about providing staff with a skill set, more importantly it is about developing the desired behaviour and culture in the institution. A culture that grows. This should not be a one off activity. That is why it is so essential that time and effort is put into developing staff to be able to continuously review and reflect on what they do to ensure that it continues to deliver what is needed in the best way possible.
Will	Any continuous improvement needs the will of the staff involved. We are here to support them and teams by facilitating process improvement work, delivering training and supporting to improve the work.
Flexible approach	Our approach should be flexible, improve and change over time. Whilst we may have a "huge" ambition to get "there" organisationally and culturally our way should be to get to the first step, then second and so on.
Knowledge	We harness staff to make change based on knowledge by supporting them to gather and analyse data on process steps, understand what it feels like for a customer and to agree measures so we know how well things are working. Everyone involved in a piece of work will gather tools and methods that they can take away with them and start to apply in their own day-to-day work. We ensure that lessons learnt are shared across the University.

FIGURE 23.5
Continuous Improvement Narrative part 2.

CASE STUDY 1: STUDENTS, NOT SYSTEMS "IT'S THE STUDENTS NOT THE SYSTEMS!"

The Continuous Improvement Team worked with Team A (responsible for Continuing Professional Development language course delivery) at the request of a leader to support new system requirements to improve course administration. The Continuous Improvement Team scoped the work with Team A and refined the boundaries whereby the work itself was prioritised above system considerations; Team A wanted to identify improvements to enable better workload and inbox management. Facilitated sessions enabled Team A to perform demand analysis with the student perspective as the focus for value/failure categorisation. Improvements were developed and prioritised based on the resulting data including ensuring the relevant website (notoriously difficult to navigate across the University!) was user-friendly for public customers, immediately reducing failure demand by 10% through delivering the right course materials at the right time for the students, and making registration easier to understand for students by making information accessible and resolving technical application form issues. The data provided useful baseline measures and the impact of improvements could be measured via tallies in the same timeframe during the next academic year.

Team A utilised the principle of putting the student at the centre which yielded both local and strategic success because acting on what matters to students ensures an improvement in their experience. Confidence in change is also promoted which generates a cultural shift in favour of learning and experimentation, for example Team A were equipped to employ the Leicester approach in other pieces of work – ensuring improvement is indeed continuous. Furthermore Team A's participation demonstrates the benefit of involving staff as the meaningful work was defined and well-bounded during scoping, and focus and commitment was agreed upon as necessary and beneficial. Measures were also important as Team A felt empowered to make changes based on evidence, and also understood their team's purpose from the student perspective.

CASE STUDY 2: WISH YOU WERE HEAR

The Continuous Improvement Team worked with Team B (staff and leaders from various central service areas plus student representatives) to make efficiency improvements to the HEAR (Higher Education Achievement Report) process for students and staff without requiring fundamental system changes, and to inform long-term HEAR plans. Process mapping showed the steps, unnecessary work (waste), common queries and data in the "as-is" process for all represented areas – consequently Team B understood the end-to-end process in its entirety and could see the evidence for change in a visual manner wherein unnecessary work would be identified and removed. The unnecessary work included duplication and over-processing, such as disproportionate touchpoints and the superfluous submission and verification of student timesheets.

The HEAR process mapping with Team B upheld the principle of focussing on flow and removing unnecessary work which ensured that efficiency improvements, such as time saved for students and staff, would manifest in the "to-be" process. Moreover unifying students, staff and leaders to question the purpose of the process for the first time since the HEAR was implemented at the University of Leicester in 2012, was paramount in identifying unnecessary work and establishing smooth process flow. The leaders helped to remove barriers by allocating appropriate staff time and ensuring efficiency in action planning, decision making and process ownership. The approach in ensuring change was well-bounded but also easy to understand, for example in referring to unnecessary work instead of waste, ensured that learnings were readily understood which further enabled a development of the change culture for the numerous areas within Team B.

CASE STUDY 3: ONE SCOPE, TWO SCOPE, THREE SCOPE, FOUR...

The Continuous Improvement Team contacted Team C (leaders responsible for academic support in the research lifecycle) following a senior leader's direction to review the division. Members of Team C narrowed the work's focus to a particular area, though the boundaries remained undefined due to the conflicting requirements of multiple stakeholders. A dedicated scoping session with additional Team C representatives explored processes and issues in order to agree the scope. However, the debate highlighted confusion over roles and process owners resulting from a recent restructure. In addition, other change initiatives were active and presented a risk of overlap: an assessment of staff roles and a communications project. Team C also challenged the reason for our intervention and noted the unfruitful nature of previous external change directives. Further scoping attempts revealed other barriers including some hesitancy in considering the customer's perspective but also difficulties in committing time for facilitated sessions, although isolated observations were possible.

Scoping extended beyond eleven weeks and four versions of a scoping document. Barriers originated from the top-down approach as members of Team C were both unprepared and unsupported to make decisions and guarantee commitment. Furthermore, Team C comprised only leaders – staff involved in the processes were not consulted, therefore the work was not shaped by staff with day-to-day expertise and remained unfocussed. Through this practical experience the Continuous Improvement Team learned that key ingredients for success included engagement of leaders both in the formulation and initiation of change, early involvement and commitment of staff in the piece of work, work should be well-bounded, and that of course improvement should be guided by customer need.

EMBEDDING IN THE ORGANISATION

Being involved in improvement pieces as illustrated in the case studies mentioned started to earn the team a good reputation. As a next step we once more considered our strategic position. To achieve a more strategic position we established a Continuous Improvement Board which included members of the Senior Leadership Team and a Lean Subject Matter Expert. The Board was set up to provide direction, guidance and decision-making to support the successful delivery of the Leicester approach to continuous improvement and its impact. The existence of a Board did not make us strategic but having the Board has strengthened our position and has enabled the approach to be shared at more senior levels in the institution. In addition the Board provides a framework for prioritisation in alignment with strategic objectives.

To develop the ability to link other change pieces or projects across the organisation we set up the Change Operational Group – a group which meets every two months and has representatives from Organisational Development, Human Resources, Information Technology, Finance, Corporate Portfolio Management Office, Student Lifecycle Change Programme and Student Success Teams. Setting up this group has been beneficial because it gives visibility of what is going on, reduces any duplication of effort and provides intelligence on the culture of the organisation. It has helped position us better within the wider change setting and builds both our reputation and confidence. It is also an attempt to mitigate the "archipelago" approach to change. Through the group we have learned those "islands" are more likely to join up.

We have connected with an existing leadership training programme to deliver continuous improvement workshops to share practical tools which work well. This has been beneficial in embedding continuous improvement in the everyday activities of staff, rather than being seen as another initiative. The workshops can lead to further support for leaders should they need it. The training programme is university-wide and draws on staff from all areas. Many of these areas are new and provide us with more intelligence about what is going on. In addition we recognise that not all staff will attend workshops and therefore we have created a Continuous Improvement Toolbox.

The objective for the toolbox is to provide information on theory, examples, tools, games and activities. The tools can be used to gather knowledge and evidence for change which is woven into the narrative.

Effective communication is critical to help embed an approach and we have learned that our reputation is building because of what we are doing and not what we say we can do. Therefore we have capitalised on existing communication networks, participating in staff talks to keep telling staff our story and showcasing what we have done. We contribute and support a team of Change Partners which has been established to support the programme of work for the student lifecycle. We have also facilitated some one-off workshops to support change.

REASSESSING THE CULTURE

This chapter started with learning about where we were as an organisation before developing the approach to continuous improvement. We have illustrated some case studies where we have tested the approach and further developed it and explored our strategic position to help endorse it. In this last section we will reflect on the impact of the approach.

We have shown how we used observation for learning about culture. We have continued to do this but we also frequently reflect as part of our routine using the following questions to form a learning review:

1. What have we set out to do?
2. What are we learning?
3. What do we want to do next?

We can draw out the learning from all the work we have done so far which include both successes and hurdles. From these reviews we have now distilled the following ingredients for successful work:

- The work is well-bounded.
- Leaders are involved.
- Staff are involved.
- Commitment is agreed – People are willing to put time and effort in.
- There is an obvious customer.
- There is agreement and willingness to take measures.

Although these ingredients may look like they have been lifted directly from other lean and continuous improvement research, these have in fact been proven at the University of Leicester via our own learning. We now use these ingredients as a checklist to start or not to start pieces of work. This has also been demonstrated in Case Study 3.

In building our approach we included measures to assess the impact. Measures for improvement work are derived and collected from the staff involved with some support from us to guide them. Staff involvement is key for all elements of the approach. We knew right at the start, however, that it was not just about the numbers but also about culture. From reflecting on the work we have done we could see how people changed in work we did to support improvement.

There has already been much written about evidencing benefits and measures from improvement work. In line with our ethos we wanted to develop a way to measure culture change in the organisation. The result was the Cultural Thermometer which can be used to chart the progress of a cultural shift per piece of work or as a whole. The guide is as follows:

a) Observation by the Continuous Improvement Team is completed at the start of a piece of work to examine how interested the team seems in the improvement work.
   The following questions are used (score 1–5):
   1. How committed do they appear to the improvement work?
   2. How open minded are they to use the approach/tools for future work?
   3. How enthusiastic are they to engage in change?

b) At the end of the piece of work we examine how likely they are to continue with the improvement.
   The following questions are used (score 1–5):
   1. How committed are they to continue with the improvement work?

2. How likely are they to use the approach/other tools for future work?
3. How enthusiastic are they about the amount of change in the work?

c) After a few months we examine whether they have started something themselves after finishing the improvement.
   The following questions are used (score Yes/No):
   1. Have the actions been completed?
   2. Have they identified another piece of improvement work?
   3. Have they used any tools from the Continuous Improvement Toolbox?

We shaped the Leicester approach by using learning and reflection to understand the culture of our organisation. We designed the approach which we wanted to test out. The use of learning reviews, which we build both into work we support and the way we reflect as a team, has shaped the approach and embedded it more in the organisation. The testing is important. In this chapter we have described a cycle of improvement to the approach. Designing an approach is not a quick fix as it is about gradual culture change which is long term.

Our principles will not change but what we do, how we engage and how we gather evidence for our impact and intelligence about our culture will. We have learned a great deal from both successes and failures and these have given us those vital ingredients which we know work for us at the University of Leicester. In conclusion we believe that any organisation developing their own approach must firstly understand their organisation and develop something which fits their unique culture.

The key to the shaping and development of the approach is learning.

Theory comes from practice, practice comes from theory: learning is the glue between theory and practice.

REFERENCE

Johnson, G. 2009. Culture and strategy. In: *Fundamentals of Strategy*, K. Scholes, and R. Whittington (ed.), pp. 121–142. Pearson Education.

24

What If We Knew the Future Could Be Different!

Radka Newton

CONTENTS

Lean is about creating value for the end-user as well as being about respect for people. Understanding of our own organisational culture and its impact on improvement initiatives that result in change, cultural and organisational, goes hand in hand with any lean initiative. Yet we sometimes underestimate those who are at the heart of the lean initiatives. Lean in HE calls for the importance of a sensitive human-centered approach in lean leadership because it is people who implement these improvements for people, students and other staff. Awareness and reflection are key stages of any lean project. However, often here we are, starting from an uncomfortable position that something is wrong. A good value stream map will show all our mistakes and rework, waste very visibly. How scary!

No wonder we just sometimes want to close our eyes and go into a mode of denial. It is ok. Nobody likes to hear – "your work is waste". But what if we took a bit of thinking time before we launch ourselves into continuous improvement practice? What if we gave ourselves some time to think?

In this chapter I will propose a framework for lean initiatives that will build on the Gestalt cycle of experience that is used in coaching to get to the bottom of fundamental life issues faced by an individual. But in a way, it is still an improvement initiative moving towards greater awareness and real mobilisation of forces and aimed at making sustainable change in a challenging situation. Just like lean. In any lean initiative or in process improvement we strive to makes things better, move on towards the new future and abandon the old cumbersome ways of doing. That takes guts and what we try to achieve is a real change. Change of working, change of behaviour, change of pace and often change of systems and even people's roles. This fundamental shake up needs some thinking through and the framework proposed in Figure 24.1 will introduce three additional initial steps to our usual lean cycle that starts with identifying value.

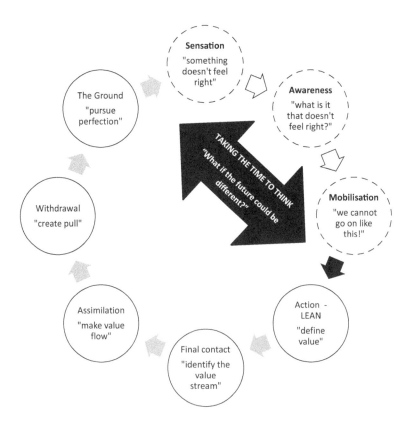

FIGURE 24.1
Gestalt and lean cycles of experience.

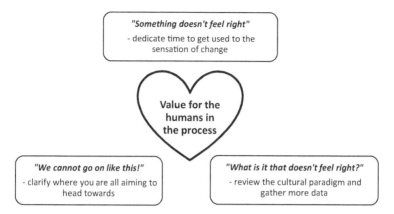

FIGURE 24.2
The initial triad of steps.

The initial triad of steps (Figure 24.2) creates the space for thinking about the sensation of change and it provides time to get used to the sensation of change, raise people's awareness of what you are planning to achieve, and brings about the questions about the value for the team or teams that are involved in the process delivery.

There may be frustration, anger and tiredness and it is worthwhile to acknowledge all of this before we launch into any further actions. The sensations accompanying a broken process may be negative to start with and the awareness rising of what lies behind it all is crucial. Is it a poor IT system that is ruling the process or could it be the organisational culture that is interfering with smooth operations? The awareness stage requires more research, data gathering and understanding of what is happening, who is involved and what are the potential hurdles to overcome. Only then we can start mobilising the energy and acknowledging the need to act, to start the change with a shared vision. What comes after? We are all very familiar with the next steps. That's when lean kicks in and we can roll up our sleeves and get things moving.

So let's take a closer look at the initial triad that puts the respect for people at its heart. It brings the value for anybody in the process to the forefront. It engages the head and heart.

"SOMETHING DOESN'T FEEL RIGHT"

The very first step every lean training will teach you is to identify value. In the HE context this is not as straightforward as in a traditional production setting where value is usually associated with throughput time and the focus of lean initiatives is on speed and smoothness of operation. The dimensions of value in education are multifaceted – the value for the end-user, the value for the process owner and the value for multiple stakeholders including student families and graduate employers. The respect for people that is central to lean applies to both end-user or customer and the people who are involved in the process. Lean initiatives usually come about as a result of some urgency. Something doesn't work, we need to fix it. The lean teams launch into actions far too fast underestimating the impact on those who are key to the process delivery. In the initial stage, lean leaders can learn a lot from coaching practice where identification of the root of the problem goes hand in hand with raising awareness of the sensation around the issue we are trying to tackle and a better understanding of our own assumptions and fears.

Giving ourselves some time to think as described by Nancy Kline (1999) can provide some powerful tools that the lean practice could benefit from. "Time to think practice" offers a concept of "incisive questions" that can help us and our teams break free from assumptions.

- If our team was not held back by our organisation's poor communication, what would we be doing?
- If we could trust our experiment or a new initiative would be a success, what would we do next?
- If we knew we were the experts to make a big difference in our organisation, how would we present it to our Dean?
- If we knew that our stories could reveal what may be wrong with the processes, what stories would we tell our managers?

The "time to think" creates ease and readiness for the change. It helps the teams understand the purpose of improvement and gives them some space for discussing aspirations but also facing fears.

We often hear that the majority of lean initiatives fail and processes revert back to what they used to be. The initial identification of the value for those who will be implementing the lean initiative helps to set the boundaries and parameters of the planned change. It helps the teams to get onto the same page. This initial stage requires strong leadership and the lean leader should appreciate the importance of being a coach as well as a process improvement enthusiast. This applies to the team members who ought to be empowered to demonstrate lean leadership with a "time to think" hat on, acknowledging sensations associated with change.

Let's now meet Sarah, a senior HE leader with passion for lean.

SARAH'S STORY

Sarah was a member of a senior leadership team in a highly ranked business school. She was in charge of international student recruitment and on her travels around the world, she has developed a great sense of empathy for those young people and their families taking the leap into the unknown to embark on a prestigious degree in the UK. Sarah understood the applicant journey extremely well as she had gone through the same process several times herself. She knew how scary and exciting at the same time that journey could be. She felt for every single candidate who came to her exhibition stand or attended an interview with her. It was up to her to paint that picture of the unknown and create that dream future vision of studying abroad. At times she felt the pressure and she knew she had to be true and honest, yet positive and also fast in responding to any little query that came to her inbox.

The sense of urgency met with Sarah's dedication to making the application process as smooth as it could be. She was just freshly out of her MBA and was looking for a new challenge. One day she decided to ask for more responsibility and her manager was delighted when Sarah put herself forward to lead the admissions team. "I will turn this around, no more endless waiting for a response, the applicants will hear in less than 10 days!" From four weeks to less than ten days became her motto and her drive. Her focus was fully on delivering the best value for applicants. She cared about nothing else but to provide the best applicant experience, as she saw it.

You may be thinking that she was a perfect example of a lean enthusiast driven by the value for the end-user of the admissions process. She would be really pleased if you thought so as she was a lean maniac. Her house was organised in a lean way even so far as to prevent any shortage of a nicely chilled glass of white wine. Post-it notes and flowcharts dominated her office walls and she would not hesitate to preach lean to practically everybody in the business school. Sarah's recruitment team loved her. She carefully selected every single of them and created that team from scratch. Her empathy for applicants and the importance of fast response was drummed into the team from the early stages. Many of them came from outside the education sector and brought customer service experience with them. If you imagine a group of happy, innovative and upbeat individuals, that was Sarah's team. Lean never featured on their agenda. They were breathing change on a daily basis. They had open conversations about things that went wrong, and they celebrated their successes. Sarah was often the first one to come clean and own up to a messed-up innovation that she was happy to scrap and rethink.

The culture Sarah and the team co-created was focused on the value for the applicants and the value for the academic teams they supported in recruiting the best students for their programmes. They put a lot of emphasis on relationship building and understanding what their support should look like. They worked on the planes, in the hotel lobbies, in the taxi journeys to the airports. The time difference meant that their applicants were awake 24/7, and so were they. Sarah knew that the organisational culture was an important aspect of any effective operation and she put a lot of effort into building the ethos of openness and trust with constant ideation and review of the processes.

The admission team had just lost their manager and inundated by thousands of applications flooding the CRM system, they had no option but to put their heads down and wade through the treacle. The CRM system was cumbersome and the automatic messages sent to the applicants would put off anybody who has a tiny bit of sensitivity in them. Your application has been deactivated! You haven't paid the deposit! You no longer exist! Sarah couldn't wait to fix this. She felt invincible. Equipped with her fresh MBA degree where she specialised in operations management, her many successes with her recruitment team and her own ability to achieve almost anything, she set off on a new lean journey that was going to become a crusade. Her focus never slipped off the applicants' experience. She was ready to combat the CRM, the long queues, the negative tone of automated emails, the lot! She knew the future could be different...

"WHAT IS IT THAT DOESN'T FEEL RIGHT?"

Sarah created a culture in her team that enhanced creativity and the underlying condition was trust of the team members who were at ease about admitting mistakes and constantly reviewing their practices. These characteristics fit perfectly with continuous improvement but they are not as common in Universities as we may think.

Organisational culture provides a context to the team behaviour and cannot be ignored when considering service delivery and process improvement. It has also been recently debated as one of the main obstacles to lean initiatives. The definition of organisational culture is complex and multiple authors offer a variety of perspectives. For our purpose, culture will be taken from a perspective as a set of shared knowledge that gives a shared meaning and sense making to the taken-for-granted for the members who see the world through the lens of this knowledge. It is something an organisation is rather than has and is manifested in the language, symbols, rituals, organisational structure, power distribution and the way the decisions are made (Johnson, 2001; Smircich, 1983). The expectations and rules within which Universities as organisations exist are determined by the societal context, which reduces ambiguity but constrains their totality of freedom of existence and sets boundaries within assumptions of what is acceptable. In the context of educational organisations, there will be therefore some common features to all universities regardless of their internal set of beliefs and values.

Teams and departments create their own subcultures, which is even harder to navigate. As in Sarah's case, the two interdependent teams, student recruitment and admissions, operated two very different cultures driven by the objectives of their remits. Understandably the admissions team where mistakes can cost a UKVI licence (the UK governmental approval to host overseas students, and therefore critical) are much more risk averse and often petrified of making or admitting an error. In the HE sector there are further complexities between the academic culture and the culture of professional administrative teams. The HE sector therefore is very heterogeneous from a cultural perspective and research from the financial sector by Maul et al. (2001) points out that in this cultural climate it is rarely possible to introduce homogeneous quality improvement programmes.

Morgan and Murgatroyd (1994), in Billing (1998: 151), related the desirable culture characteristics to service quality and customer satisfaction. They propose six aspirational cultural characteristics that enhance service quality:

1. Innovation is valued highly.
2. Status is secondary to performance and contribution.
3. Leadership is a function of action, not position.
4. Rewards are shared through the work of teams.
5. Development, learning and training are seen as critical paths to sustainability.
6. Empowerment to achieve challenging goals supported by continued development and success provide a climate for self-motivation.

Now how do you know your team has these characteristics and how can you raise your awareness of the context you operate in?

PAUSE, RAISE YOUR OWN AWARENESS OF THE CULTURE AROUND YOU

Before we start thinking about how the future can be different by implementing a lean initiative, an awareness of the culture we operate in will be essential. Sarah took it for granted that the new team will be just the same as her innovative and highly reflective student recruitment team. She skipped the importance of the initial pause and evaluation of what was around her. A very useful and intuitive framework – *Cultural web* – developed by Scholes and Johnson (2011) can help any lean enthusiast with the first steps towards a successful lean project. This simple but powerful way of looking at the world around you will give you the starting point and will set you in the right direction towards one of the key lean mantras – respect for people: meaning the colleagues you are about to invite to your lean party. And as a good party host, you will do your best to know what makes them tick and what music will get them onto the dance floor.

Here is what Sarah was surrounded by but could not see. As an advanced lean practitioner you know that "go and see" is essential. So let's do the cultural Gemba walk first (Figure 24.3).

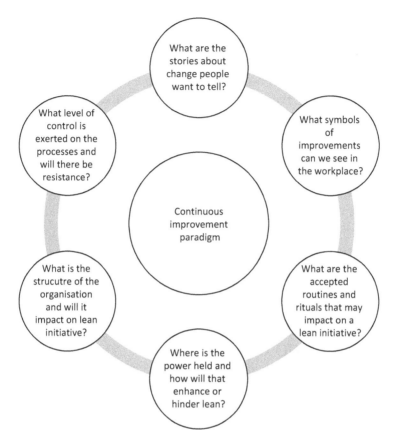

FIGURE 24.3
Cultural web adapted to lean initiatives.

WHAT SARAH DID NEXT...

I know you want to know what happened with Sarah. She did have a bumpy journey, you guessed correct. Her previous experience with the recruitment team meant that she was prepared to openly admit that processes were not fit for purpose and she expected the team just to get on with improvements. Not this time. At one of her presentations of an admissions value stream map full of red crosses symbolising process failure, one of the team members who normally rarely spoke, put his hand up and said: "Most of the red crosses are pointing out the areas of my day-to-day work. If we get rid of those tasks, what will I do?" Sarah paused and cheerfully said: "Well, you can do something more exciting, like taking part in calling campaigns. You will love it, you will actually get to talk to people rather than just staring at the screen." She was pleased with her answer and moved on with her visionary presentation. The same hand went up again: "But it is not a part of my job to do that. I don't want to talk to applicants on the phone. I am trained to review applications on the system. That's what I do." Sarah's lean world full of positivity and never-ending change collapsed in front of her. She finished her presentation and went back to her office. She felt angry, tearful and frustrated. But this was the reality of her lean initiative. Some of the team's comforts were to be replaced by innovations or simply got rid of if they brought no value to the applicants. It made perfect sense, you couldn't argue with her faultless and detailed analyses. But as her operations management teacher pointed out to her, "these processes are delivered by people, not machines. You cannot just switch them off."

"WE CANNOT GO ON LIKE THIS!"

The lesson Sarah learnt changed her approach to lean and she decided to pause a bit. She abandoned the processes and improvements and organised a team away day. She took the team to a beautiful old manor house in the mountains where the air was clear of improvement speak. As the team members walked and talked, she listened. They talked about their children, hobbies, pets, house extensions, and she listened. She allowed the team time to get to know one another and time to think. She allowed herself a luxury of getting to know her new team as human beings, not as broken cogs in a broken process.

The away day gave the team some space to think about who they are, what they want their day-to-day work to be and feel like, what they are worried about and what they love about their jobs. It gave them the time to think about what if the future could be different. The team came away with their own understanding of the value of their work and a clear team charter detailing their values and behaviours they wish to live by at work.

They reinstated respect for one another, which brought about much higher respect for applicants. Sarah realised that resistance to change meant that they cared. They showed commitment and dedication and also exposed their fears of the unknown. The process improvement was about to change their jobs, their routines and their known was about to be challenged. Appreciation of a lean initiative as change has been beneficial for Sarah. She has since always focused on value for both the end-user and the process owner. She is still a lean enthusiast but she has found better head and heart balance. She is still seeking perfection.

CONCLUSION: PAUSE, CREATE EASE

You have now read the whole book or hopefully you just jumped straight to this chapter. Well done! It is time to pause and digest what you have learnt. Where is your own awareness now about lean in HE? It is certainly much higher now and hopefully the book will have given you a lot to think about. Even though the HE sector is in a constant state of urgency, creating space and time to think does pay off. People at ease perform much better, are happier and a joy to be around. Many lean practitioners start with a clear voice of the customer in their head. That voice becomes their focus and so it should be. However, as we have seen from Sarah's story, lean is also about respecting the people who deliver the service and every lean initiative follows an organisation change pattern.

The organisation culture assessment and the readiness for change is a useful initial indicator of how the people will react and embrace the change. The feelings and stories around change will disclose the organisation's memory of change and the appetite for lean. The dilemma between prioritising the voice of the customer and the people involved is a common conundrum for all lean practitioners and there is no straightforward answer. The combination of coaching techniques and lean may be one of the approaches that could facilitate potential tension. Coaching brings a non-judgmental and exploratory angle to process improvement and explores the human feelings and anxieties in an open and positive way.

Lean as originally designed in the manufacturing context is very process oriented and even though it does emphasize respect for people, making the process flow well and effectively is a priority. In our educational context we are surrounded by processes but all these are designed by people for people and it is paramount to see the human element behind the process. The definition of value in this context becomes multifaceted and it will add an emotional dimension to any educational lean initiatives.

If you are itching to get stuck into a lean initiative, we are proud that with this book we have enthused you. But, please, pause... allow yourself time to think about what if the future could be different, for you, your colleagues and most importantly for your students.

REFERENCES

Billing, D. 1998. Quality management and organisational structure in higher education. *Journal of Higher Education Policy and Management*, 20(2), 139–159.

Johnson, G. 2001. Mapping and re-mapping organisational culture: A local government example. In: *Exploring Public Sector Strategy*, Harlow et al. (Eds.), Pearson Education, pp. 300–316.

Kline, N. 1999. *Time to Think: Listening to Ignite the Human Mind*. London: Octopus Publishing Group Ltd.

Maull, R. Brown & Cliffe. 2008. Organisational culture and quality improvement. *International Journal of Operations & Production Management*, 21(3), 302–326.

Smircich, L. 1983. Concepts of culture and organizational analysis. *Administrative Science Quarterly*, 28(3), 339–358.

Scholes, K., & Johnson, Gerry. 2008. *Exploring Public Sector Strategy*. Harlow, UK: Prentice Hall.

Index